Moon Sig

discover your true self

Alexander Kolesnikov

Moon Sign

discover your true self

Alexander Kolesnikov

This book is for sale at http://leanpub.com/moonsign

This version was published on 2013-08-18

ISBN 978-1491274613

This book is a part of the Lunarium project. If you are interested in the book's subject, you will find more information at http://www.lunarium.co.uk

©2013 Alexander Kolesnikov

Contents

About the Moon Sign 1
    What is the Sun Sign 1
    You Are Not Your "Star Sign"! 3
    As Above So Below 3
    What is the Moon Sign 3
    What's the Difference Between the Sun Sign and the
        Moon Sign 5
    How to Find Out Your Moon Sign 8
    The Signs of the Zodiac 9
    What Comes Next 16

The Moon in Aries 17
    Hot Emotions 18
    Plenty of Energy 18
    Speed 19
    Pioneers 20
    Fighting Spirit 23
    Moon in Aries in the Family 23
    Recovering from Stress 24
    Health and Diet 24
    A Surprise Moment 26

The Moon in Taurus 29
    Exaltation 29
    The Soul 30
    Beauty 31

CONTENTS

- Voice 32
- Storytelling 33
- The Magic of Cooking 36
- Money, Economy, and Politics 37
- Moon in Taurus in the Family 38
- Recovering from Stress 38
- Health And Diet 39
- A Surprise Moment 40

The Moon in Gemini **43**
- Changeable 43
- Scientists, philosophers, intellectuals 44
- Commerce 45
- Quick 46
- Always on the move 46
- Charming 47
- Musicians 48
- Versatile 48
- Humor 49
- The Moon in Gemini in the Family 49
- Recovering From Stress 50
- Health and Diet 50
- A Surprise Moment 52

The Moon in Cancer **55**
- Mysterious 55
- Fast and Unexpected 56
- Deep 56
- Scientists 58
- Writers and poets 59
- Musicians 60
- Actors 61
- Politicians 61
- The Moon in Cancer in the Family 63
- Recovering From Stress 64

Health and Diet	65
A Surprise Moment	66

The Moon in Leo — 67

Actors	68
Writers and Poets	69
Composers and Musicians	70
Scientists	71
Artists	72
Born Celebrities	73
World Leaders	74
Gamblers	75
Stars	75
The Moon in Leo in the Family	76
Recovering From Stress	77
Health and Diet	78
A Surprise Moment	79

The Moon in Virgo — 81

Attention to Detail	81
Writers	82
Arts and Crafts	84
Scientists	85
Actors and Actresses	86
Engineers and Inventors	88
Industrialists	88
Politicians	89
Adventurers	91
The Moon in Virgo in the Family	91
Recovering from Stress	92
Health and Diet	93
A Surprise Moment	94

The Moon in Libra — 97

Both Sides	97

CONTENTS

    Relationships 98
    Scientists and Inventors 98
    Actors and Actresses 100
    Artists 101
    Authors 103
    Musicians, Singers and Dancers 104
    Fashion 105
    Other Creative People 106
    The Moon in Libra in the Family 106
    Recovering from a Stress 107
    Health and Diet 107
    A Surprise Moment 108

The Moon in Scorpio 111
    The Moon in Fall 111
    Intense 111
    Sexy 112
    Extreme 112
    Secrets 113
    Actors and Directors 114
    Scientists 116
    Singers and Other Musicians 116
    Authors 118
    Power 119
    The Moon in Scorpio in the Family 121
    Recovering from a Stress 121
    Health and Diet 122
    A Surprise Moment 123

The Moon in Sagittarius 125
    Enthusiastic and Philosophical 125
    Discoverers and Adventurers 126
    Sports People 126
    Actors 127
    Authors 128

    Musicians 130
    Artists 131
    Scientists and Philosophers 132
    Outworldly 133
    Spicing Up 134
    The Moon in Sagittarius in the Family 134
    Recovering From Stress 135
    Health and Diet 136
    A Surprise Moment 136

The Moon in Capricorn 139
    The Detriment 139
    Old When Young, Young When Old 140
    Traditional 140
    Politicians and Career People 140
    Engineers and Industrialists 142
    Musicians 143
    Scientists 145
    Designers 146
    The Moon in Capricorn in the Family 147
    Recovering From a Stress 148
    Health and Diet 148
    Artists 149
    Authors 149
    A Surprise Moment 150

The Moon in Aquarius 153
    Rebels 153
    Social Reformers 155
    Scientists and Inventors 156
    Authors 157
    Industrialists and Entrepreneurs 159
    Actors and Directors 159
    Chefs 160
    Aviators 161

CONTENTS

    Musicians 162
    The Moon in Aquarius in the Family 163
    Recovering From a Stress 164
    Health and Diet 164
    A Surprise Moment 164

The Moon in Pisces 167
    Politicians 168
    Healers and Mystics 169
    Movie People 170
    Artists 171
    Musicians, Dancers and Singers 172
    Scientists 174
    Authors 174
    The Moon in Pisces in the Family 175
    Recovering From a Stress 176
    Health and Diet 177
    A Surprise Moment 178

The Moon Sign Compatibility 179
    Why the Moon Sign Compatibility is Very Important . . 179
    A Note For Astrologers 180
    Levels of Compatibility 181
    The Same Moon Sign 182
    The Moon Sign of One Partner is the Sun Sign of Another
        Partner 183
    The Same Element 184
    Friendly Elements 185

The Moon Sign and the Sun Sign - How They Work Together 187
    The Moon and the Sun are in the Same Sign 188
    The Moon is in the Second Sign From The Sun 189
    The Moon is in the Third Sign From The Sun 190
    The Moon is in the Fourth Sign From The Sun 191
    The Moon is in the Fifth Sign From The Sun 193

The Moon is in the Sixth Sign From The Sun	194
The Moon is in the Seventh Sign From The Sun	195
The Moon is in the Eighth Sign From The Sun	196
The Moon is in the Ninth Sign From The Sun	197
The Moon is in the Tenth Sign From The Sun	198
The Moon is in the Eleventh Sign From The Sun	199
The Moon is in the Twelfth Sign From The Sun	200
More About the Natal Phase	201

The Moon Signs in Daily Life 203
    When the Transiting Moon is in Your Own Moon Sign . . 204
    How to Find Out the Transiting Moon's Sign 205
    The Universal Lunar Calendar at Lunarium 207
    iLuna 211
    The Transiting Moon in Aries 216
    The Transiting Moon in Taurus 217
    The Transiting Moon in Gemini 217
    The Transiting Moon in Cancer 218
    The Transiting Moon in Leo 219
    The Transiting Moon in Virgo 220
    Transiting Moon in Libra 220
    The Transiting Moon in Scorpio 221
    The Transiting Moon in Sagittarius 222
    The Transiting Moon in Capricorn 223
    The Transiting Moon in Aquarius 223
    The Transiting Moon in Pisces 224
    The Phases of the Moon 225
    The Waxing and the Waning Moon 229
    More About Your Personal Phase of the Moon 230

The Moon and Surgery 235
    The Anatomical Correspondences of the Signs of the Zodiac 236
    The New Moon, the Full Moon, and the Eclipses 238
    Other Factors 239

CONTENTS

The Void-of-Course Moon **241**
    What the Void-of-Course Moon Is 242
    What the Void-of-Course Moon Isn't 246
    The Meaning of the Void-of-Course Moon 247
    How to Find Out When the Next Void-of-Course Period Is 249
    Do You Like Happy Ends? 250

Appendix A. How to Find Out Your Moon Sign **255**
    If No Birth Time Is Available 255
    The Limitations of the Moon Sign Calculator, and of the
        Moon Sign App 258
    A Precise Method of Finding Out Your Moon Sign 259

Appendix B. How to Find Out Your Sun Sign **261**

Appendix C. Moon Sign Celebrities **263**
    Aries 263
    Taurus 266
    Gemini 268
    Cancer 270
    Leo 271
    Virgo 272
    Libra 274
    Scorpio 276
    Sagittarius 277
    Capricorn 278
    Aquarius 280
    Pisces 281

About the Moon Sign

Most people know about astrology just one thing: they have a "star sign". In fact, "star sign" is just a marketing term introduced by newspapers and magazines, it doesn't exist in real astrology. The astrological feature misnamed as "star sign" is actually the **Sun Sign**, i.e. the Sign of the Zodiac in which the Sun was situated at the moment of a person's birth.

What is the Sun Sign

Have a look at the picture on the next page.

At the moment when you were born, the Sun was somewhere in the sky. It might have been below the horizon if you were born at night, but still it was somewhere, in relation to the Earth and to the starry sky. But where exactly?

Astrologers measure the movement of the lights and the planets against the starry sky, to figure out where those are located at any specific moment, and to make that task easier, they put an imaginary ruler along the path of the Sun through the stars. That ruler is the zodiac, and it consists of twelve sections, the signs of the zodiac.

The whole zodiac is a circle, and so it has in it 360°. There are twelve signs in the zodiac, and each sign has in it 30° of that zodiacal circle. If an astrologer wants to specify where the Sun (or indeed any other celestial body) was situated at a specific moment in time, he or she will use the zodiac as a ruler and say: the Sun was in the 11th degree of Aries, or the Sun was in the 28th degree of Sagittarius. Or, to keep things as simple as possible, one can mention only the section of the ruler: Sun in Aries, Sun in Taurus, Sun in Gemini, and so on.

Sun Sign can usually be easily figured out from the date of birth, and if you didn't already know that, Appendix B will offer a popular table showing which date belongs to which Sun Sign. The same Appendix B will tell you, however, that such popular tables aren't actually 100% reliable; in certain cases, they can lie. Read it yourself, if you are interested, but the Sun Sign isn't actually the topic of this book.

What is the Sun Sign

You Are Not Your "Star Sign"!

An important thing to understand is that you shouldn't really totally associate yourself with your "star sign" (it's actually your Sun Sign, okay?), like saying: *I am an Aries*, or *I am a Libra*. The Sun Sign is just one of your astrological features, albeit one of the most important ones. So the correct way to say it is: *my Sun is in Libra*, or *my Sun is in Aries* - leaving space for something else. You will soon see why this is important.

As Above So Below

According to this ancient adage, whatever was prominent in the sky at the moment of one's birth will be also prominent in the newborn's life. Two objects are always very prominent in the sky: the luminaries, the Sun and the Moon. The presence of the Sun is always obvious during the day while the Moon dominates the night, and as there is no day without night, we are all well aware of both the Sun and the Moon.

In Western Astrology, the Sun is considered to be the most important factor in a person's natal chart, but in Indian Astrology (Jyotish) with its rich uninterrupted tradition it is the Moon which is the most important factor.

So if you **really** want to know a little bit of astrology about yourself, you have to understand that plus to your Sun Sign (do you still call it "star sign"?), you also have your Moon Sign, and these two are equally important.

What is the Moon Sign

The Moon moves across the starry sky in the same way as the Sun does but much faster, making the whole circle in approximately 27 days. In the same way as with the Sun, the Moon's position among the stars at any particular moment can be measured in the signs of the zodiac, and at the moment when you were born the Moon was somewhere in one of the twelve signs:

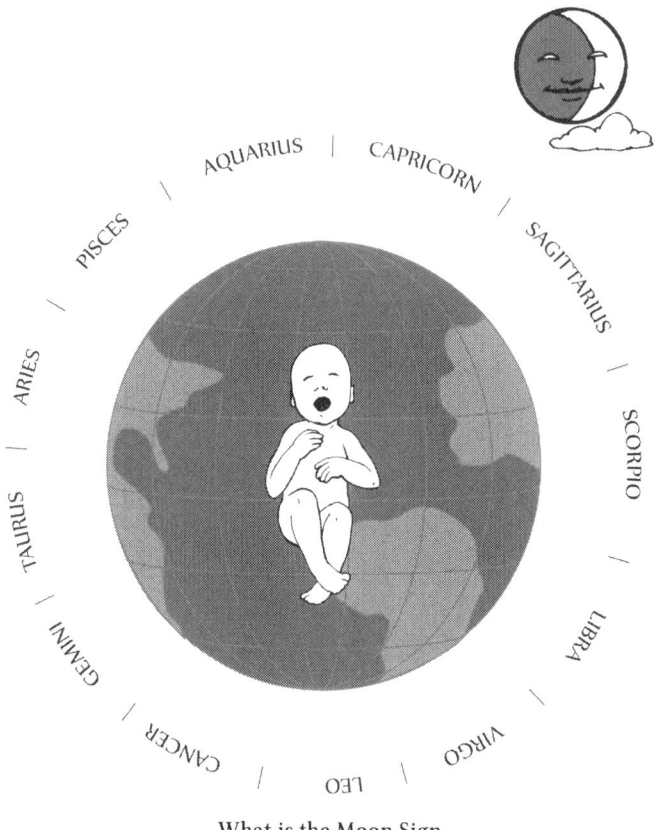

What is the Moon Sign

The sign of the zodiac where the Moon was at the moment of your birth is your Moon Sign. It is important to understand that in most cases the Sun Sign and the Moon Sign are different. If you have Aries, for example, for your Sun Sign, your Moon Sign can be Libra, or Sagittarius, or Gemini, or indeed any of the 12 signs, including of course Aries as well.

What's the Difference Between the Sun Sign and the Moon Sign

Everyone's personality has two sides: the Yang side and the Yin side, the conscious side and the unconscious side, the active side and the passive side, the day side and the night side.

The Sun is associated in astrology with consciousness, and this is why it is given such an importance, especially in the West. We believe that we control our life consciously; that whatever we have in our mind is the most important thing in the world. The Sun Sign therefore describes quite well the conscious, day side of the person, how one positions him or herself in the world, what he or she wants to achieve, and in which particular way he or she prefers to conquer the world.

On the other hand, the Moon is associated in astrology with the subconscious, intuitive side of personality. The Moon is responsible for our emotions, instincts, memory, and pretty much everything else which goes on automatically, without conscious control. All these aspects of the person's life are described by the Moon Sign.

Consciousness vs Subconsciousness

Now, let's think which part of our daily life is controlled by our consciousness. Say, you woke up in the morning and you are walking to the kitchen, to have your coffee. You probably don't have much in your consciousness, perhaps some vague thoughts about the day ahead, or maybe an inner dispute on whether to have a full breakfast or just cereals will be enough.

At the same time, your body is very busy. Complex groups of muscles contract and relax in a precise rhythm so that you could walk. Your stomach, in anticipation of breakfast, is already busy preparing a complex mixture of chemicals, which will digest any food you might have. And there is a lot of other extremely complex processes throughout the body: checking numerous important levels and taking measures if something is out of norm, guarding against infection, curing any problems you might have, filling your lungs with fresh air, and so on.

All these numerous complex activities are happening automatically, your consciousness has no idea about them. Indeed, if you tried to control your body consciously, you would immediately collapse: human consciousness is so weak and helpless against the complex machinery of the human body. Only subconsciousness, associated with the Moon, is powerful enough to take care of such a complexity.

Therefore, your Moon Sign can help you to understand how your body works, what it needs, how to properly take care of it, what are its potential weak spots and which natural healing agents will be most appropriate for your body type. Some parts of the body are especially strongly associated with the Moon, such as stomach, or women's breasts and womb.

The Moon Sign can be clearly visible in the way the person recovers from a significant stress. We used to involve ourselves in stressful situations by acting consciously, and the body has to activate all the vital functions to cope with the problem. But as soon as the crisis is over, and we are probably sitting somewhere in an armchair pretty much absent-minded, the Moon gets the chance to return back to normal, to restore the proper functioning, and this is where you can often clearly see what the person's Moon Sign is.

Those with their Moon in Gemini feel the need to chat, as if to speak out their recent stress; for a Taurus Moon Sign, eating something tasty will help to calm down, while Moon in Scorpio will prefer some good sex, or a strong drink, or a very hot shower - or maybe all of this together. We'll discuss the peculiarities of different Moon Signs in the coming chapters.

Women, Children, Mothers, and Emotions

In astrology, the Moon is also associated with women in general, and with little children, from toddlers and to the age when they become less dependent on their mother.

Because of this, I would say that for women and children it might be more important to know their Moon Sign than their Sun Sign, in order to fully understand their character, potential talents, as well as vulnerabilities.

It doesn't mean however that the Moon Sign isn't important for men. The Moon rules our emotions, and if you think of how many of our actions are ultimately driven by emotions, you will understand that the Moon is important for everyone. A man's Moon Sign shows his attitude to women and children in general, and to his mother in particular. Very often men with the Moon in Cancer, for example, worship their mother, compare to her all the other women in their lives, and and chances are they will choose a partner similar to their mother.

In fact, the Moon is strongly associated with the image of the mother both in case of men and women. For a woman, her Moon Sign can tell what kind of mother she is: maybe she is like a friend to her children, or maybe she is a powerful matriarch type. It will also say a lot about how she sees her own mother; and the Moon Sign of a child will help to understand how he or she sees his or her mother.

The Spiritual Viewpoint

No matter whether you believe in reincarnation or not, some of the world's greatest religions teach us that human soul is travelling from one life to another, learning lessons in each life, developing and fine-tuning its abilities, with the ultimate goal to perfect itself and join again with the Absolute.

From this point of view, the Sun is the sparkle of the eternal light, which travels through numerous incarnations. Therefore *Sun Sign* can help us to understand the person's ultimate goal, what kind of important lesson he or she is going to learn in this life, and other very important things.

The Moon then is the material shell, which is given to the divine sparkle of the Sun in this specific life. This "shell" can mean many things: the body, the parents who gave birth to the child, the general circumstances of the person's life, and the whole life in general. So the Moon's message is more specific, it tells us something we need to know in our daily life, while the Sun's role is more esoteric.

When doing research for this book, I was often amazed by how aptly different stages of a person's life were described by the symbolism of his or her Moon Sign. You will see many examples in the next chapters of this book.

How to Find Out Your Moon Sign

Well, this is a little bit difficult. With the Sun Sign, you can easily find it out from your date of birth (in most cases), just because the calendar we use was created in such a way that it fits precisely the movement of the Sun against the stars.

The movement of the Moon however is quite complex, and there are no simple recipes that could help us. It actually takes a few pages of astronomical formulas to figure out the Moon's location in the sky at any specific moment. Fortunately, there are many easy to use services and applications that will help you to find out your Moon Sign given the date, the time and the time zone of your birth.

The most easily accessible is the free online Moon Sign calculator at the Lunarium website[1].

---

[1] http://www.lunarium.co.uk/moonsign/calculator.jsp

Also, I created an iPhone app named Moon Sign[2] that will calculate your or your friend's Moon Sign quickly and easily. Just make a search on the Apple App Store for "Moon Sign".

Not so long ago, I created a version of the Moon Sign app for Android. You can obtain it both from the Google Play[3] and Amazon App Store[4].

There are also other ways to find out your Moon Sign, some of them easier than the others. For example, is it possible to figure out the Moon Sign for a person who doesn't know his or her time of birth? You will find all the relevant information in the Appendix A.

The Signs of the Zodiac

Now that you know your Moon Sign, how do you figure out what it means? I've written twelve chapters, one for each sign of the zodiac, to help you answer this question. However, the Moon has so many meanings and responsibilities, and each sign of the zodiac has such a rich character that there is an endless variety of ways how the Moon can show herself in one or another sign. Therefore, it is important to understand how to recognize in the kaleidoscope of daily events and moods those which are in tune with your Moon Sign.

You already know the most important things the Moon is responsible for. Now I want to give you some idea about what the signs of the zodiac are, what kind of energy they offer. To understand how a Moon Sign can manifest itself, you can just take into account different associations of the Moon and color them with the energy of the sign the Moon is in.

These are the brief characteristics of the signs of the zodiac, to get you started:

---

[2]http://appstore.com/moonsign
[3]https://play.google.com/store/apps/details?id=com.siriuslab.moonsign
[4]http://www.amazon.com/Alexander-Kolesnikov-Moon-Sign/dp/B00DPSXLS2/

Aries

Energy, impulsiveness, impatience; an urge to act despite obstacles. Full of initiative, proactive but is typically unable to finish what was started. Aspires to be the first, has a strong preference for simple solutions, and an inability to appreciate workarounds — "brakes were invented by cowards".

Taurus

Practicality, deliberation, constancy and patience. In many cases, Taurus gives a talent in dealing with plants. What Aries started but abandoned, Taurus can continue for eternity. High capacity for work, especially if there is no need to do several things at once. Loves comfort and has the ability to create it. Possesses thriftiness, and a good understanding of the value of things.

Gemini

An ability to make contacts, flexibility, adaptability, and an ability to do several things at the same time. Has an interest in any kind of information, from newspapers and soap operas to books on math and physics. Talent in languages, wide range of interests, and is changeable, with an inability to concentrate on a single matter.

Cancer

Deep emotions, hidden from the others. Needs security, with a private, protected space. Possesses prudence, has a desire and ability to care, nurture and foster. Takes initiative, especially in matters related to home, family, and household. Unpredictable, because their emotions — the main driving force behind their actions — are thoroughly hidden.

Leo

Brightness, expressiveness, with a desire to show off, to be noticed and praised. High creative potential, with an ability for significant achievements under the influence of inspiration. Desires to be a leader, exhibits pride and egocentricity, but also generosity.

Virgo

Displays interest in numerous tiny details in the world around them. Has the ability to be captivated by work that would seem unbearably boring to just about everyone else. Loves collecting, studying the inner workings of different mechanisms, and desires diversity in everything, with a need for constant variance when it comes to their sensations. Tend to seem very critical as the result of being able to take note of the tiniest faults. Quite often, has an interest in making healthy lifestyle choices.

Libra

Has an interest in partner relationships, communication, and an exchange of opinions. Possesses an inherent need to share joys and troubles with someone else, otherwise joys will seem imperfect and troubles will feel especially bitter. Desires fairness and objectivity, with a tendency to balance everything according to its opposite: black vs white, white vs black; hence, they are often indecisive and hesitant.

Scorpio

Has an intense inner life hidden under a veneer of impassivity. Negative feelings like envy, jealousy, or greed can be especially strong and might require an effort in order to control them and prevent them from over-complicating one's life. They experience increased sexuality, and have a magnetic influence on others that gives them an ability to manipulate them. Interested in everything secret, mysterious, with a desire to penetrate beyond the external shell of events in order to understand their hidden moving forces.

Sagittarius

Has a very wide range of interests, talents and opinions, with a great desire to experience everything the world has to offer. Has an interest in anything foreign and exotic, from far away. Sagittarius wants to get everything at once, instant gratification, and that can create problems. On the other hand, no other sign can reach the scale of knowledge and the breadth of activities that Sagittarius has.

Capricorn

Serious, orderly, ambitious, has an intuitive understanding of the structure of society. Capricorn, even blindfolded, will quickly find the closest social ladder and will immediately try to climb it as high as possible. Has the ability to organize and to be an administrator, loves to make plans and schedules. They possess a respectful attitude towards their seniors and are rather strict with their juniors.

Aquarius

Displays some eccentricity in combination with a deep, constant interest in some specific area of knowledge or sphere of activity. Loves everything new, unusual, original, and is focused on the future. Inventive, often having an innate ability to deal with technical stuff. Interested in the laws that rule society, and unwilling to be bound by any obligations.

Pisces

Separation from reality, emotional openness, ability for compassion and empathy. Spirituality, sensitivity for music, intuition, ability to understand another person without words. Innate mystical understanding, religiousness, philanthropy, ability to sacrifice. Lack of practical sense, tendency to create chaos and drift with the current.

Elements and Qualities

The descriptions above are very brief, but still it would require an effort if you decided to memorize them and use for your understanding of people's Moon Signs. There is however another, easier way to figure out what each sign of the zodiac is about. First of all, each of the signs belongs to one of the four Elements.

Fire signs are Aries, Leo, and Sagittarius. Their most important characteristics are *energy, activity, enthusiasm, and idealism.*

Air signs are Gemini, Libra, and Aquarius. They are about *communication, information and connectedness.*

Water signs are Cancer, Scorpio, and Pisces. Their main qualities are *emotionality, mysteriousness, synthesis and a strong interest towards the hidden side of life.*

Earth signs are Taurus, Virgo and Capricorn. They are *practical, pragmatic, and materialistic.*

Also, each sign of the zodiac belongs to one of the three Qualities: Cardinal, Fixed or Mutable.

Cardinal signs are Aries, Cancer, Libra and Capricorn. They are impulsive, full of initiative, like to make the first step. For their dynamism, the initial strong impulse is very typical. Dealing with something, they push it strongly, make it moving, but since the movement has started they don't really care what happens next.

Fixed signs are Taurus, Leo, Scorpio and Aquarius. They are obstinate, stubborn, like to stand on their own, and if they are doing something, they will just go on and on and never stop. However, in order to actually start doing something, Fixed signs need an impulse of a Cardinal sign.

Mutable signs are Gemini, Virgo, Sagittarius and Pisces. They are flexible and changeable, easily orient themselves in the surrounding world, notice every change in the environment and help all the other signs not to lose the sense of reality.

Now, if you'll remember what different Elements and Qualities mean, you will be able to easily figure out the main theme of any of the signs of the zodiac. For example, Aquarius is an Air sign, so it deals with information and communication, but it is also a Fixed sign, so it has some strong opinions and interests and doesn't really want to change or question them.

Try constructing descriptions for different signs from their Element and Quality, and see how your descriptions will match the people who have either their Moon or Sun in that sign of the zodiac.

The Signs of the Zodiac and Planets

To even better understand the nature of the signs of the zodiac, it is good to know that each of them is ruled by one of the planets. It can be also seen the other way around: each planet has its "home" in one or two signs of the zodiac, or "owns" those signs, or rules them. The planet shares its qualities with the home signs, and knowing the character of the planet-owner is useful for understanding what its signs are about.

There is a traditional scheme that shows how the signs of he zodiac are distributed between planets. This scheme exists from time immemorial and is used in both the Traditional Western Astrology and Jyotish (Hindu Astrology). According to it,

- **the Sun** rules the sign of Leo;
- **the Moon** rules the sign of Cancer;
- **Mercury** rules Gemini and Virgo;
- **Venus** rules Libra and Taurus;
- **Mars** rules Aries and Scorpio;
- **Jupiter** rules Sagittarius and Pisces;
- **Saturn** rules Aquarius and Capricorn.

(This traditional scheme doesn't take in consideration Uranus, Neptune, and Pluto, but it is sufficient for our purposes).

I could write a whole book discussing the qualities of planets and how they interact with the signs, but here I can only allow myself to give brief characteristics of the planets. If a planet has two signs, then the first sign as listed is its "day home", where the qualities of the planet are manifested in a Yang way - outwardly, visibly, actively - while the second sign is the "night home", and the planet manifests itself there in a Yin way - inwardly, deeply, passively.

- **The Sun** is bright, proud and generous.
- **The Moon** is caring, nurturing and deeply emotional.
- **Mercury** is curious, agile and discriminating.
- **Venus** is attractive, sympathetic and appreciating.
- **Mars** is active, energetic, with combative spirit.
- **Jupiter** is optimistic, expansive and philosophical.
- **Saturn** is pessimistic, strict and responsible.

Again, it will make a great exercise to look at the people you know, to find out their Moon Sign, to figure out the planet which rules that sign, and to notice how that planet shows itself in the people's characters.

What Comes Next

In the following chapters, one for each Moon Sign, I will offer my opinion on how different Moon Signs manifest themselves in life, giving examples from the lives of different people. Some of those people will be famous, others - simply interesting. You will see that the same Moon Sign can manifest itself in very many different ways, but if you know the symbolism of the Moon and of the signs of the zodiac, you'll be able to recognize those manifestations easily.

I will also give an advice on the life style and kinds of healing that are appropriate for each Moon Sign.

Note: the great majority of examples in this book, the birth details for them and some facts from the people's biographies were taken by permission from Astro-Databank, a great resource of astrological information for any researcher. If some quotation is given without mentioning its source, the source is always Astro-Databank, and I have linked the names of all the people I use in my examples to their Astro-Databank page. I recommend you to visit that page when you have time as you will find there some additional interesting facts and details.

The first sign of the zodiac is Aries, and so the next chapter is about the Moon in Aries.

The Moon in Aries

Aries is a Fire sign ruled by Mars, and so it has an abundance of energy. It is also a Cardinal sign, and therefore impulsive, able to concentrate an enormous amount of energy in a short period of time. The energy of Aries is powerful but it can be difficult to control.

When a person is born with his or her Moon in the Sign of Aries, everything associated with the Moon gets filled with the powerful energy of the sign, and this energy wants to be spent. If it is not spent for any good purpose, then it will be splashed out as conflicts or dissipated in the body creating various health problems.

Moon-in-Aries people are a bit like an adventurer who has just landed in a new unknown country. They enjoy freedom, desire to go ahead and bravely experience whatever life can offer to them. As some people would say, they rush in where angels fear to tread. But feeling themselves in an uncharted territory, they are self-sufficient, resourceful, and are used to relying primarily on themselves.

People born with the Moon in Aries like challenges, as they see in them an opportunity to test how good they are. And of course they always want to be the first and the best, to excel in everything they do. Easily excitable, they welcome all innovations. They would hate a routine, predictable and boring life.

They are full of creativity and initiative, very good at starting new projects, but usually they don't have enough stamina to bring all their started projects to completion.

Hot Emotions

The Moon rules emotions, and the Moon-in-Aries person's emotions can "go over the top" from time to time, and can be difficult to hide. Even in less extreme cases, the emotions of such a person are so powerful that everything he or she thinks about is literally written on their faces, and it can be difficult for such people to deceive or to pretend that they have in mind something different.

Moon-in-Aries people can quickly become angry or irritated, but not for long. Unless they are not contradicted or attacked, they will calm down very quickly. By nature, they are honest and direct - sometimes too much so, and other people might occasionally perceive them as rude and lacking political wisdom.

Plenty of Energy

The Moon is closely associated with the human body, and Moon-in-Aries people need to be able to perform some physical activity to feel good. Many of them choose as their hobby some kind of sport, from jogging to martial arts, or they might push and urge everyone around them to do this or that, to do it faster, to move. A Moon-in-Aries person can become quite a nuisance for those less-energized individuals!

Aries Moon individuals want to be busy all the time, and if there is a problem, they tackle it without delay or, if the problem is long-existing, they might provoke a crisis to try and get rid of it.

One stunning example of a Moon-in-Aries individual is Ron Ely[5], an American actor who was playing Tarzan on TV. According to Astro-Databank[6], "he insisted on doing all his own stunt work, from wrestling tigers to swinging on vines to riding zebra-back. Known

---

[5]http://www.astro.com/astro-databank/Ely,_Ron
[6]http://www.astro.com/astro-databank/Main_Page

for his daredevil ways, at one point he was considered television's most injured actor, suffering burns, animal bites and falling off vines".

In fact, these burns and bites are attributes of Mars, the ruling planet of Aries. The influence of Mars can move Moon-in-Aries people into activities that require courage and fighting spirit. They might find themselves in sports, in the Army, in search and rescue or firefighting teams, or in similar occupations associated with speed, risk and danger.

Speed

Moon-in-Aries folks adore doing things as quickly as possible, in a "fast and furious" way. One reason for this is that the energy of Aries comes in impulses, and when the impulse is over, one might find it difficult to complete what was started. Not surprisingly then that among people who were born with the Moon in Aries we can find many men and women who pursue activities where speed is of utmost importance, such as car racing for instance.

A good example here is Richard Petty[7], an American race-car champion, "a famous driver considered *The King* because of winning over 200 races and setting a record he shared with only one other driver of seven Winston Cup titles".

The same need for speed can also show itself as impatience: the Moon-in-Aries people hate waiting, they want everything to happen right now, immediately, and they often won't be too shy to let everyone know about their expectations.

Speed is a general attribute of most Moon-in-Aries individuals. They do everything quickly, they walk quickly, they cook food quickly (and can burn it from time to time), and they also develop quickly. When looking for celebrities with the Moon in Aries, I met

---

[7] http://www.astro.com/astro-databank/Petty,_Richard_Lee

many prodigies: they developed so quickly that achieved a very high level in one or another occupation very early in their life.

One interesting example is Willard R. Espy[8], an American writer and reporter who was reading from age three and "decided he wanted to make people laugh and began writing his *Encyclopedia Anonymica* at four".

Another example is Gisele MacKenzie[9] who played the piano by two, and was also taking violin and voice lessons.

Pioneers

Aries is the first Sign of the Zodiac, and those who were born with the Moon in Aries often become pioneers in their field, they open new doors for humanity. They have for that all the necessary qualities, as they are full of initiative, can devote themselves completely to one important thing, and they are very independent. Although most people would enjoy some support from the others, Moon-in-Aries people don't usually need much of support or approval. They just go ahead and do whatever they consider to be right, while the others are welcome to follow.

Some of the famous Moon-in-Aries pioneers explored the physical world. A few examples are:

- Umberto Nobile[10], an Italian explorer and Air Force General, the pioneer in Arctic aviation who in 1926, with the Norwegian explorer Roald Amundsen and Lincoln Ellsworth of the United States flew over the North Pole in the dirigible Norge (see an article about him in Encyclopaedia Britannica[11]).

---

[8]http://www.astro.com/astro-databank/Espy,_Willard_R.
[9]http://www.astro.com/astro-databank/MacKenzie,_Gisele
[10]http://www.astro.com/astro-databank/Nobile,_Umberto
[11]http://www.britannica.com/EBchecked/topic/416930/Umberto-Nobile

- Edmund Hillary[12], an adventurer from New Zealand, who was one of the first two men to climb to the top of Mount Everest in 1953 and return.
- James Doolittle[13], an American Air Force general, aeronautical engineer, scientist, boxer, stunt pilot and Vice-President of Shell Oil Co. He was the first to fly coast-to-coast in under 24 hours, the first to fly "blind," relying only on instruments.
- Steve Fossett[14], an American billionaire and adventurer, and also "a record-breaking aviator, balloonist and sailor, accomplished mountain-climber, tri-athlete and swimmer. With 116 record-setting achievements to his name, Fossett was the first person to fly a solo, nonstop flight around the world" (Astro-Databank[15]).

Other Moon-in-Aries pioneers paved new ways in science and religion:

- Galilei Galileo[16], an Italian astronomer, physicist, inventor of the first telescope and founder of modern experimental science.
- Enrico Fermi[17], an Italian-American physicist who discovered uranium fission.
- Samuel Hahnemann[18], the founder of Homeopathy.
- Martin Luther[19], who created the Reformed Church in 1525.
- F.M. Alexander[20], the creator of the "Alexander Technique" of body training.

---

[12]http://www.astro.com/astro-databank/Hillary,_Edmund
[13]http://www.astro.com/astro-databank/Doolittle,_James
[14]http://www.astro.com/astro-databank/Fossett,_Steve
[15]http://www.astro.com/astro-databank/Main_Page
[16]http://www.astro.com/astro-databank/Galileo,_Galilei
[17]http://www.astro.com/astro-databank/Fermi,_Enrico
[18]http://en.wikipedia.org/wiki/Samuel_Hahnemann
[19]http://www.astro.com/astro-databank/Luther,_Martin
[20]http://www.astro.com/astro-databank/Alexander,_F.M.

- Jose Silva[21], the founder of "Silva Mind Control".

There are also two most amazing pioneers of the computer age, both born with the Moon in Aries:

- Steve Jobs[22], the founder of Apple, one of the initiators of computer revolution.
- Bill Gates[23], the founder of Microsoft, the company whose software is synonymous with computing for most people in the world.

A good example of the ability of the Moon-in-Aries people to start from nothing and to achieve very quickly a lot, sometimes with very little or no support, is Elizabeth Arden[24]. "Born in poverty, she started with $6,000 borrowed money in 1910 and built an industrial empire".

Another example is Diane Von Fürstenberg[25]. "After moving to New York, her first design show was in April 1970. Two years later, with a loan of $30,000, she opened her own showroom and went on to a sweeping success within months. Wholesale by 1976 estimated at $20 million, in less than five years, she had built a fashion empire. In 1976 she landed on the cover of Newsweek magazine after selling more than five million of her signature wrap dresses".

Moon-in-Aries people are good at doing things in an unusual way, which is actually a byproduct of their pioneering approach. If that unusual way resonates well with the other people, they can achieve a great success. An example of this is Salvador Dali[26], a Spanish surrealist painter who is described as being "original and eccentric, truly one of a kind".

---

[21] http://www.astro.com/astro-databank/Silva,_Jose
[22] http://www.astro.com/astro-databank/Jobs,_Steve
[23] http://www.astro.com/astro-databank/Gates,_Bill
[24] http://www.astro.com/astro-databank/Arden,_Elizabeth
[25] http://www.astro.com/astro-databank/Furstenberg,_Diane_Von
[26] http://www.astro.com/astro-databank/Dali,_Salvador

Fighting Spirit

The energy of Mars, the ruler of Aries, moves those who were born with the Moon in Aries to achieve, to win, to conquer. They will fight for whatever they believe is right.

Since the Moon is strongly associated with women, from the astrological point of view, many of Moon-in-Aries women display the fighting spirit of Aries very strongly, Elizabeth Arden and Diane Von Fürstenberg, both mentioned above, being just two bright examples.

They are the commanders, the generals of their lives, and therefore when choosing a partner they'd better find someone milder and less energetic than themselves, otherwise there can be a clash of wills.

Moon in Aries in the Family

Moon-in-Aries girls are often tomboys, and a good example here is Angelina Jolie[27], the movie star who is doing most of her stunts herself, is comfortable with guns, martial arts and guy-flicks.

The fact that someone was born with the Moon in Aries often shows that they had a very active parents' family, typically (but not necessarily) with the mother playing the leading role, where the child was taught how to achieve, to win, to fight. The mother was probably a commander type woman, strong, brave and self-sufficient, maybe good with tools and machines, well capable of changing her tires and fuses. She could often be angry, not very patient and not very attentive to the small child's needs. She taught her children primarily to be brave, self-sufficient, and could show very well how interesting and exciting this world is.

After growing up, this Moon-in-Aries child will most probably have a similar attitude to his or her own children, teaching them first of

---

[27] http://www.astro.com/astro-databank/Jolie,_Angelina

all how to find their path in life, and maybe giving less attention to such boring things as feeding, caring or nurturing. Quite often, children born with the Moon in Aries leave their parents' home early to seek independence.

As an interesting example, Jon Voight[28], the father of Angelina Jolie, also has his Moon in Aries.

Recovering from Stress

To recover from a significant stress, people born with the Moon in Aries often feel the need to hit something (or someone), to run, to jump, to do something in which they can invest a huge amount of their difficult energy. Going to a gym or doing martial arts can provide a more controllable outlet for such a relief.

Many years ago, I've read that in some Japanese companies there existed a special rubber doll resembling the boss of the company. After leaving the bosses' office, if an employee was particularly unhappy, he or she could go and beat the doll as much as they wanted. Then, after releasing their conflicting energy, they could go and continue to work calmly.

I don't know if this story is true or not, but this way of recovering after stress would be perfect for many Moon-in-Aries individuals.

Health and Diet

Health of those who have their Moon in Aries can suffer when energy is not spent freely but is instead stagnated - like when people are forced to work 9 to 5 in the office, to be nice, to do things slowly and patiently. It is very important for this kind of people to find an outlet for their energy. Anything will do: jogging, cycling,

---

[28]http://www.astro.com/astro-databank/Voight,_Jon

yoga, but the most natural fit for the kind of energy offered by the sign of Aries is something where plenty of energy can be spent very quickly, something which doesn't require a lot of stamina or patience. Games like squash or badminton can be very good in this respect, I believe.

Another kind of problem can arise if a Moon-in-Aries person doesn't understand the impulsive nature of his or her energy. When the impulse is on, such people can do a lot, but when it is over, trying to squeeze from themselves the very last drops of energy can only lead to exhaustion, and can be detrimental for health.

The healthy approach would be to let the energy flow freely when it is abundant, and to have enough of rest and relaxation in between the high energy waves.

The typical problem for the Moon in Aries is inflammation, and the affected areas are often those primarily associated with the Moon: stomach, digestion, skin, reproductive system. Head is a generally sensitive area for people with the Moon in Aries.

One sad historical example here is Leopold, Prince of England[29], a hemophiliac who had his Moon in Aries and died after striking his head.

In addition to a good control of energy, an appropriate diet is very important for Moon-in-Aries individuals.

They tend to eat very quickly, and engage in a stressful activity very soon after a meal. This is why their food should be lightweight, easily digestible, but also high in calories. The digestive system should not spend much time assimilating the food, but the body should get plenty of energy at the same time.

It is also important for those who have their Moon in Aries not to be restricted by the established meal times. They should eat whenever they feel hungry, and their own intuition will be the best guide in choosing the most appropriate food.

---

[29]http://www.astro.com/astro-databank/Leopold,_Prince_of_England

Unfortunately, too many of the Moon-in-Aries people don't pay enough attention to what they eat. They will just have any snack in the middle between two activities, and swallow it as quickly as possible. The words "fast food" are very symbolically appropriate for the Moon in Aries.

This is a very wrong attitude, which can ultimately result in various digestive troubles. Those who have the Moon in Aries should be very attentive to what they eat. The food should be very natural, adequately cooked for easier digestion, and it is very important to enjoy the meal, even in those few minutes that it takes.

It is also important to avoid a very spicy food. The Moon already feels quite hot in the fire sign of Aries, there is no need to add more heat. On the other hand, the food that is too cold will contradict the nature of the Moon in Aries and can be difficult to digest.

One of the consequences of the Moon's position in the hot sign of Aries is that the Moon-in-Aries folks need a lot of liquids to keep their body working smoothly. However, too much of strong tea, coffee, chocolate and other stimulants is also undesirable for the Moon-in-Aries people, especially in the middle of a stressful activity, as over-stimulating themselves can make the control over their energy more difficult.

A Surprise Moment

I was surprised to find out that many famous painters were born with the Moon in Aries. The ruler of Aries, Mars, isn't that much associated with beauty or harmony.

However, according to the rules of astrology, the Sun is very strong and prominent in Aries, and so the Moon-in-Aries people have a strong solar creativity in their disposal. Typically, those painters with the Moon in Aries achieve success in the directions where creativity and originality are of utmost importance, such as surrealism, impressionism, or cubism.

In addition to Salvador Dali, who was already mentioned above, other examples are:

- Pierre-Auguste Renoir[30], a French impressionist artist.
- Georges Braque[31], a French painter, the founder of Cubism.

There are many more examples of very creative individuals with the Moon in Aries, here are only a few of them:

- Benvenuto Cellini[32], an Italian renaissance artist.
- Louis Armstrong[33], an American jazz trumpeter.
- Luciano Pavarotti[34], an Italian superstar operatic tenor who eclipsed even Caruso.
- Jean-Michel Jarre[35], a famous French musician and song-writer.
- Stevie Wonder[36], an American musician, singer and performer.

You will find quite a number of the Moon-in-Aries people examples, as well as their dates of birth, in the Appendix C. As for the people mentioned in this chapter, if you want to also know their time and place of birth, as well as some additional biographical details, you can click on the name of the person in the text to be redirected to the appropriate page of the Astro-Databank.

---

[30]http://www.astro.com/astro-databank/Renoir,_Auguste
[31]http://www.astro.com/astro-databank/Braque,_Georges
[32]http://www.astro.com/astro-databank/Cellini,_Benvenuto
[33]http://www.astro.com/astro-databank/Armstrong,_Louis
[34]http://www.astro.com/astro-databank/Pavarotti,_Luciano
[35]http://www.astro.com/astro-databank/Jarre,_Jean-Michel
[36]http://www.astro.com/astro-databank/Wonder,_Stevie

Taurus is the next sign after Aries in the zodiacal order. These two signs are very different in so many ways: Aries is fast and impulsive while Taurus is slow and steady. The next chapter will tell you many interesting things about the Moon in Taurus.

The Moon in Taurus

Taurus is a fixed Earth sign ruled by Venus, and so those people who were born with the Moon in Taurus are patient, persistent, practical and are more than able to enjoy all the good things in life: the beauty of nature, tasty food, comfortable living, sensual pleasures. To truly enjoy all these things, you need to take your time, and so the Moon-in-Taurus people don't like to be in a hurry, and they don't like changes. If it is so pleasant and cozy where they are, why should they go somewhere else?

The Moon-in-Taurus individuals are usually serene, loyal, calm, but they can also sometimes be quite stubborn. They like to do something practical, be it cooking, gardening, building something, or any kind of DIY. Due to the fixed nature of Taurus, they might find it difficult to start something new, but once they are committed to the project, they will make sure that the job will be done.

People born with the Moon in Taurus don't mind dealing with the routine. In fact, they really like when things are stable, predictable and are going according to a plan. On the other hand, major changes in life often make them stressed and unhappy.

They are usually not very fast and prefer to take time doing something. They hate to be hurried and to be given an advice they haven't asked for.

Exaltation

According to astrological rules, the Moon in Taurus is in the sign of its exaltation. This means that the attributes of the Moon are manifested very strongly in this sign. The Moon-in-Taurus individuals are very good with children, it is natural for them to care about other people, to feed them; their emotions are stable and strong; their body is typically strong, efficient and not susceptible to the adverse outside influences.

The Moon is the symbol of the feminine, and everything related to women can be very important for those who were born with the Moon in Taurus. One example is Jane Addams[37], an American social worker and feminist who "devoted her life to social welfare and the rights of women and children".

As a side note, I was pleased to say that I was able to find more female celebrities with the Moon in Taurus than in any other sign of the zodiac.

The Soul

The Moon is also associated with the soul, and although our materialistic science denies the existence of the soul, the Moon-in-Taurus individuals often feel intuitively that there is something else in the human beings, not just the physical body. As a result, they might devote themselves to psychology or psychiatry, perhaps the closest to the soul things you can find in the modern science. A good example is Alfred E. Adler[38], an Austrian neurologist and psychiatrist who was the director of the first child psychology clinic in Vienna.

Another excellent example is the famous Carl Gustav Jung[39], a Swiss psychiatrist and author, "noted as being an outstanding influence in the development of the theory and practice of analytical psychiatry, synchronicity, introvert-extrovert types, individuation and the personal-collective unconscious".

Or, here is a non-scientific example of a Moon-in-Taurus person

---

[37] http://www.astro.com/astro-databank/Addams,_Jane
[38] http://www.astro.com/astro-databank/Adler,_Alfred_E.
[39] http://www.astro.com/astro-databank/Jung,_Carl_Gustav

who cared very much about the soul: Mother Teresa[40], who through her service of universal love as a nun and missionary devoted her life to the poor and sick.

Beauty

Venus, the ruler of Taurus, often gives the Moon-in-Taurus people a talent in arts, a good understanding of beauty and value and an ability to create beautiful things. It is not surprising then that many of these people become famous painters, sculptors, or they might find some other way to make our world more beautiful. To give you just a few examples,

- Jean-Paul Gaultier[41], a French haute couture fashion designer.
- Marius Petipa[42], a French dancer and choreographer who "established the supremacy of the Imperial Russian Ballet, giving final polish to technique of the form known as classical ballet".
- Franz Lehar[43], a Hungarian writer and composer of light operas.
- Camille Saint-Saens[44], a French composer, organist and pianist who, as a child prodigy, was composing at the age of six and performing as a pianist by the age of ten.
- Agnes Anne Abbot[45], a German-American painter.
- Rene Charles Acht[46], a Swiss artist, painter, sculptor and art teacher.

---

[40] http://www.astro.com/astro-databank/Teresa,_Mother
[41] http://www.astro.com/astro-databank/Gaultier,_Jean-Paul
[42] http://www.astro.com/astro-databank/Petipa,_Marius
[43] http://www.astro.com/astro-databank/Lehar,_Franz
[44] http://www.astro.com/astro-databank/Saint-Saens,_Camille
[45] http://www.astro.com/astro-databank/Abbot,_Agnes_Anne
[46] http://www.astro.com/astro-databank/Acht,_Ren%C3%A9_Charles

- Michaelangelo Antonioni[47], an Italian film director who "had a profound impact on film sensibilities since the 60s".
- Demi Moore[48], an American actress and model.
- Greta Garbo[49], a Swedish-American actress, "one of the most magical and famous of the stars of the silver screen".
- Cameron Diaz[50], an American actress.

This list can go on and on, but I will leave the other examples for the Appendix C, go and explore it on your own.

Not only these people create beauty in the world but also, since the Moon is strongly associated with the body, they can be beautiful or physically attractive themselves. This is why a list like the one above will always contain many actresses, actors and models.

Voice

In the body, Taurus is associated primarily with the neck and throat, and this is exactly the area where vocal cords are located. It is not surprising then that the Moon in Taurus, in the sign of its exaltation (which is also ruled by Venus), very often gives a deep, beautiful voice. Just have a look at this list of famous singers who were born with the Moon in Taurus:

- Elton John[51], a British musician and rock superstar of immense appeal of the '70s, '80s, and '90s. "His frenetic, bisexual lifestyle has almost eclipsed his extravagant costuming and dynamic concert performances around the world".

---

[47]http://www.astro.com/astro-databank/Antonioni,_Michaelangelo
[48]http://www.astro.com/astro-databank/Moore,_Demi
[49]http://www.astro.com/astro-databank/Garbo,_Greta
[50]http://www.astro.com/astro-databank/Diaz,_Cameron
[51]http://www.astro.com/astro-databank/John,_Elton

- Mireille Mathieu[52], a French singer, "more than 120 million records sold worldwide".
- Diana Ross[53], an American singer and "Academy-Award nominated actress who was one-third of the elegant Supremes trio in the '60s and went on to become a superstar stylist on her own".
- Christina Aguilera[54], an American singer, a superstar by the age of 18. "In mid-2000, she appeared on the covers of both Rolling Stone and Seventeen magazines".
- Bob Dylan[55], an American musician, songwriter and poet, "called the Robert Burns of the pop revolution, and the most influential figure in the history of rock outside of Elvis Presley with over 36 albums and 300 songs".
- Mick Jagger[56], a British guitarist, musician and lead singer superstar with The Rolling Stones.
- Iggy Pop[57], an American musician, a punk rocker.

Storytelling

To be honest, I was surprised to see how many famous authors have their Moon in Taurus. Following astrological stereotypes, it would be more natural for all these authors to have their Moon in, say, communicative Gemini, or maybe in Aquarius, which has more patience to express complex ideas or scenarios. But no, it is the Moon in Taurus that gave the world some of the most prominent writers and poets:

---

[52]http://www.astro.com/astro-databank/Mathieu,_Mireille
[53]http://www.astro.com/astro-databank/Ross,_Diana
[54]http://www.astro.com/astro-databank/Aguilera,_Christina
[55]http://www.astro.com/astro-databank/Dylan,_Bob
[56]http://www.astro.com/astro-databank/Jagger,_Mick
[57]http://www.astro.com/astro-databank/Iggy_Pop

- F. Scott Fitzgerald[58], an American writer, a novelist, screenwriter and short story writer of the 1920s. Given that Taurus is strongly associated with wealth and money, it is interesting that "Totally charming with a strong desire for approval, he was always preoccupied with wealth and social status. His stories and novels dealt mainly with the rich whose intrigues and decadence fascinated the middle class".
- O. Henry[59], an American author, "one of America's favorite short story writers and one of the top selling writers of the early 20th century". Again, money played a role in his life too. O. Henry adopted this pen name, didn't allow to publish his photo and used to provide false biographical information because he wanted to hide from the world, and especially from his daughter, that he had a criminal record. According to Astro-Databank[60], "He had been indicted for embezzlement of bank funds in Austin, Texas and sent to a prison in Columbus, Ohio 1898 to 1901. He spent his three years in prison writing so he could earn money to support his daughter". Those who know a little bit more of astrology will be fascinated to find that O. Henry had his Moon in the 12th house of secrets and imprisonment.
- Marcel Proust[61], a French writer who is "classified as one of the greatest French novelists of the 1900's. An author of complex style, he was called immoral and decadent for several decades before he was recognized".
- Michel de Montaigne[62], a French writer and Renaissance man.
- Novalis[63], a German Romantic poet, author and philosopher who greatly influenced later Romantic thought.

---

[58] http://www.astro.com/astro-databank/Fitzgerald,_F._Scott
[59] http://www.astro.com/astro-databank/O._Henry
[60] http://www.astro.com/astro-databank/Main_Page?midx=2
[61] http://www.astro.com/astro-databank/Proust,_Marcel
[62] http://www.astro.com/astro-databank/Montaigne,_Michel_de
[63] http://www.astro.com/astro-databank/Novalis

- Hans Christian Andersen[64], a Danish writer of fairy-tale stories, plays, novels, poems and travel books.
- Ian Fleming[65], a British writer of adventure fiction, the creator of "James Bond".
- George Bernard Shaw[66], an Irish writer, novelist, critic and dramatist who was awarded the Nobel Prize for Literature in 1925.
- Alexandre Dumas[67], a French writer, one of the great French novelists and dramatists.
- Henrik Ibsen[68], a Norwegian writer, a dramatist considered to be the father of modern drama as he introduced realism into the theatre.
- John Milton[69], a British writer and poet who is best know for his "Paradise Lost", 1667. "His work is generally regarded as surpassed only by Shakespeare".
- Jean Jacques Rousseau[70], a Swiss philosopher, the most influential of the 18th century in political and social theory and in literature.

Another very interesting, although less famous, example is Queen Silver[71], an American prodigy, world famed by 14 for being an orator, philosopher, scientist and writer. "Brilliant, she wrote and delivered a series of science lectures explaining Einstein's theories". She also grew to become a feminist. Quite amazingly, Queen Silver seems to be her real name, and it is very much resonating with the Moon in Taurus. Indeed, the Moon is in exaltation in this sign (the queen), and the metal associated with the Moon is silver.

---

[64]http://www.astro.com/astro-databank/Andersen,_Hans_Christian
[65]http://www.astro.com/astro-databank/Fleming,_Ian
[66]http://www.astro.com/astro-databank/Shaw,_George_Bernard
[67]http://www.astro.com/astro-databank/Dumas,_Alexandre
[68]http://www.astro.com/astro-databank/Ibsen,_Henrik
[69]http://www.astro.com/astro-databank/Milton,_John
[70]http://www.astro.com/astro-databank/Rousseau,_Jean_Jacques
[71]http://www.astro.com/astro-databank/Silver,_Queen

Hindu Astrology (Jyotish) can help to understand why the Moon in Taurus is good for writing. According to Jyotish, the second house (and Taurus is the second sign of the zodiac, so it is similar to the second house) is associated with everything that comes out of the person's mouth, like speech and ability to transfer knowledge orally. Writers are actually storytellers, and the persistence and patience of the fixed sign Taurus gives them an ability to write thick books, while the ruler of Taurus Venus makes their words beautiful.

The Magic of Cooking

Moon-in-Taurus people enjoy their food, and very often they make great cooks. It is not clear how, but they always manage to do something wonderfully tasty from the simplest of the ingredients. The Moon is associated with the food while the ruler of Taurus Venus represents everything that is pleasant, beautiful and harmonically balanced, hence the talent to create delicious food.

An example of a Moon-in-Taurus celebrity chef is Giada De Laurentiis[72], an Italian-born American chef, writer, television personality, and the host of the current Food Network television program *Giada at Home*.

To be honest, you won't find many famous cooks with the Moon in Taurus. This is because the Moon-in-Taurus kind of food is typically simple, natural, home-made, like the simple Italian food for which Giada de Laurentiis became so famous. For most world-renown chiefs, it is more typical to have their Moon in the other Earth signs: Virgo (the mastership of ingredients, the technology of cooking), or Capricorn (career in cooking). Many of them also have their Moon in Aquarius (inventiveness in cooking) or Aries (quick cooking).

---

[72]http://en.wikipedia.org/wiki/Giada_De_Laurentiis

Money, Economy, and Politics

Taurus is strongly associated with values and money, and financial success and stability are very important for the Moon-in-Taurus individuals. Having enough money for the comforts that they value so highly is one of the top priorities in their lives. Also, this gives them the feeling of stability that they value very much.

On the greater scale of things, the sign of Taurus is associated with the economy. Quite naturally, one of the most prominent economists in human history, Karl Marx[73], was born with the Moon in Taurus.

Another Moon-in-Taurus individual, Conrad Hilton[74], can show an example of what to do with the money. He was an American entrepreneur, author and hotel magnate who "parlayed a $5,000 investment in 1918 into a hotel chain worth more than half a billion dollars".

There are also some negative examples, such as Bernie Madoff[75], a former American businessman, stockbroker, investment advisor, and financier. He is the former non-executive chairman of the NASDAQ stock market, and the admitted operator of a Ponzi scheme that is considered to be the largest financial fraud in US history.

The Moon is also associated with population in general and with public opinion, and since it is so strong in Taurus, we can find quite a few Moon-in-Taurus individuals who became prominent in politics. Some examples are:

- Samuel Adams[76], an American statesman, a founding father of the US and a signer of the Declaration of Independence.

---

[73] http://www.astro.com/astro-databank/Marx,_Karl
[74] http://www.astro.com/astro-databank/Hilton,_Conrad
[75] http://www.astro.com/astro-databank/Madoff,_Bernie
[76] http://www.astro.com/astro-databank/Adams,_Samuel

- Ronald Reagan[77], an American politician, elected US President on November 1980.
- Bill Clinton[78], a US President in whose career women (the Moon) played an important, although not always positive role.

Moon in Taurus in the Family

If your Moon is in Taurus, then most probably your parents' home is a place where you are happy to return again and again because you always felt yourself very comfortable there. Chances are that you have a strong connection with your mother and that your childhood was comfortable and happy.

Your mother made sure that you are well fed, comfortable and have everything you need, even if she didn't have plenty of money. You might have learnt cooking from one of your parents, and now you enjoy cooking for your own family too.

Becoming an adult, people born with the Moon in Taurus tend to recreate the best of what they experienced in their parental home in their own family. It is typical for them to have a strong family with plenty of attention given to the upbringing of children. Moon-in-Taurus parents like to care, feed, hug and kiss.

Recovering from Stress

When recovering from a significant stress, it is usually very important for a Moon-in-Taurus individual to eat something tasty. It can be also very helpful to physically relax in a comfortable environment, forget about the outside world and, ideally, have a relaxing massage. A good sex can be very helpful too.

---

[77]http://www.astro.com/astro-databank/Reagan,_Ronald
[78]http://www.astro.com/astro-databank/Clinton,_Bill

Shopping is another kind of therapy that can do miracles for Moon-in-Taurus people, especially if they can allow themselves something beautiful, valuable, or very tasty, something they always wanted to buy.

Health And Diet

Neck and throat are the sensitive areas of those born with the Moon in Taurus, so they should be careful eating an ice cream or having a cold drink on a hot summer day. In general, the Moon-in-Taurus physiology is a bit on the chilly side, so people born with the Moon in Taurus should always make sure that they are dressed warmly enough for the weather.

Also, although the Moon in Taurus is quite resistant to negative influences and so typically gives a stronger health than it would be otherwise, the taurean physiology is prone to stagnation. This is why it is important for those who were born with the Moon in Taurus to ensure that they have enough movement in their lives. It would be also very good and healthy for them to have some kind of massage regularly.

Spa treatment or sauna can also be very good for Moon-in-Taurus people. They are close to nature, often have a talent for gardening, and so regularly spending some time in the garden, or maybe walking in a field or forest will be highly desirable for maintaining and improving their health.

The ideal food for the Moon in Taurus should be tasty, very natural, with plenty of fruit and vegetable, and not too heavy. It is very important to not over-indulge in savoring food as the body typical for Moon in Taurus can gain weight easily, and then won't want to get rid of that extra weight no matter what.

Green salad should be a regular dish, and ideally the proportion of fruits and vegetables in a Moon-in-Taurus diet should be much higher than that of meat.

Dairy products are also usually very beneficial for the Moon in Taurus, but they should be fresh and natural. By natural, I mean that whole milk and proper butter will be much more desirable for such people than skimmed milk and a "healthy" imitation of butter, while popular in the West products with 0% fat should better be avoided.

A Surprise Moment

You will often read in astrological books that the Moon-in-Taurus people are very practical, pragmatic and down-to-earth, that they are generally skeptical and will be the last to believe in astrology or other subjects that don't fit into the procrustean bed of materialistic worldview.

It might come as a surprise then that some of the world's most prominent mystics were born with the Moon in Taurus:

- Edgar Cayce[79], an American mystic known as "The Sleeping Prophet". "While in a sleep state he could discuss history, geology, metaphysics, philosophy and medicine".
- Carlos Castañeda[80], a Peruvian-American anthropologist and mystic, the author of "The Teachings of Don Juan".
- Emanuel Swedenborg[81], a famous Swedish mystic, writer and educator, brilliant and eclectic student of fields that ranged from physics and astronomy to the Bible, seeking to find a Key to Everything.
- Jane Roberts[82], an American mystic, the author of the "Seth" books, dictated by a discarnate entity.

---

[79] http://www.astro.com/astro-databank/Cayce,_Edgar
[80] http://www.astro.com/astro-databank/Casta%C3%B1eda,_Carlos
[81] http://www.astro.com/astro-databank/Swedenborg,_Emanuel
[82] http://www.astro.com/astro-databank/Roberts,_Jane

Another interesting example that fits here well is Baruch Spinoza[83], a Dutch writer and philosopher, historically one the world's great minds. "Deeply religious, his pantheistic views upset both Christians and the Jews of his day; in many ways he was a mystic".

It is also interesting to note that Carl Gustav Jung, who was very interested in different aspects of esotericism, also had a psychic mother (and you remember that the Moon is strongly associated with the mother, don't you?), who had a major influence on him.

My understanding here is that the exaltation of the Moon in Taurus greatly amplifies all the attributes of the Moon, and since the Moon is strongly linked to the human unconsciousness, the link between intellect and the subconscious mind is very strong in Moon-in-Taurus people. Their intuition is powerful, and although unconsciously, they are strongly aware of the existence and reality of the invisible side of the world.

As a side note, I was fascinated to find that Louis de Broglie[84], the physicist and Nobel Prize winner who developed the Wave Theory and discovered the wave nature of the electron (thus proving that matter is just a form of energy) was born with the Moon in Taurus.

The next in the order of the zodiac comes Gemini, a sign which is very different from Taurus, so the next chapter will discuss what the Moon in Gemini is famous for.

---

[83]http://www.astro.com/astro-databank/Spinoza,_Baruch
[84]http://www.astro.com/astro-databank/Broglie,_Louis_de

The Moon in Gemini

Gemini is a mutable Air sign, ruled by Mercury, curious, changeable and adaptable, and if a person was born with the Moon in Gemini, this makes him or her witty, bright and genuinely interested in numerous things.

Mercury gives versatility, and the Moon-in-Gemini individuals can easily switch between a number of very different occupations, or even do them all simultaneously, in parallel. They are witty, communicative and are especially good in everything that requires quick mind and an ability to grasp information on the fly. They are eternal students, always studying this or that, or sometimes several subjects at once, through the whole their lives.

They are also often called eternal children, because irrespective of their age, they manage to keep a very youthful attitude to life: they are interested in everything, they want to know everything and everyone, they want to try everything, they are playing with things and people, they are joking about problems which would make other people seriously depressed. They also often look much younger than their peers.

On the other hand, being adult, they can easily establish a good contact with younger people, and therefore can become excellent teachers.

Changeable

The Moon-in-Gemini people are easily influenced by everything and everyone: news, rumors, other people's emotions and opinions. As a result, they can easily understand everyone and appreciate every point of view. However, they might find it difficult to figure out what's exactly *their own* point of view, or to concentrate on a complex subject for an extended period of time.

Scientists, philosophers, intellectuals

Mercury rules the intellect while the Moon is strongly connected to the subconscious, and when Mercury and the Moon cooperate, like in the case of people born with the Moon in Gemini, a sign ruled by Mercury, these two can give above the average mental abilities, good memory, excellent capacity for handling information. Such people prefer an analytical, logical approach to life, and so it isn't surprising that many scientists, philosophers and other intellectuals were born with the Moon in Gemini. Here are several examples from my collection:

- Johannes Kepler[85], a German author, mathematician, scientist, astronomer, court astrologer and teacher. *Known as "the father of modern astronomy", he discovered the three laws of planetary motion that paved the way a half century later for Newton's laws of universal gravitation. The leading astronomical theorist for over 400 years, he was regarded as having "one foot in medieval mysticism and one foot in the scientific method".*
- Sigmund Freud[86], an Austrian psychiatrist, known as the father of psychoanalysis. Quite interestingly, psychoanalysis is symbolically very appropriate for the Moon in Gemini, as it is an intellectual, verbal, analytical (Mercury, Gemini) approach to analysing the contents of the soul (the Moon).
- Pierre Teilhard De Chardin[87], a French paleontologist and Jesuit priest known for scientific and genetic research and

---

[85] http://www.astro.com/astro-databank/Kepler,_Johannes
[86] http://www.astro.com/astro-databank/Freud,_Sigmund
[87] http://www.astro.com/astro-databank/Teilhard_De_Chardin,_Pierre

for philosophical works on the meaning of evolution and the future of mankind.
- Edward Teller[88], a Hungarian-American theoretical physicist, known colloquially as "the father of the hydrogen bomb".
- Christopher Wren[89], a British architect, one of the most famous, who designed Saint Paul's Cathedral and more than 50 other London churches after the great London fire of 1666.
- Nicholas Culpeper[90], a British physician of the 17th century who is best remembered for his "Culpeper's Herbal", a compendium of natural healing that remained the standard text for over three centuries. This book was written in plain English and was addressed to common people, unlike most of the medical books of Culpeper's time that were available only in Latin. We can sense the prominence of Mercury and Gemini here (language, communication).

Commerce

Mercury is the god of trade and commerce, and the Moon-in-Gemini people can indeed be very good in those areas. John D. Rockefeller Sr.[91] is a great example here. He was an American industrialist and founder of Standard Oil enterprise and of the first great American oil fortune. "The son of a penniless, bigamous con man and patent-medicine salesman, he turned his shady family name into a synonym for prodigious wealth and worldly success".

---

[88]http://www.astro.com/astro-databank/Teller,_Edward
[89]http://www.astro.com/astro-databank/Wren,_Christopher
[90]http://www.astro.com/astro-databank/Culpeper,_Nicholas
[91]http://www.astro.com/astro-databank/Rockefeller_Sr.,_John_D.

Quick

The Moon-in-Gemini folks usually do everything quickly: they think quickly, they react and move quickly, they are agile and flexible. Naturally, many of them select an occupation in which they can put their abilities to good use. Here are a few examples:

- Jackie Chan[92], a Chinese master of martial arts.
- Jose Raul Capablanca[93], a Cuban chess master and a champion.
- Steffi Graf[94], a German tennis phenomenon, winning 11 of 13 tournaments in 1987 to become the top ranking woman tennis player.

Always on the move

It is typical for the Moon-in-Gemini individuals to move a lot in their lives. It can start from an early childhood if the parents' family had to move from place to place on some reason, or it can come later in life, but they just love having a kaleidoscope of places, faces and impressions around them, so they might prefer to keep moving on and on. They might also choose a career or a lifestyle that will keep them always on the move. They can feel themselves at home just about everywhere. A couple of examples from my collection are:

- Amelia Earhart[95], an American aviator pioneer and author, an historic adventurer in her 16-year-career.
- Sam Abell[96], an American photographer who worked for National Geographic Society since 1970.

---

[92]http://www.astro.com/astro-databank/Chan,_Jackie
[93]http://www.astro.com/astro-databank/Capablanca,_Jose_Raul
[94]http://www.astro.com/astro-databank/Graf,_Steffi
[95]http://www.astro.com/astro-databank/Earhart,_Amelia
[96]http://www.astro.com/astro-databank/Abell,_Sam

Charming

A Moon-in-Gemini person can easily find common language with anyone, and not only at the level of words and ideas but also at the level of emotions. This is why they can often be so emotionally appealing, so easily charming, and they know very well what people want to hear and feel. Many actors, singers, artists and other creative people benefit from having Gemini for their Moon Sign. Some examples are:

- Tina Turner[97], an American singer with enormous energy and talent.
- Omar Sharif[98], an Egyptian-American actor, an elegant and handsome screen lover.
- Jean Gabin[99], a French actor, distinguished and handsome, internationally known.
- Kirk Douglas[100], an American actor, on-screen from 1946 in some 82 films: thrillers, westerns and costume epics.
- Brooke Shields[101], an American actress and model.
- Albrecht Dürer[102], a German artist, a painter, engraver and designer, draftsman and theorist, one of foremost artists of the Renaissance.
- Auguste Rodin[103], a French artist, one of the world's master sculptors whose work influenced countless other artists in the late nineteenth and early twentieth century.

---

[97] http://www.astro.com/astro-databank/Turner,_Tina
[98] http://www.astro.com/astro-databank/Sharif,_Omar
[99] http://www.astro.com/astro-databank/Gabin,_Jean
[100] http://www.astro.com/astro-databank/Douglas,_Kirk
[101] http://www.astro.com/astro-databank/Shields,_Brooke
[102] http://www.astro.com/astro-databank/D%C3%BCrer,_Albrecht
[103] http://www.astro.com/astro-databank/Rodin,_Auguste

Musicians

Writing music can be a perfect occupation for a Gemini Moon as on one hand music is akin to mathematics, while on the other hand it is addressed to people's souls. No doubt many composers and musicians were born with the Moon in Gemini, here is just a few of them from my collection:

- Antonin Dvorak[104], a Czech composer, a teacher and a violinist.
- Herbert von Karajan[105], an Austrian conductor, pianist and recording artist.
- Franz Joseph Haydn[106], an Austrian child prodigy and prolific composer. The bulk of his work from 1777-1790 included 125 symphonies and overtures, 76 quartets, 68 trios, 54 sonatas, 31 concertos, 24 operas, 14 masses, 22 arias and more.

Versatile

You might have already noticed that quite often the Moon-in-Gemini individuals achieve success in more than one field. These two are, in my opinion, great examples of Mercury's versatility:

- Miuccia Prada[107], an Italian noted fashion designer. Prada trained briefly as an actress and earned her PhD in Political Science.
- Marcel Achard[108], a French writer and director, also a playwright and screenwriter of highly popular comedies for 50

---

[104]http://www.astro.com/astro-databank/Dvorak,_Antonin
[105]http://www.astro.com/astro-databank/Karajan,_Herbert_von
[106]http://www.astro.com/astro-databank/Haydn,_Franz_Joseph
[107]http://www.astro.com/astro-databank/Prada,_Miuccia
[108]http://www.astro.com/astro-databank/Achard,_Marcel

years from his first success in 1923. Before his first play in 1922, he was a teacher and journalist.

Humor

And of course, many of the Moon-in-Gemini individuals possess a great sense of humor. One good example is Billy Connolly[109], a Scottish actor and comedian. "Originally an anarchic folk singer, Billy was too eccentric and outrageous with his humor to be acceptable on TV".

They can be very funny, and often can mock other people easily.

The Moon in Gemini in the Family

The Moon-in-Gemini people are usually born in families where there is a lot of communication between family members. There were probably plenty of friends, guests and all sorts of relatives in the house at any given time, and parents themselves, especially the mother were of such a disposition that it was very easy to discuss with them absolutely anything, no limits, no complexes.

A Moon-in-Gemini mother is actually more like a sister, she can excitedly discuss with her kids the latest computer games and gadgets, help them to do their homework, or to prepare for a date. On the other hand, she might be not that good with cooking, caring and nurturing, as those are all such boring things for a Gemini.

A Moon-in-Gemini parent is easy to speak to but he or she might find it difficult to understand the depth of feelings of some other Moon Signs. So depending on what are the Moon Signs of their kids, the deceptive easiness of communication of the Moon in Gemini can seem to them superficial and unsatisfactory. The Moon in Gemini

---

[109]http://www.astro.com/astro-databank/Connolly,_Billy

doesn't like emotional dramas and believes that everything can be discussed logically and rationally, and every problem can be resolved that way.

Nevertheless, the Moon-in-Gemini parents will teach their kids to understand other people, to be knowledgeable and interested in everything that's happening in the world, while children with the Moon in Gemini usually start speaking earlier than their peers, can have a talent in acting and foreign languages, as well as a thirst for knowledge. Many of them will find nursery school very limiting, as they will probably already know what will be taught there.

The Moon-in-Gemini kids will keep their parents busy asking them numerous questions, demanding to read them a book, but they can also be easily satisfied by a computer game or an interesting gadget.

Recovering From Stress

To recover from a significant stress, it is very important for a Moon-in-Gemini individual to have a good chat, as if to speak away the disturbing energy overfilling his or her system. Unlike many other people, they won't enjoy peace and quiet, and will instead throw a party, invite many friends and have fun.

It is also great if such an individual has a hobby or a particular interest, since switching their attention to that interesting topic will help to quickly forget a disturbing experience and to direct an excess of energy into something useful and enjoyable.

Health and Diet

Fresh air is of utmost importance for the Moon-in-Gemini people as their lungs and air passages are typically quite sensitive. Living in a countryside would be very healthy for them, but unfortunately it isn't possible in a village to achieve the intensity of information exchange desired by these individuals. They will definitely prefer to live somewhere in the city with a super-fast wi-fi connection permanently available and all kinds of transport within an easy reach. If that's the case, then they should still find a way, as frequently as possible, to take with them all their friends and go for a weekend to a place with an unspoiled atmosphere. A fresh sea breeze or the fragrant air of a forest will have a miraculous healing effect on them.

Needless to say that smoking is even more detrimental for those born with the Moon in Gemini than for most other people.

The wellbeing of their nervous system is also very important for the Moon-in-Gemini people. They can usually function very well in highly stressful situations when the main workload is about handling some kind of information. However, if the atmosphere is highly emotionally charged, or there is some threat, or something else that makes them uncomfortable, these usually very capable people can become surprisingly vulnerable and prone to nervous breakdowns. If that happens, they might require a lot of time (and fresh air) to recover. Their system isn't very strong physically, it's just very flexible and highly adaptable.

Breathing exercises, like those of Pranayama, can be very important for the Moon in Gemini people, although it should be mentioned that to really succeed in Pranayama one should have a qualified and experienced instructor.

Diet-wise, the Moon-in-Gemini individuals can be very adaptable, and their inborn curiosity can move them to try many different kinds of food. It would be good for them to prefer warm, nutritious kinds of food with substantial amounts of natural fat. Dry, cold, processed foods can make these people more nervous, worried and generally unhappy.

A Surprise Moment

There is a common stereotype that people with strong Gemini (which includes those having their Moon in Gemini) are quite superficial, and too changeable to do something large-scale, something that requires a prolonged effort and ability to coordinate complex plans. It can come as a surprise then how many Moon-in-Gemini individuals became prominent politicians, and not just politicians but world leaders who left a very important trace in the history of their countries and nations. Just have a look at the list of examples that follows:

- Simon Bolivar[110], a Venezuelan military hero called "The Liberator". Bolivar led revolutions against the Spanish in New Granada (renamed Colombia in 1819, it included Venezuela and Ecuador), Peru and Upper Peru (Bolivia). He was president of Colombia from 1821-30 and Peru from 1823-29.
- Barack Obama[111], an American President elected in 2008, and then again in 2012, lawyer, and civil rights activist.
- Catherine the Great[112], a Prussian-Russian Empress, one of the most powerful and memorable in history.
- Giuseppe Garibaldi[113], an Italian military leader, born in France, who was instrumental in winning the freedom of Italy.
- Giulio Andreotti[114], an Italian politician, prime minister seven times, high-ranking minister to most of Italy's 50-odd Cabinets since WW II, devout acquaintance of five Popes, and close acquaintance of American presidents from Eisenhower to Bush.

---

[110]http://www.astro.com/astro-databank/Bolivar,_Simon
[111]http://www.astro.com/astro-databank/Obama,_Barack
[112]http://www.astro.com/astro-databank/Catherine_the_Great,_Empress
[113]http://www.astro.com/astro-databank/Garibaldi,_Giuseppe
[114]http://www.astro.com/astro-databank/Andreotti,_Giulio

- Bernard Baruch[115], an American financier and statesman, a political power-broker who served as an unpaid advisor to seven U.S. Presidents.
- David Ben-Gurion[116], an Israeli politician, one of the founders of the country and the first Prime Minister in 1973.
- Helmut Kohl[117], a German politician and chancellor of Germany, with 16 years of service. Kohl reached his peak in 1990, nicknamed "King Kohl", and is considered to be the father of German reunification.

In fact, the enormous influence gained by some Moon-in-Gemini politicians shouldn't be surprising. The Moon is strongly associated with the public, with population in general, and Gemini helps to understand very well the feelings and emotions of the masses of people, as also gives an ability to speak to people simply and convincingly.

In the next sign of the zodiac the Moon has its home - that will be the Moon in Cancer.

[115] http://www.astro.com/astro-databank/Baruch,_Bernard
[116] http://www.astro.com/astro-databank/Ben-Gurion,_David
[117] http://www.astro.com/astro-databank/Kohl,_Helmut

The Moon in Cancer

Cancer is a cardinal Water sign, ruled by the Moon itself, so the Moon is at home in this sign, and its qualities and attributes work here most powerfully and naturally.

Mysterious

To better understand the element of Water, imagine a body of water - a lake, or a sea, or an ocean. There isn't usually much happening at the surface, if only some waves, but you can be sure that there is a significant depth, and plenty of life below the surface.

Similarly, people born with the Moon in a Water sign can seem calm and serene from the outside while there is always a lot of what is happening inside of them. They might be daydreaming, or they might be struggling with some complex powerful emotions - you never know. They are mysterious, and they are definitely not the type of people with whom "what you see is what you get".

The Moon-in-Cancer people are quite sensitive to the natural rhythms, especially those of the Moon, and so can be subject to unexpected changes of mood and behavior that don't seem to be caused by any external events. It would be good for them to know about the Moon's phases, at the very least, and plan their life accordingly. See a later chapter *The Moon Signs in Daily Life* for more information on the daily influences of the Moon.

The Moon is deeply rooted in the subconscious, and so these individuals are strongly influenced by traditions and old memories, even perhaps - who knows? - the memories of their ancestors, or the memories from the past lives.

It is believed that the Moon in Cancer can give some people mediumistic abilities, and I do know one medium with the Moon in Cancer.

Fast and Unexpected

Cancer is a cardinal sign, which means it tends to do something actively in the outside world. Since the motivations of Water are always hidden below the surface, the Moon-in-Cancer individuals often act unexpectedly for the surrounding people, and their actions might seem irrational (as they usually are, since they are driven by deep and complex emotions rather than logical reasoning).

One example of how fast a Moon-in-Cancer individual can be is the famous Michael Schumacher[118], a German race car driver, the pilot of a Ferrari in Formula One.

The Moon-in-Cancer kids can develop quicker than their peers. For example, Shakira[119], a Colombian singer-songwriter and a world famous pop star, wrote her first poem at the age of four, and her first song at the age of eight. She was strongly influenced by her father in her early life. As you'll find out in a later section, it is very typical for Moon-in-Cancer children to be strongly influenced by at least one of their parents.

Deep

The Moon is tightly linked to the subconscious, and since she is so strong in her own sign in Cancer, the life of those born with the Moon in this sign is strongly influenced by the contents of the collective and individual subconscious: past memories, suppressed desires, archetypal images. These people understand and intuitively

---
[118]http://www.astro.com/astro-databank/Schumacher,_Michael
[119]http://www.astro.com/astro-databank/Shakira

feel a lot, but it is often difficult for them to fully express their understanding in words. Nevertheless, strong Moon can give them deep knowledge and unusual abilities. Here are a few interesting personalities, to illustrate the point:

- Padre Pio[120], an Italian healer, a Capuchin monk and stigmatic. "He was a special, unique case as he was the first priest 'marked by God' in two thousand years. Nuns, monks and even lay persons have experienced the stigmata but never a consecrated priest. His phenomena was witnessed and reported by tens of thousands of people".
- Sri Sathya Sai Baba[121], an Indian traditional guru, a healer known for his remarkable physical manifestations.
- Ramana Maharishi[122], an Indian mystic of the Hindu religion who, after a mystical experience at age 17, left his parents to become an ascetic.
- Annie Besant[123], a prominent British theosophist, author and feminist. I've noticed that prominent feminists often have a very strong Moon, such as the Moon in Cancer, in its home, or in Taurus, its exaltation. This is symbolically very appropriate as the Moon is a symbol for the feminine.
- Steve Wozniak[124], an American entrepreneur, a self-taught computer engineer who designed virtually the entire product line that enabled Apple Corporation to go from a two-man garage operation to a half-billion dollar a year business in six years.

Whatever they do (and you can certainly find some distinguished Moon-in-Cancer individuals in every profession) is deep, and often has a strong connection to some kind of mystery.

---

[120] http://www.astro.com/astro-databank/Pio,_Padre
[121] http://www.astro.com/astro-databank/Sai_Baba,_Sri_Sathya
[122] http://www.astro.com/astro-databank/Ramana_Maharishi
[123] http://www.astro.com/astro-databank/Besant,_Annie
[124] http://www.astro.com/astro-databank/Wozniak,_Steve

Scientists

Contemporary science is all about logic, statistics and objective proof, so can really some Moon-in-Cancer individuals, with their deep, intuitive, irrational understanding, achieve anything in this kind of science? Let's see:

- Isaac Newton[125], a British astronomer, physicist, mathematician and astrologer who showed how the universe is held together. Newton is often described as one of the greatest names in the history of human thought. He is considered to be the father of mechanics, perhaps the most sticks-and-stones kind of science, but at the same time he was a devoted alchemist, very active in alchemical research. Not with the purpose of making gold of course - true alchemy is all about the mysteries of nature.
- Elisabeth Kübler-Ross[126], a Swiss psychiatrist and author who is noted for her work with death and the dying. Death is the ultimate mystery for human beings, and the Moon-in-Cancer people often understand intuitively that life doesn't end with the end of the physical body.
- Robert Oppenheimer[127], an American scientist, a nuclear physicist and head of the Atomic Energy Commission's General Advisory Committee 1947-1952. He was known as the "father of the atom bomb" (which is already interesting as the Moon in Cancer is strongly associated with parental figures). Nuclear physics is perhaps the most mysterious of the modern sciences as it tells us, ultimately, that the world as we know it doesn't really exist.

---

[125]http://www.astro.com/astro-databank/Newton,_Isaac
[126]http://www.astro.com/astro-databank/K%C3%BCbler-Ross,_Elisabeth
[127]http://www.astro.com/astro-databank/Oppenheimer,_Robert

Writers and poets

Expressing their ideas in words can prove to be difficult for the Moon-in-Cancer individuals, but you can't avoid doing that if you are a writer or a poet. As a result, the writings of these people can often be unusual in one or another way, just because all the richness of content can't be easily squeezed into the Procrustean bed of words. Those writings can be somewhat quirky, or they might feel like a stream of steam from an overheated boiler, or they can be full of strange complex images rooted in the subconscious. Here are a few Moon-in-Cancer writers and poets from my collection:

- George Orwell[128], a British novelist and essayist who *won his greatest success in 1946 with his amusing and witty anti-communist satire, "Animal Farm", and in 1949 with his shocking and insightful futuristic novel, "1984".*
- Guy de Maupassant[129], a French author "of vivid and brutal short stories that made him popular to his readers. Writing with a terse, biting and impersonal style, he was richly dramatic in effect".
- Thomas Mann[130], a German writer, the author of novels, plays and essays. According to Wikipedia[131], he was "known for his series of highly symbolic and ironic epic novels and novellas, noted for their insight into the psychology of the artist and the intellectual".
- Charles Baudelaire[132], a French poet "tormented by religion and the struggle between good and evil in man, suffused with his deeply Catholic sense of sin and remorse".

---

[128]http://www.astro.com/astro-databank/Orwell,_George
[129]http://www.astro.com/astro-databank/Maupassant,_Guy_de
[130]http://www.astro.com/astro-databank/Mann,_Thomas
[131]http://en.wikipedia.org/wiki/Thomas_mann
[132]http://www.astro.com/astro-databank/Baudelaire,_Charles

Musicians

Music can be an easier way for the Moon-in-Cancer people to express their ideas as it doesn't require words, and so there are many musicians under this Moon Sign even in my limited collection. Still, music has its own rules and logic, and to make it suitable for the complexity of their images, the Moon-in-Cancer musicians might need to bend the existing rules, or push their limits by becoming geniuses. Here are some examples:

- Yo-Yo Ma[133], a French-American cellist, praised for his extraordinary technique and rich tone.
- Niccolo Paganini[134], an Italian composer and virtuoso instrumentalist who made his violin concert debut in Genoa at age nine. From the age of 13, he had one triumphant concert tour after another.
- Kurt Cobain[135], an American musician, *lead singer whose anguished lyrics helped sell millions of records featuring the gritty sound of grunge rock 'n roll of "Nirvana", a head banging punk metal band formed in 1991.*
- Igor Stravinsky[136], a Russian composer and conductor, considered by many to be one of the greatest and most versatile composers of the twentieth century.
- Claude Debussy[137], a French composer and pianist. A musical genius, his works are as fresh and current today as when he first founded the impressionist school.
- Giacomo Puccini[138], an Italian opera composer *of bold and dramatic harmonies.*

---

[133]http://www.astro.com/astro-databank/Yo-Yo_Ma
[134]http://www.astro.com/astro-databank/Paganini,_Niccolo
[135]http://www.astro.com/astro-databank/Cobain,_Kurt
[136]http://www.astro.com/astro-databank/Stravinsky,_Igor
[137]http://www.astro.com/astro-databank/Debussy,_Claude
[138]http://www.astro.com/astro-databank/Puccini,_Giacomo

- Julio Iglesias[139], a Spanish singer known as the master of the love song. The world's top selling living pop star, Iglesias has sold a Guinness record of 100 million albums worldwide.
- Jascha Heifetz[140], a Lithuanian-American musician who was a world famous violinist who played as a soloist with virtually all of the world's great orchestras.

Actors

Acting is yet another profession where the Moon is Cancer can make a great impact, as people of this Moon Sign have a powerful imagination, and they know very well how to touch other people's feelings and emotions. A few examples are:

- Bo Derek[141], an American actress.
- Luc Besson[142], a French director.
- Keanu Reeves[143], a Lebanese-American actor, "parlayed his non-communicative and dead-pan style into being one of the highest paid actors in his generation in 11 years".
- Liza Minnelli[144], an American singer and actress.

Politicians

Strong Moon is very important for politicians. The Moon is associated in astrology with large amounts of people, with population in general, and with popularity too. In addition, the Moon is both the public and the personal unconscious, and these two are connected at

---

[139] http://www.astro.com/astro-databank/Iglesias,_Julio
[140] http://www.astro.com/astro-databank/Heifetz,_Jascha
[141] http://www.astro.com/astro-databank/Derek,_Bo
[142] http://www.astro.com/astro-databank/Besson,_Luc
[143] http://www.astro.com/astro-databank/Reeves,_Keanu
[144] http://www.astro.com/astro-databank/Minnelli,_Liza

the deep level. The Moon in Cancer helps politicians to understand what people want at that deep level, to act accordingly and to become popular.

As the Moon in Cancer is also very much family-oriented, I was amazed to discover that three of some of the most prominent of the US politicians and public figures came from the same family and at the same time share the same Moon Sign: all three were born with the Moon in Cancer. Here they are:

- Theodore Roosevelt[145], the youngest, 26th President of the United States, from 1901 to 1909, a fifth cousin to the 32nd President of the United States, Franklin Delano Roosevelt, and the uncle and guardian of Franklin's wife, Anna Eleanor Roosevelt.
- Franklin D. Roosevelt[146], the 32nd US President, the only one to serve four terms.
- Eleanor Roosevelt[147], an American First Lady, the wife of Franklin D. Roosevelt.

This "family presidential business" is especially meaningful since the zodiacal sign of Cancer is very important in the astrology of the United States of America. Suffice to say that the Independence Day is celebrated on the 4th of July, when the Sun is in Cancer.

Another important US public figure with the Moon in Cancer is Condoleezza Rice[148], a government aide who became President George W. Bush's National Security Advisor on January 22, 2001. "Intelligent, articulate, self-confident, and attractive, she is the first woman and second African-American to hold that position".

---

[145] http://www.astro.com/astro-databank/Roosevelt,_Teddy
[146] http://www.astro.com/astro-databank/Roosevelt,_Franklin_D.
[147] http://www.astro.com/astro-databank/Roosevelt,_Eleanor
[148] http://www.astro.com/astro-databank/Rice,_Condoleezza

One other example of a powerful and influential Moon-in-Cancer individual can be appropriate here: Edmond de Rothschild[149], a French financier and member of the legendary Rothschild banking family. Baron Edmond was noted for working rather independently from the other members of his family, and he was rumored to be the wealthiest.

The Moon in Cancer in the Family

Being in its home sign, the Moon in Cancer gives people a very strong parenting, caring, nurturing instincts, which is especially strong in women but can be quite noticeable in men too.

The Moon-in-Cancer people are excellent parents who are especially good with small children. As children grow and develop a desire for independency, such parents' powerful love can become smothering. The time when children leave home to live their own lives can be the most challenging for a Moon-in-Cancer parent.

The strong emotional bond of the Moon in Cancer works the other way around too. Children born with the Moon in Cancer usually develop a strong dependency on their parents and might be unwilling to start living their own lives. They can select a partner who emotionally resembles one of the parents, typically the mother. They can also be looking for parent-like figures everywhere in their lives, especially if they weren't very lucky with their own parents.

One should never underestimate the power of the parenting and nurturing instinct of the Moon in Cancer, as it will always find one or another way to express itself. I know a Moon-in-Cancer man who was never kind with his children and who is now, in his late 70s, spends a large portion of his time and budget to feed stray dogs in the surrounding forests, and he shares his apartment with a bunch of those dogs.

---

[149]http://www.astro.com/astro-databank/Rothschild,_Edmond_de

The Moon-in-Cancer people are also very good with the home chores, like cooking, cleaning or washing. Their home is the most important place in their life, and they want everything to be perfect there. They are very capable carers too, and not only with kids but with elderly or disabled people as well. They assume responsibility for the whole household and become the Matriarch, or the Patriarch of it.

They are also very protective for their children and other family members and can be insanely brave fighting off an attack on them - real or imagined.

Recovering From Stress

For every Moon-in-Cancer individual, it is very important to have his or her private space, their own home which belongs only to them and to nobody else. One of my Moon-in-Cancer friends lived with his family in a tiny flat where everybody had to share the same room for the whole day. So he moved around the furniture to create some empty space behind a wardrobe, and that was his own private home where he used to hide when not feeling well or being tired or stressed.

It is very important for the Moon-in-Cancer individuals to have such a private space. This is where they can heal themselves after even the most disturbing influences. Their body and soul are usually strong enough to self-heal, they just need a safe haven where the self-healing could take place. They are actually quite good at creating a space that feels like home - even in an office - if the surroundings are friendly enough for them.

As Cancer is a Water sign, people born with the Moon in Cancer can rely on water for carrying away their troubles. A bath or a shower can be very helpful for recovering from minor stresses while in case of a major stress a spa treatment at a seaside resort can bring the desired relief.

Health and Diet

The Moon in Cancer is quite strong and efficient when it comes to keeping and restoring health but it needs a proper emotional atmosphere to unleash its powers. This is why the advice about having a private space is important here too. Emotional security is of utmost importance to the Moon-in-Cancer people.

Living by a body of water, such as a river or an ocean, can be very beneficial for them as that water will invisibly but reliably, day-by-day, carry away their emotional troubles, especially if they have a river or a sea view from their home.

Stomach and digestion in general are very sensitive areas if a person was born with the Moon in Cancer, and so having a healthy diet can be more important for such a person than it is for many other people.

The Moon in Cancer diet should be simple, natural and traditional, with plenty of dairy products if possible. Exotic, innovative, experimental dishes are not really appropriate for this Moon Sign whereas something home made, cooked by the mother or grandmother will be not only healthy from purely nutritional point of view but will also give some invisible support on a much deeper level.

The Moon-in-Cancer people can be excellent cooks themselves, especially with those dishes which are traditionally cooked in their family, but they should never cook when in a bad mood.

As the Moon is associated with both the stomach and the emotions, it can be typical for the Moon-in-Cancer individuals to compensate for the lack of pleasant emotions by the abundance of tasty food; therefore they can easily gain weight during stressful periods of their lives. It would be much healthier if they could pacify their emotions in some other way.

Meditation can be wholeheartedly recommended to those who were born with the Moon in Cancer as a way to restore their emotional balance and even, if practiced regularly, to improve health.

A Surprise Moment

There is a common stereotype about people with strong Cancer that although they certainly do appreciate beautiful things, their understanding of beauty is somewhat peculiar. Like they might adore the table cloth left from the grandmother, or a particular wallpaper design which went out of fashion a few decades ago. In short, they aren't usually trend setters when it comes to fashion and beauty.

However, I was pleased to discover that many Moon-in-Cancer people do not actually fit this stereotype. Just look at this list of the Moon-in-Cancer celebrities:

- Franco Moschino[150], an Italian fashion designer whose styles are avant-garde and popular with the rebellious pop-culture.
- Giorgio Armani[151], an Italian designer and award-winning top star who created a fashion empire in 15 years.
- Christian Dior[152], a French couturier; the creator of the "New Look" style in Parisian design after the WWII.

The next after Cancer is the regal sign of Leo, and so the next chapter will discuss the gifts and talents of those who were born with the Moon in Leo.

[150] http://www.astro.com/astro-databank/Moschino,_Franco
[151] http://www.astro.com/astro-databank/Armani,_Giorgio
[152] http://www.astro.com/astro-databank/Dior,_Christian

The Moon in Leo

Leo is a fixed Fire sign ruled by the Sun. Fire can be associated with energy, creativity, ideas, and in case of Leo this is a very stable and reliable Fire, akin to the eternal fire of the Sun itself.

When a person is born with the Moon in the sign of Leo, everything which is associated with the Moon - emotions, subconsciousness, physiology, family relationships and so on - becomes filled with the powerful energy of the Sun, and this might be not a very easy combination. In Nature, the Moon only reflects the light of the Sun - more or less of it, depending on the phase. But when the Moon is in Leo, it becomes itself a little bit like the Sun. Think about it: the symbol of the feminine, the Moon, becomes like the symbol of the masculine, the Sun.

This can be good for men, as the Moon in Leo can make them brighter, more creative and powerful. It might be also great for many women - especially those who want to prove themselves in life, to achieve a top position in society, to shine in their profession, to become a celebrity.

However, a girl born with the Moon in Leo is a queen, and a queen might find it difficult to enjoy occupations that are traditionally considered as feminine: caring for children, doing the household chores, cleaning, washing... And if there is more than one queen in a family or a team, that can become a real problem!

The Moon-in-Leo people are creative. Their mind is full of bright images and sparkling ideas. They are generous, affectionate, but they also have a very important need - to be loved! If they are not loved and appreciated, they feel miserable, can be prone to depression and might even develop physical problems.

They are also proud, and they want to be praised for what they do.

As a result, they will never do something formally, just to get rid of it, but will rather put their soul into every accomplishment, make it very special, truly of their own.

Actors

Most Moon-in-Leo individuals adore being on the stage or in front of a camera - this is where their talents can be noticed, finally! Therefore, we can find many actors and actresses who have Leo for their Moon Sign. Here is a small selection of them:

- Clint Eastwood[153], an American actor in tough-guy roles (you remember that the ruler of Leo, the Sun, is a symbol of the masculine, right?).
- Marlene Dietrich[154], a German-American actress and singer who "achieved 62 years of international fame as an immortal screen goddess in German and American films". Well, "an immortal goddess" resonates with the Moon in Leo very well.
- Tom Hanks[155], an American actor and film producer. I was interested to find out that among many of his awards there are a few Golden Globes - that sounds very much like the Moon in Leo, considering that gold is the metal of the Sun!
- Peter Ustinov[156], a British actor who won two Best Supporting Actor Oscars for his roles. He was also a writer, a dramatist, a filmmaker, theatre and opera director, stage designer, screenwriter, comedian, humorist, newspaper and magazine columnist, radio broadcaster and television presenter. Such a fountain of creativity!

---

[153]http://www.astro.com/astro-databank/Eastwood,_Clint
[154]http://www.astro.com/astro-databank/Dietrich,_Marlene
[155]http://www.astro.com/astro-databank/Hanks,_Tom
[156]http://www.astro.com/astro-databank/Ustinov,_Peter

- Barbra Streisand[157], an American singer-songwriter and actress, as well as writer, film producer, and director. According to Wikipedia[158], she is "one of the few entertainers who have won an Oscar, Emmy, Grammy, and Tony Award".
- Jane Fonda[159], an American actress who "at times has been a sexpot, a feminist, a political activist, a maker of exercise videos, businesswoman, philanthropist and wife to famous men". What a wonderful collection of different manifestations of the Moon in Leo!

Writers and Poets

Love is so important for the Moon in Leo, and who can better speak about love if not poets. Many of the Moon-in-Leo writers and poets are also dramatists or playwrights, or they can be very interesting personalities, and there might be some other way how the light of the Sun ruling Leo shines through them. Here are some examples from my collection:

- Paul Verlaine[160], a French poet "famous for symbolism, subtle tenderness and delicate quality".
- Oscar Wilde[161], an Irish-British writer, poet and dramatist who had a great wit.
- Jack London[162], an American writer of 46 adventure tales and hundreds of short stories.
- Kurt Vonnegut[163], an American writer, a master of science fiction.

---

[157] http://www.astro.com/astro-databank/Streisand,_Barbra
[158] https://en.wikipedia.org/wiki/Barbra_Streisand
[159] http://www.astro.com/astro-databank/Fonda,_Jane
[160] http://www.astro.com/astro-databank/Verlaine,_Paul
[161] http://www.astro.com/astro-databank/Wilde,_Oscar
[162] http://www.astro.com/astro-databank/London,_Jack
[163] http://www.astro.com/astro-databank/Vonnegut,_Kurt

- Antoine de Saint-Exupéry[164], a French pilot and writer who influenced the world of aviation literature with his novels.
- Friedrich von Schiller[165], a German playwright and poet, ranking next to Goethe as the greatest dramatist of his time.
- Alexandre Dumas, fils[166], a French playwright and novelist.
- Richard Bach[167], an American writer who "published four books on his life passion, flying, with moderate success. He leaped to fame with his simple, short and inspirational allegory, 'Jonathan Livingston Seagull', first published in August 1970, with a small print run and little promotional efforts. It became a runaway best seller by word of mouth, though Bach, reportedly a direct descendant of Johann Sebastian Bach, insisted it was more of a visionary gift than something he personally wrote".

Composers and Musicians

Music is a great way to express one's creativity and to allow one's soul sing, and of course, many Moon-in-Leo individuals chose music for self-expression. Note that there are two of the Beatles who had Leo for their Moon Sign, and one of them was the co-author of "All You Need Is Love"!

- Jean Sibelius[168], a Finnish composer, the best-known symphonic composer of Scandinavia and one of the most original musical figures of the 20th century.
- George Michael[169], a Greek-British singer and songwriter, "always bearded with stubble and a tough-guy persona". Yet another tough guy with the Moon in Leo!

---
[164]http://www.astro.com/astro-databank/Saint-Exup%C3%A9ry,_Antoine_de
[165]http://www.astro.com/astro-databank/Schiller,_Friedrich_von
[166]http://www.astro.com/astro-databank/Dumas,_Alexandre_fils
[167]http://www.astro.com/astro-databank/Bach,_Richard
[168]http://www.astro.com/astro-databank/Sibelius,_Jean
[169]http://www.astro.com/astro-databank/Michael,_George

- Paul McCartney[170], a British musician who is most widely known as being a member of the mega-star group "The Beatles", and the co-author of "All You Need Is Love" song.
- Ringo Starr[171], a British musician, drummer, actor and superstar with "The Beatles".
- Antonio Vivaldi[172], an Italian famous violinist, a composer of concertos for various instruments.
- Claudio Abbado[173], an Italian conductor. He has served as music director of the La Scala opera house in Milan, principal conductor of the London Symphony Orchestra, principal guest conductor of the Chicago Symphony Orchestra, music director of the Vienna State Opera, and principal conductor of the Berlin Philharmonic orchestra.
- Carlos Santana[174], a Mexican-American musician, leader of the band "Santana".

Scientists

The ruling planet of Leo, the Sun, is a symbol for the rational mind and consciousness. It illuminates the darkness of the unknown, makes things comprehensible. This is why people born with the Moon in Leo can become great scientists or inventors, as the following examples show:

- Friedrich Bessel[175], a German mathematician, astronomer, and systematizer of the Bessel functions.

---

[170]http://www.astro.com/astro-databank/McCartney,_Paul
[171]http://www.astro.com/astro-databank/Starr,_Ringo
[172]http://www.astro.com/astro-databank/Vivaldi,_Antonio_Lucio
[173]http://www.astro.com/astro-databank/Abbado,_Claudio
[174]http://www.astro.com/astro-databank/Santana,_Carlos
[175]http://www.astro.com/astro-databank/Bessel,_Friedrich

- Louis Braille[176], a French blind organist who invented a transcription system for the blind in 1824. I mentioned him here as a scientist because his creation was of a scientific nature, but in fact he was a musician - notice the creative nature of his profession. Also please notice an interesting symbolism: the Sun is associated with light and vision, and a person with the Moon in sunny Leo created a system that helps people to less suffer from blindness.
- Jacques-Yves Cousteau[177], a French oceanographer, inventor, filmmaker and author who studied the sea and all forms of life in water and co-developed the aqualung.
- Alexandre Becquerel[178], a French physicist. He researched the nature of light and its chemical effects on phosphorescence, conductivity and the magnetic properties of many substances, making important discoveries. Please notice that a scientist with the Moon in Leo was studying light!
- Guglielmo Marconi[179], an Italian scientist and physicist who invented wireless telegraph and radio signal transmission in 1895.

Artists

As the Sun helps us to see the beauty of the surrounding world, a person with the Moon in Leo might decide to be an artist, in order to do pretty much the same for the other people. Photographic artists are especially interesting in this respect as they are using sunlight instead of paint! These are some of the Moon-in-Leo artists from my collection:

[176]http://www.astro.com/astro-databank/Braille,_Louis
[177]http://www.astro.com/astro-databank/Cousteau,_Jacques
[178]http://www.astro.com/astro-databank/Becquerel,_Alexandre
[179]http://www.astro.com/astro-databank/Marconi,_Guglielmo

- Ansel Adams[180], an American photographic artist, "the most significant figure in photography in the 20th century and one of the finest technicians in the history of photography, known since 1930. As a dedicated conservationist, his interpretation of natural scenes are breathtaking for their grandeur and beauty".
- Claude Monet[181], a French painter who was "the initiator, leader, and unswerving advocate of the Impressionist style". I've noticed that Impressionism as a style is often chosen by those having the Moon in a Fire sign.
- Maurice Vlaminck[182], a French artist. "Without any academic studies he started to paint using a brilliant orange, red, and blue palette; between paintings he also wrote novels and articles". Note the mentioned colors: they are so typical for the Sun in the sky.

Born Celebrities

I've noticed that the Moon in Leo can often belong to people who were born into wealth and popularity, which is typically the case with the children of celebrities. No matter what are their personal talents then, they have a very high start in life, and they emerge in the limelight, for better or worse, without doing anything for that. I believe that Paris Hilton[183], an American actress and socialite, a child of a noted hotel family, can be an example of such a person.

---

[180]http://www.astro.com/astro-databank/Adams,_Ansel
[181]http://www.astro.com/astro-databank/Monet,_Claude
[182]http://www.astro.com/astro-databank/Vlaminck,_Maurice
[183]http://www.astro.com/astro-databank/Hilton,_Paris

World Leaders

Leo is a royal sign, and those who were born with the Moon in this sign have inborn qualities, talents and instincts that naturally make them a central figure in a group of people. It isn't a surprise then that many of the most prominent of the World's leaders have Leo for their Moon Sign. Here are some of them for an illustration:

- Herbert Hoover[184], an American politician, the President of the United States from 1929 to 1933, during the Great Depression. During his lifetime, he received some 500 medals, honors and awards.
- Mohandas Gandhi[185], more popularly known as Mahatma Gandhi (Mahatma meaning a great soul), an Indian lawyer and civil rights champion, the spiritual and political leader of India through her "tempestuous birth of independence". He began the freedom movement in 1919 with nonviolent disobedience.
- Cosimo de Medici[186], an Italian nobility, the first of the powerful Medici political dynasty, *de facto* rulers of Florence during much of the Italian Renaissance. According to Wikipedia[187], he was also known as "Cosimo *Pater Patriae*" (Latin for *father of the nation*). Note that the Sun, the ruler of Leo, is an important symbol for the father figure.
- Benjamin Disraeli[188], a British politician, the Prime Minister, the only man with a Jewish heritage who ever held that post. He served in government for forty years, twice as Prime Minister of Great Britain, and played a central role in the creation of the modern Conservative Party.

---

[184]http://www.astro.com/astro-databank/Hoover,_Herbert
[185]http://www.astro.com/astro-databank/Gandhi,_Mohandas
[186]http://www.astro.com/astro-databank/Medici,_Cosimo_de
[187]http://en.wikipedia.org/wiki/Cosimo_de'_Medici
[188]http://www.astro.com/astro-databank/Disraeli,_Benjamin

- Margaret Thatcher[189], a British politician who became the first female Prime Minister of the United Kingdom, and was one of the most powerful women in the world in the latter part of the 20th century.

Gamblers

Leo is a sign which is strongly associated with games, especially games of chance, with gambling and related to them excitement. Therefore when people are born with the Moon in Leo, they can often have this gambling spirit as an inseparable part of their soul. Not necessarily it will lead them to actual gambling though, they can find some other exciting, somewhat risky ways in life. However, I do have an example of a gambler with the Moon in Leo:

- Joe Adonis[190], an Italian-American gambler and mafia boss. He was a leader of the US underworld, convicted of violating New Jersey gambling laws in 1951 and deported. He died, allegedly, of a heart attack, which does correlate with the fact that heart is a sensitive organ in case of the Moon-in-Leo people.

Stars

The Sun is the single most prominent celestial body, as seen from the Earth, and when a person is born with the Moon in Leo, the sign of the Sun, he or she has a potential to become a star, or a luminary in some field, someone who can bring to other people illumination, show them a purpose in their lives, or do something extraordinary, which nobody thought could be possible. I have several of such people in my collection:

---
[189]http://www.astro.com/astro-databank/Thatcher,_Margaret
[190]http://www.astro.com/astro-databank/Adonis,_Joe

- Paramahansa Yogananda[191], an East Indian author, mystic and founder of the Self-Realization Movement. He spent his youth hoping to find an illuminated teacher to guide him in his spiritual quest and met his Guru when he was 17.
- Frater Albertus[192] (aka Dr. Albert Richard Riedel), a German alchemist, occultist, author; he founded the Paracelsus Research Society in Salt Lake City, Utah.
- Evangeline Adams[193], an American astrologer with a clientele of nearly 100,000 people including the Prince of Wales, Mary Garden, J.P. Morgan and Enrico Caruso. "In 1914 she was accused of fortune telling and taken to court. At the trial she demonstrated her vocation by reading the chart of an unknown person who turned out to be the Judge's son. The Judge dismissed the case, saying that 'Adams raises astrology to the dignity of an exact science'".
- W.D. Gann[194], a legendary stock market trader who developed the technical analysis tools based on geometry, astronomy, astrology and ancient mathematics. According to Wikipedia[195], "he was believed to be a religious man by nature who believed in religious as well as scientific value of Bible as the greatest book ever written".

The Moon in Leo in the Family

When it comes to the Moon-in-Leo parents, there can be at least two typical scenarios.

One of them is when parents want to be proud of their children. They buy for the kids the most fashionable clothes, the best toys and

---

[191] http://www.astro.com/astro-databank/Yogananda,_Paramahansa
[192] http://www.astro.com/astro-databank/Albertus,_Frater
[193] http://www.astro.com/astro-databank/Adams,_Evangeline
[194] http://www.astro.com/astro-databank/Gann,_W.D.
[195] http://en.wikipedia.org/wiki/William_Delbert_Gann

games, arrange for them the most prestigious school, make sure that their talents are noticed, supported and appreciated. They might play with the kids to encourage their creativity and enjoy seeing their own talents reflected in the little ones.

The other possibility is that a Moon-in-Leo parent can be so preoccupied by his or her own success and popularity that no time is ever left for the kids. In this case, the kids might still have expensive toys and clothes, and probably a great nanny, but they severely lack their parents' love which they crave for so much.

As for a child born with the Moon in Leo, he or she definitely has some creative talents that should be discovered and supported. Such a child usually has a strong character, loves his or her parents and wants to be proud of them, but also needs plenty of encouragement and appreciation. He or she is usually generous, optimistic and tends to occupy the central position in a group of peers. The Moon-in-Leo kids crave for love and praise.

A typical Moon-in-Leo home is a place for frequent parties and celebrations. There has to be something posh about it; it should be very special, one if a kind, a little bit like a palace, even if it's only a studio apartment.

Recovering From Stress

To quickly recover from a significant stress, a Moon-in-Leo person needs to be loved and praised and told that she or he is the best person in the world.

Anything that can make their inner fire burning brighter will also be very helpful, as that fire will quickly burn to ashes any troubles. Pursuing a hobby, playing a game, watching a performance, gambling - anything that can make them excited - is vey much advisable for a Lunar Leo.

Sunshine is an important source of vital energy for Moon-in-Leo people, so a few days on a beach or a trip to a sunnier place can quickly erase any traces of stress from the soul and the body.

Health and Diet

The heart and the circulation are the sensitive areas of those born with the Moon in Leo, and in order to be healthy, it is of utmost importance for them to be loved. Lonely, neglected, unloved Moon Leos are not simply unhappy, they are putting their physical health at risk as well.

Developing the inner source of creativity by doing something very interesting, the Moon-in-Leo people can compensate for the lack of love, to some degree, but then again they can't be really happy unless the results of their creativity are praised and appreciated.

So the best advice for those Moon Leos who are unloved and unappreciated, and who are having problems with health at the same time, is to think how they can change their life to become happier. Without that, medical treatment of health problems might be less effective than expected.

As it was already mentioned, sunshine is very important for the Moon in Leo, so living in a location with plenty of sunny days will be definitely good for the health of those who have Leo for their Moon Sign.

From a Moon-in-Leo individual's point of view, food isn't just a fuel for the body; it also has to be interesting, and maybe a little bit posh. He or she likes to eat out in good restaurants, and if this person will invite guests (which probably happens quite often), he or she will make sure that the meal is cooked and served not worse than in those restaurants.

Meat or other food with high content of protein is well suited for Moon-in-Leo-type physiology, and it should be moderately spicy, to help the fire burn, - but not too spicy, to not overheat the Moon.

A Surprise Moment

I found that some Moon Signs have an affinity with certain occupations, and this affinity isn't always obvious from the symbolism of the sign. Writing and the Moon in Taurus is one example, but I've also noticed that a few of the Moon Signs are strongly associated with designing and manufacturing cars. One of those car-related Moon Signs is Leo, and here is a couple of examples to demonstrate the point:

- Jean Pierre Peugeot[196], a French industrialist, an automobile maker and one of the "Big Three" of French entrepreneurs.
- Battista Pininfarina[197], an Italian industrialist, the original creator of a car body design.

I won't tell you right now the other Moon Sign that is strongly associated with cars, just keep reading!

After dramatic and bright Leo, the next sign of the zodiac is the nitpicking and hard-working Virgo, and the next chapter will tell you about the talents and abilities of those who were born with the Moon in Virgo.

---

[196]http://www.astro.com/astro-databank/Peugeot,_Jean_Pierre
[197]http://www.astro.com/astro-databank/Pininfarina,_Battista

The Moon in Virgo

Virgo is a Mutable Earth sign ruled by Mercury. The Moon in Virgo is somewhat similar to the other combination of the Moon's and Mercury's energies, the Moon in Gemini, but since Virgo is an Earth sign, the Moon in Virgo is more down to earth, more practically minded, interested in everything tangible, not just all sorts of information.

Attention to Detail

The Moon-in-Virgo people can be very scientific in their attitude to life. They want to know by all means what things are made of, how healthy or not they are. Buying food, they will always check the 'use by' date, and what are the ingredients. They prefer everything clean, and pure, and natural, but not necessarily simple. Simplicity can be boring for the Moon in Virgo; these people prefer complexity and multiplicity.

They want to try and touch and taste as many things as possible, they are the collectors of objects, and tastes, and feelings, and sensations. They are curious and sensual.

The Moon-in-Virgo individuals usually have a good memory; they like to know many things and to impress others with their knowledge. Because of their attention to details, they can usually find lots of fun in occupations which other people would consider extremely boring.

My sister, for example, as soon as she could write, started writing different notes on different subjects on pieces of paper, and over the years she collected a massive paper database of all sorts of information (we didn't have any computers yet in those years).

Also, in each of the many books in her library, on many random pages inside the book, she left her signature, and name, and address, so that if someone borrowed the book one day, they had absolutely no doubt regarding the true owner of the book. She now works in the pharmaceutical industry and can quote by heart all the recent developments in the world of antibiotics.

Another side of the typical for the Moon in Virgo attention to detail is that these people can be very critical and nitpicking. They know exactly what is right and what is wrong, and will list three hundred reasons of why it is so.

Writers

Virgo is not only a home sign of Mercury, it is also the sign where Mercury is exalted, which means Mercury becomes very prominent and noticeable in Virgo. This is why many of those who were born with the Moon in Virgo choose a Mercury-related occupation, such as writing.

It might be also interesting to note that the palms of hands are one of the anatomical projections of Virgo, and writing is done by palms, whether it is actual writing on paper or typing on a keyboard. So being a writer or a journalist is very natural for a Moon-in-Virgo individual. Typically, his or her writings are somewhat Virgo-specific. They might be full of curious details like the "Hitchhiker's Guide to the Galaxy", or they might be very sensual, like "Lolita", or they can be numerous. Have a look at my small collection of the Moon-in-Virgo writers (no, my Moon is *not* in Virgo, this is why my collection is so small!):

- Douglas Adams[198], a British sci-fi writer "known for his wacky 'Hitchhiker's Guide to the Galaxy', a 1979 cult favorite.

[198]http://www.astro.com/astro-databank/Adams,_Douglas

It has turned into a book, which sold 14 million copies around the world, and later into a television series. His 'Dirk Gently's Holistic Detective Agency' embraces time travel, ghostly possession, quantum mechanics, musical theory, computer modeling, cellular communications and other galaxies. At one point his philosophy supplied the answer to 'the ultimate question of life, the universe and everything'. The answer was 42".

- Georges Simenon[199], a Belgian-French novelist, "whose prolific output included more than 400 novels, 84 detective novels, 100 psychological novels, and numerous articles, short stories and novellas. His books sold more than 600 million copies in 57 languages and spawned many movies".
- Vladimir Nabokov[200], a Russian-American writer, scholar, translator and lepidopterist (if you don't have time to look up this word, it means "a person who studies or collects butterflies and moths"). He received an Oscar nomination for the screen adaptation of his greatest novel "Lolita", which also brought him notoriety and financial independence.
- William Wordsworth[201], a British writer, one of the great British poets of the Romantic era, best known for his nature poems and sonnets. The Moon-in-Virgo people love nature.
- Ivan Bunin[202], a Russian poet and novelist and one of the best of Russian stylists.
- Stendhal[203], a French writer, considered to be one of the great literary figures of the 19th century. Wikipedia[204] mentions that he was known for his acute analysis of his characters' psychology. "Acute analysis" sounds very much like Virgo, while the Moon is closely related to psychology.

[199]http://www.astro.com/astro-databank/Simenon,_Georges
[200]http://www.astro.com/astro-databank/Nabokov,_Vladimir
[201]http://www.astro.com/astro-databank/Wordsworth,_William
[202]http://www.astro.com/astro-databank/Bunin,_Ivan
[203]http://www.astro.com/astro-databank/Stendhal
[204]http://en.wikipedia.org/wiki/Stendhal

- Maurice Druon[205], a French novelist. He was a member of several academies, like those of Athens, the kingdom of Morocco and the Romanian Academy.
- Thomas Carlyle[206], a Scottish writer, journalist, biographer and novelist. "The eldest of nine kids, he was a prodigy and genius who attended university at age 14. Too independent to remain a teacher, he became a magazine writer".
- William Faulkner[207], an American popular novelist, winner of the Nobel Prize in 1949 and the Pulitzer Prize in 1955. He became famous for his long, complicated stories.

Arts and Crafts

People who have Virgo for their Moon Sign can also be very good in using their palms for many other things, not just for writing novels. They can also play piano, paint, create sculptures and do very thoroughly many, many other things. Typically, they don't limit themselves to just one occupation but have a collection of them. Here are a few of distinguished individuals of this kind:

- Paul Gauguin[208], a French artist, painter, sculptor and ceramist. "Considered one of the best Post-Impressionist painters to come out of France, Gauguin was best known for his brilliantly colored works depicting primitive life in Polynesia".
- Akira Kurosawa[209], a Japanese director and producer, as well as an artist, a painter and an author.
- Benjamin Britten[210], a British foremost composer. He was a central figure of the 20th-century British classical music, and wrote music in many genres.

---

[205] http://www.astro.com/astro-databank/Druon,_Maurice
[206] http://www.astro.com/astro-databank/Carlyle,_Thomas
[207] http://www.astro.com/astro-databank/Faulkner,_William
[208] http://www.astro.com/astro-databank/Gauguin,_Paul
[209] http://www.astro.com/astro-databank/Kurosawa,_Akira
[210] http://www.astro.com/astro-databank/Britten,_Benjamin

- Felix Mendelssohn Bartholdy[211], a German composer, pianist, organist and conductor of the early Romantic period.
- Jean Cocteau[212], a French artist, poet, novelist, critic, playwright, painter, and illustrator, as well as stage and screen designer and producer, "a multi-faceted and brilliant talent".

Scientists

I've already mentioned the scientific aptitude of the Moon in Virgo, and you might be even wondering why haven't I proceeded then straight to a list of prominent Moon-in-Virgo scientists. Well, I just wanted to show you that the Moon-in-Virgo people are very versatile and can do many different things (sometimes simultaneously). But here is finally the list you were waiting for so patiently. Just note that there are two astronomers in this short and random list. I believe that astronomy, with its numerous stars and constellations, resonates with Virgo very well.

- Roberto Assagioli[213], an Italian psychiatrist; founder of psychosynthesis, which included both psychoanalysis and the wisdom of spiritual traditions. Note again that, as with Freud's Moon-in-Gemini, an interest to a kind of scientific analysis (Mercury) of the soul's content (the Moon) is prominent when the Moon is in a sign of Mercury.
- Arthur Schopenhauer[214], a German philosopher and writer known for his fine prose style and pessimistic philosophies. At some point in his life he was deeply involved in the study of Buddhist and Hindu philosophies and mysticism.

---

[211]http://www.astro.com/astro-databank/Mendelssohn_Bartholdy,_Felix
[212]http://www.astro.com/astro-databank/Cocteau,_Jean
[213]http://www.astro.com/astro-databank/Assagioli,_Roberto
[214]http://www.astro.com/astro-databank/Schopenhauer,_Arthur

- Rudolf Steiner[215], an Austrian-Hungarian mystic, philosopher, scientist, artist, educator and author. He developed an extraordinary system of agriculture called biodynamics, in which the Moon's rhythms play an important role.
- Camille Flammarion[216], a French scientist and astronomer in charge of an observatory near Paris in 1882. As an author, his works included "The Wonder of Heaven" and "Dreams of an Astronomer." Later in life, Flammarion turned to controversial work on psychic research. ̄
- Tycho Brahe[217], a Danish astronomer and scientist who originated the technique of systematic observations, and "disproved the concept that no change could occur in the heavens. Some of his work allowed his assistant and successor, Johannes Kepler, to formulate the laws of planetary motion. His work also provided important links between the theories of Copernicus and those of Sir Isaac Newton".

Actors and Actresses

Yet again, we can see here a similarity with the Moon in Gemini. Whenever the Moon is in a sign of Mercury, this gives a person some special charm and attractiveness. My explanation for this is that the Moon-in-Virgo (as well as the Moon-in-Gemini) people possess an intuitive understanding of how to communicate their feelings to the other people, how to touch other people's souls. The earthy nature of Virgo adds to this some special sensuality and sexuality, a deep physical attractiveness that works so well for many actors and actresses. A few of them from my collection are:

[215]http://www.astro.com/astro-databank/Steiner,_Rudolf
[216]http://www.astro.com/astro-databank/Flammarion,_Camille
[217]http://www.astro.com/astro-databank/Brahe,_Tycho

- Gina Lollobrigida[218], an Italian actress who made her debut in 1947 after winning a beauty contest. "She was the sexy star of some 60 films".
- Madonna[219], an American singer and actress who was originally dubbed "The Queen of Punk", primarily because of her outrageous attire and tacky image. "She eventually became a top superstar due to her unerring instinct for exhibitionism with the ability to shock the public and grab the attention of the media".
- John Travolta[220], an American actor on stage, film and TV. "A one-man acting industry, he has effortlessly played such diverse roles as a lusty angel, simple genius, star struck thug, FBI agent, presidential candidate and egocentric lawyer".
- Patricia Kaas[221], a French singer and actress. According to Wikipedia[222], "stylistically her music is not classical chanson, but is closer to a mixture of pop music, cabaret, jazz and chanson".
- Michelle Pfeiffer[223], an American actress "seen in five consecutive critical, if not commercial hits".
- Dustin Hoffman[224], an American actor who "has created some of the most unforgettable characters in the history of cinema, winning two Oscars and five Oscar nominations plus an Emmy in his 30 years of work".
- Sean Connery[225], a Scottish actor and film icon for the role of agent 007 in the "James Bond" series. "Known on movie sets as a hard-working actor, he demands and expects professionalism from every actor, director, and crew member".

---

[218] http://www.astro.com/astro-databank/Lollobrigida,_Gina
[219] http://www.astro.com/astro-databank/Madonna
[220] http://www.astro.com/astro-databank/Travolta,_John
[221] http://www.astro.com/astro-databank/Kaas,_Patricia
[222] http://en.wikipedia.org/wiki/Patricia_Kaas
[223] http://www.astro.com/astro-databank/Pfeiffer,_Michelle
[224] http://www.astro.com/astro-databank/Hoffman,_Dustin
[225] http://www.astro.com/astro-databank/Connery,_Sean

- Jean-Claude Van Damme[226], a Belgian-American actor who did stints in European commercials and low-budget French films before moving to Hollywood in 1981. He was a son of a florist and an accountant. See below about how Moon-in-Virgo individuals perceive their parents, and you will understand why the latter fact is quite curious.

Engineers and Inventors

Practicality, attention to detail, interest in complex structures and ability to make things with their own hands - all these qualities can make a Moon-in-Virgo individual a great engineer, mechanic, or inventor. Here are a few examples of such individuals:

- Clement Ader[227], a self-taught French engineer, inventor, and aeronautical pioneer.
- Auguste Lumière[228], a French pioneer of cinematography and color photography.
- Alexander Graham Bell[229], a Scottish-born American audiologist best known as the inventor of the telephone at age 29 and founder of AT&T.

Industrialists

In astrology, the Moon is associated with large masses of people, while the symbolism of Virgo includes work, efficiency, technical and technological abilities. When all these are brought together, we have an enterprise where many people are working to produce a large-scale practical result.

[226]http://www.astro.com/astro-databank/Van_Damme,_Jean-Claude
[227]http://www.astro.com/astro-databank/Ader,_Clement
[228]http://www.astro.com/astro-databank/Lumière,_Auguste
[229]http://www.astro.com/astro-databank/Bell,_Alexander_Graham

Many of the Moon-in-Virgo people find such an industrial environment perfectly suitable for their skills and talents, and some of them can achieve a great success, like these several examples from my collection:

- Pierre Samuel DuPont[230], an American politician and noted family as the DuPont Corporation owns the country's largest chemical company.
- Alfred Heineken[231], a Dutch industrialist who built an Amsterdam brewery into one of the world's biggest brewing companies.
- Jack Welch[232], an American business executive, perhaps the most touted CEO in America over the past 20 years. "The head of General Electric from 1981, Welch retired in 2001 with a record of returning more value to shareholders than even Bill Gates or Sam Walton, an increase of more than 3,000% during his tenure".
- Willy Messerschmitt[233], a German industrialist, an aircraft engineer and designer who designed his first plane in 1916 and organized his own manufacturing company by 1923.
- Sergio Pininfarina[234], an Italian industrialist, the son of entrepreneur Battista Pininfarina. He carried on the car design business that his dad established and was active in his civic involvement.

Politicians

The cooperation of the Moon and Mercury can be very important for politicians, as it gives the ability to understand what people

---

[230]http://www.astro.com/astro-databank/DuPont,_Pierre_Samuel
[231]http://www.astro.com/astro-databank/Heineken,_Alfred
[232]http://www.astro.com/astro-databank/Welch,_Jack
[233]http://www.astro.com/astro-databank/Messerschmitt,_Willy
[234]http://www.astro.com/astro-databank/Pininfarina,_Sergio

need, and to tell people the exact words they want to hear. We've seen several very prominent politicians with the Moon in Gemini; the Moon in Virgo is similar, but adds an ability to handle the nitty-gritty of economical problems, an interest in health matters, or a desire to sort out imperfections and to get things working. Here are some prominent politicians who were born with the Moon in Virgo:

- Caspar Weinberger[235], an American political aide who was key to President Nixon's program to trim federal spending. Having served as the Secretary of Health, Education and Welfare he also served as the Director of Management and Budget from 1970. In addition, he served on a state legislature in 1952.
- Rajiv Gandhi[236], an Indian politician and noted family, the eldest son of Indira Gandhi. "He was struggling against a tide of corruption, scandals, local-election defeats, the defection of ministers and worsening communal violence".
- Oliver Cromwell[237], a British statesman, the Parliamentary General of the English civil war who was later named Lord Protector. "From a prominent family, he was a wealthy land owner with an iron will and high moral purpose".
- Helmut Schmidt[238], a German politician, Chancellor of West Germany since 1974. "Enormously popular for putting Germany on its feet with less inflation and unemployment than any European country".
- John F. Kennedy[239], an American author, politician and the 35th U.S. President from 1961 to 1963.

---

[235]http://www.astro.com/astro-databank/Weinberger,_Caspar
[236]http://www.astro.com/astro-databank/Gandhi,_Rajiv
[237]http://www.astro.com/astro-databank/Cromwell,_Oliver
[238]http://www.astro.com/astro-databank/Schmidt,_Helmut
[239]http://www.astro.com/astro-databank/Kennedy,_John_F.

Adventurers

A desire to experience everything our world has to offer can move some Moon-in-Virgo individuals to really spectacular achievements. Their attention to detail and ability to make things working can make a significant difference, whatever they choose to do. Here is just a couple of these mind-boggling people:

- Reinhold Messner[240], an Italian pioneer adventurer and film maker, "leader of an expedition to climb the Mt. Everest and film the conquest of the mighty peak with his Austrian partner. On 8/05/1978, they climbed the 29,028 ft. mountain without the aid of oxygen. Two years later he returned, alone, becoming the first to conquer Everest solo".
- Amy Johnson[241], a British pioneer airwoman who "took flying lessons and aircraft maintenance with the reluctant support of her father". This is a great example of the Moon in Virgo: a woman capable of aircraft maintenance!

The Moon in Virgo in the Family

Being a mutable sign, Virgo has two tendencies that contradict each other, but at the same time both reflect the true nature of the sign. One of these tendencies is about cleanliness and tidiness, keeping things in perfect order, getting everything right. The other one is a desire to fully enjoy all the numerous things life offers. Somehow, both these tendencies manage to coexist in a typical Moon-in-Virgo home.

There can be a perfect order in the whole house but at the same time a complete mess in one's personal room, or at least somewhere in a

---

[240]http://www.astro.com/astro-databank/Messner,_Reinhold
[241]http://www.astro.com/astro-databank/Johnson,_Amy

wardrobe, or in the study. The Moon in Virgo will be most happy if it will find place for both perfect order and total chaos.

Those who were born with the Moon in Virgo typically see their parents as people with good practical sense, able to do many things with their hands. They could also be scientifically minded or interested in the healthy way of living.

As Mercury, the ruler of Virgo, is the god of commerce, Moon-in-Virgo parents can be good with buying and selling things, and can teach their kids how to see the difference between the real thing and a low quality imitation of it. They can also be critical and nitpicking at times, and might require their child to keep his or her room tidy.

As a parent, a Moon-in-Virgo individual will make sure that his or her kids are clean and tidy, that they keep their things in order, and that they can do things with their hands, like knitting or helping the father to repair the car.

But don't think that Moon-in-Virgo people are just strict and critical and formal. They can be very loving, and they enjoy hugging and kissing very much!

Recovering from Stress

To recover from a significant stress, many Moon-in-Virgo individuals might want to release their conflicting energy by cleaning, and washing, and tidying everything up feverishly. On the other hand, if the stress was caused by a very formal environment with strict requirements, they might find a great relief by creating a total chaos around them.

Eating or doing something that they know is very good for their health might be helpful too. But if nothing helps, one should know that Valerian is a herb of Mercury, and a little bit of its tincture can have a magical effect on an over-stressed Moon-in-Virgo person.

Same as with the other Earth signs, gardening can bring a significant relief, but in case of specifically Virgo some DIY, knitting, or some other occupation allowing to do something monotonous with the hands can be helpful.

Health and Diet

The Moon-in-Virgo people are usually quite attentive to their health and interested in various ways of improving it. Depending on their personal preferences, they can do yoga, or try different diets, or experiment with fasting, or pay regular visits to their GP, or maybe do all of these together.

An important thing to remember for these individuals is that many health problems can originate in one's mind, and that constant worrying about real or imagined troubles can do more harm than the problems themselves. Keeping an optimistic and positive outlook is very important for everyone, but especially for the intellectually driven people like those born with the Moon in Virgo.

As for the diet, many of the Moon-in-Virgo individuals have a strong idea about what they do eat and what they don't. They can spend plenty of time over an unfamiliar dish, separating those bits that look suspicious from those that seem to be okay. To some degree, this can be a reflection of their selective, discriminating mind, but on the other hand the Moon-in-Virgo's digestive system is really very sensitive to the quality of food, and can sometimes be quite unforgiving. If other people can allow themselves to eat something not very fresh, or looking strange, or of a suspicious quality, a Moon-in-Virgo person will often end up with one or another digestive problem.

So if you were born with the Moon in Virgo, please make sure that you feed your body only with fresh, natural, highest quality food.

Speaking about the food, I've noticed that many of the world's famous chefs were born with the Moon in Virgo. My understanding is that Virgo helps them to know many different ingredients, and to understand how to put them together to achieve a perfect combination.

Many Moon-in-Virgo people become so interested in the healthy ways of living that they can choose a health-related profession. One great example is Deepak Chopra[242], an East Indian-American author, physician and healer, and an inspirational leader in holistic health.

A Surprise Moment

According to the astrological rules, Virgo, being the sixth sign of the zodiac, is somewhat similar to the sixth house, and that one deals with subordinate people, helpers, aides and those doing some kind of service. They work a lot, they do very important things, but their efforts aren't always visible, and they are very seldom praised for their work.

I've noticed that there are more than a few prominent Moon-in-Virgo individuals who, although quite distinguished by themselves, lived an worked in a shadow of another, even more prominent person.

One typical example is Friedrich Engels[243], a German co-founder, with Karl Marx, of modern Communism and Socialism. "After Marx, Engels was the finest scholar and teacher of the modern proletariat in the whole civilized world". Have you noticed that "after Marx"? This is exactly how Engels's name is always mentioned.

Another example, already mentioned above, is Auguste Lumière. According to Astro-Databank, "although it is his brother Louis who is generally acclaimed as the "father of the cinema", Auguste

---

[242]http://www.astro.com/astro-databank/Chopra,_Deepak
[243]http://www.astro.com/astro-databank/Engels,_Friedrich

Lumière also made a major contribution towards the development of the medium, He not only helped with the invention and construction of the cinematographer (the world's first camera and projection mechanism), but he made a number of improvements in photographic techniques".

Yet another example is Caspar Weinberger (see above under Politicians), who was a prominent politician, but in the role of an aide.

Interesting, isn't it?

Finally, this long and tedious Moon-in-Virgo chapter came to an end. The next chapter should be much nicer, as it will be about the Moon-in-Libra people.

The Moon in Libra

Libra is a cardinal Air sign ruled by Venus, and those who were born with the Moon in Libra inherit many of the attributes of Venus. They love everything beautiful and valuable and have a developed aesthetic perception. They are interested in music, art and dance and might be actively involved in some of the artistic activities. They prefer peaceful agreements and compromises to cruel victories - although the nature of Libra can make them somewhat argumentative and competitive.

From the sign of Libra, these people inherit a strong desire to maintain a balance in everything, and since it is a cardinal sign, it's usually them who makes the first step and takes the initiative. If someone around them is saying only bad things about a third party, they'll intervene and add something good; however, if they only hear that someone is being praised, they'll intervene again and add something negative. This happens automatically, they don't really want to say anything bad about anyone, they want to always be nice! But they also want to be objective and truthful no matter what.

Both Sides

Their ability to see both sides of a problem can sometimes get the Moon-in-Libra people into a trouble, especially when they have to make an important decision. They don't like making decisions. They will endlessly oscillate between all the available options, then, at the very last moment, they'll make a random choice, and they'll immediately regret then that they made exactly *that* choice and not the other one. It's an agony!

On the other hand, once a decision is made, a Moon-in-Libra person is usually responsible and reliable enough to carry it out. Saturn has its exaltation in Libra, which gives these people persistence and tenacity.

Relationships

Those who were born with the Moon in Libra are very much relationships oriented. They feel a strong need to have someone in their life with whom they can share everything. They just can't fully enjoy life without such a person. As for problems, even if these people are completely capable of handling a situation, they can find it unbearable unless someone is supporting them, even if purely symbolically.

Being an Air sign, same as Gemini, Libra gives an interest in information and communication. Unlike Gemini though, Libra people are more selective as to the sources of information. Rather than consuming everything they can get, the Moon-in-Libra individuals prefer the opinions of those people whom they trust, or established authorities supported by the society. They are very much society oriented and like to follow the society's trends.

Scientists and Inventors

The Moon-in-Libra people try to be very objective, and because of the strength of Saturn in Libra, they like different laws and rules and prefer to follow them whenever possible. These qualities can attract them to science, and there are indeed several Moon-in-Libra scientists in my collection, you'll see the list of them in a moment.

What's interesting is that most of these scientists are physicists. I explain it to myself like this: many of the laws of physics are about various balances and equilibriums; therefore, the Moon-in-Libra scientists are naturally attracted to physics.

What's even more interesting, most of those Moon-in-Libra physicists work or worked in the area of nuclear or atomic physics and elementary particles. Again, I have an idea why that could be so: remember the duality of the electron? Is it a wave or a particle? It is both! The deepest areas of physics are full of such paradoxes, when two seemingly mutually exclusive facts are both true, and this is exactly what makes that part of science so attractive for a Moon-in-Libra intellectual.

Finally, here is my list of the Moon-in-Libra scientists:

- Ernst Abbe[244], a German physicist, optometrist, entrepreneur, and social reformer. Together with Otto Schott and Carl Zeiss, he laid the foundation of modern optics. He wasn't a nuclear physicist, of course, but he was very active in the society, which is yet another way how the Moon in Libra can manifest itself.
- Niels Bohr[245], a Danish physicist who was awarded the Nobel Prize in 1922 for the investigation of atomic structure and radiation.
- Werner Heisenberg[246], a German scientist who, as an atomic physicist, won the Nobel Prize in physics in 1932 for his creation of quantum mechanics and was acknowledged as "the greatest German theoretical physicist".
- Alois Alzheimer[247], a German pathologist, appointed professor in Breslau, 1912. He investigated the pathology of senile and pre-senile dementia that became known as Alzheimer's Disease, named after his studies.
- Paul Dirac[248], an English theoretical physicist. Dirac is widely regarded as one of the world's greatest physicists, who was

---

[244]http://www.astro.com/astro-databank/Abbe,_Ernst
[245]http://www.astro.com/astro-databank/Bohr,_Niels
[246]http://www.astro.com/astro-databank/Heisenberg,_Werner
[247]http://www.astro.com/astro-databank/Alzheimer,_Alois
[248]http://www.astro.com/astro-databank/Dirac,_Paul

one of the founders of quantum mechanics and quantum electrodynamics.
- Nikola Tesla[249], a Serbian-American inventor and engineer who was "a master of electricity at a time when it was changing American life".

Actors and Actresses

Partnership is very important for the Moon-in-Libra people, and therefore wise Nature gave them a gift, an innate ability to attract other people's attention, some special kind of charm. They can be physically attractive, or they can move or speak in such a way that they naturally attract attention and please other people's eye or ear, or if none of these is the case, they might still have some incomprehensible power to attract other people.

Quite naturally, many of the Moon-in-Libra individuals develop their innate charm into a profession, and one of the ways how they can do it is by becoming an actor or an actress. Here is a list of some of the prominent Moon-in-Libra actors and actresses:

- Neile Adams[250], an American actress and dancer on stage, film and TV.
- Jean-Paul Belmondo[251], a French actor "hailed as cinema's new anti-hero in 1957, an overnight success in 'A Bout de Souffle'. A former boxer, he has rough features including a broken nose, a rakish grin and gruff sex appeal".
- Isabelle Adjani[252], a French actress and international film star; first accepted by Comedie-Francaise at 15 due to her extraordinary talent.

---
[249]http://www.astro.com/astro-databank/Tesla,_Nikola
[250]http://www.astro.com/astro-databank/Adams,_Neile
[251]http://www.astro.com/astro-databank/Belmondo,_Jean-Paul
[252]http://www.astro.com/astro-databank/Adjani,_Isabelle

- Leonardo DiCaprio[253], an American actor, lead in a film that was the most outstanding commercial and popular success of all times, "Titanic".
- Sylvester Stallone[254], an American actor who made a huge break-through to overnight success with writing and starring in "Rocky", 1976, an Oscar winning picture.
- Steven Seagal[255], an American actor, director, producer and Aikido expert, often seen in roles that are highly physical.
- Nicolas Cage[256], an American actor and noted family, the son of August Coppola, a professor of comparative literature and dancer Joy Vogelsang (see a section about a Moon-in-Libra family below). "He was born with that certain something that the camera captures, that invisible magic that makes him impossible to ignore, that makes him hauntingly memorable".
- Henry Fonda[257], an American actor, a top star of stage and screen for many years.

Artists

The ruler of Libra Venus gives the Moon-in-Libra people a great natural appreciation of the beauty of the surrounding world, and since Libra is an Air sign, they feel an urge to somehow tell other people about that beauty, to share their adoration of the world. That's why you will find many famous artists who were born with the Moon in Libra. In the list below, I've included not only actual artists but also other people who use their skills to share their appreciation of the world's beauty and harmony.

---

[253] http://www.astro.com/astro-databank/DiCaprio,_Leonardo
[254] http://www.astro.com/astro-databank/Stallone,_Sylvester
[255] http://www.astro.com/astro-databank/Seagal,_Steven
[256] http://www.astro.com/astro-databank/Cage,_Nicolas
[257] http://www.astro.com/astro-databank/Fonda,_Henry

- Scott Adams[258], an American cartoonist, the creator of Dilbert, one of the most successful syndicated comic strips in history.
- Ingmar Bergman[259], a Swedish film director, a "prestigiously productive and creative artist whose lens focused darkly on landscapes of tormented guilt and neurosis with only the occasional smile on a summer night".
- Henri Toulouse-Lautrec[260], a French artist and painter whose great influence on Post-impressionist French art came after his death.
- Walt Disney[261], an American cartoonist who created Mickey Mouse in 1928 and later made the first feature-length cartoon ever filmed, "Fantasia", a visual interpretation of orchestral music.
- Antoni Gaudi[262], a Spanish architect with a highly original, three-dimensional art style.
- Joan Mitchell[263], a French-American artist, "recognized as one of the finest painters of her generation from the time of an exhibition in May 1951. An abstract expressionist, she often confounds critics searching for the meaning of her paintings". There aren't many female artists in my collection, and it is very appropriate that this rare example has the Moon (the symbol of feminine) in Libra (the sign strongly associated with art and beauty).

---

[258] http://www.astro.com/astro-databank/Adams,_Scott
[259] http://www.astro.com/astro-databank/Bergman,_Ingmar
[260] http://www.astro.com/astro-databank/Toulouse-Lautrec,_Henri
[261] http://www.astro.com/astro-databank/Disney,_Walt
[262] http://www.astro.com/astro-databank/Gaudi,_Antoni
[263] http://www.astro.com/astro-databank/Mitchell,_Joan

Authors

All Air signs are communicative and have something to say, but if for the Moon-in-Gemini people it would be typical to chat about everything to everyone, the Moon-in-Libra folks are more selective. This is why they can make great writers who are true to their preferred topic, and the list below mentions some of the well-known Moon-in-Libra authors. You will notice that ladies make a substantial part of the list. This is quite interesting, because the two strongly masculine planets, Mars and the Sun, are not comfortable in Libra (Mars is in detriment here and the Sun is in fall). Does this mean that the Moon in Libra give more chances for women to succeed?

- Agatha Christie[264], a British writer of some 67 detective mystery books that are universally popular.
- Bertold Brecht[265], a German playwright and poet, one of the leaders of the "epic theatre movement".
- Bertrand Russell[266], a British-Welsh writer, mathematician, logician, philosopher, social critic, one of the founders of analytic philosophy; he is considered to be one of the twentieth century's most important liberal thinkers.
- Madame De Staël[267], a French writer, an essayist and great supporter of the French revolution. "She occupied herself with politics for her whole life and had a varying fortune, up and down".
- Charles Leadbeater[268], a British author, priest and occultist, a remarkable clairvoyant and author of many books.

[264] http://www.astro.com/astro-databank/Christie,_Agatha
[265] http://www.astro.com/astro-databank/Brecht,_Bertold
[266] http://www.astro.com/astro-databank/Russell,_Bertrand
[267] http://www.astro.com/astro-databank/De_Sta%C3%ABl,_Madame
[268] http://www.astro.com/astro-databank/Leadbeater,_Charles

- Helena P. Blavatsky[269], a Russian spiritualist and mystic, the founder of the Theosophical Society.
- Jane Austen[270], a British writer, the first renowned female novelist of England.
- Maurice Maeterlinck[271], a Belgian dramatist, essayist, poet, playwright, philosopher, lawyer and naturalist, winner of the 1911 Nobel Prize for Literature.

Musicians, Singers and Dancers

Venus has many gifts for those who were born with the Moon in one of her signs, Libra, and here is a selection of the Moon-in-Libra individuals who helped to make our world more pleasant and beautiful.

- Vincenzo Bellini[272], an Italian composer of operas who was celebrated for lyric beauty and dazzling vocal embellishments, a repertory of the Bel Canto school.
- Dr. Dre[273], an American rap musician in the gangsta' rap genre. He is a successful business man, founder of Aftermath Entertainment, a record production company.
- Billy Joel[274], an American singer inducted into the Songwriters Hall of Fame in 1992 after 15 years of preparation for success as a singer and songwriter.
- Dalida[275], a World-famous singer and actress.
- Michel Legrand[276], a French composer, arranger, conductor, and pianist.

---
[269]http://www.astro.com/astro-databank/Blavatsky,_Helena_P.
[270]http://www.astro.com/astro-databank/Austen,_Jane
[271]http://www.astro.com/astro-databank/Maeterlinck,_Maurice
[272]http://www.astro.com/astro-databank/Bellini,_Vincenzo
[273]http://www.astro.com/astro-databank/Dre,_Dr.
[274]http://www.astro.com/astro-databank/Joel,_Billy
[275]http://www.astro.com/astro-databank/Dalida
[276]http://www.astro.com/astro-databank/Legrand,_Michel

- Rudolph Nureyev[277], a Russian ballet dancer who had an outstanding technique and a compelling stage presence.
- Hélène Grimaud[278], a French pianist who as a teenager took first prize in piano at the Paris Conservatory.
- Susan Boyle[279], a Scottish singer who rose to fame on a British talent show.
- Edward Elgar[280], a British composer best known for "Pomp and Circumstance", a set of five marches. Largely self-taught, he brought new life to the choral form and also wrote two symphonies, a violin concerto and a cello concerto.
- Sergei Prokofiev[281], a Russian composer of marches, army songs, opera and symphonies.

Fashion

With their inborn aesthetic perception and taste, the Moon-in-Libra people can certainly make good fashion designers, and a couple of the most well known of them are:

- Hubert de Givenchy[282], a French fashion designer and entrepreneur, one of the greatest names in haute couture.
- Tommy Hilfiger[283], an American fashion designer, known for innovative styles that appeal to people of all ages, races and sexes.

---

[277]http://www.astro.com/astro-databank/Nureyev,_Rudolph
[278]http://www.astro.com/astro-databank/Grimaud,_H%C3%A9l%C3%A8ne
[279]http://www.astro.com/astro-databank/Boyle,_Susan
[280]http://www.astro.com/astro-databank/Elgar,_Edward
[281]http://www.astro.com/astro-databank/Prokofiev,_Sergei
[282]http://www.astro.com/astro-databank/Givenchy,_Hubert_de
[283]http://www.astro.com/astro-databank/Hilfiger,_Tommy

Other Creative People

There are definitely many other ways, not mentioned here, how the Moon-in-Libra people can express their appreciation of the nice things of the world. One example is Julia Child[284], an American chef and writer of over nine cookbooks, appearing in more than three hundred television shows. She achieved celebrity status with her book "Mastering the Art of French Cooking". One of the symbolic associations of the Moon is cooking, and food in general, and when the Moon is in Libra, she helps people to cook nice food, and make a show from cooking.

The Moon in Libra in the Family

The Moon is quite perceptive to the influences of other planets, and Libra is somewhat contradictive by nature, so the family experience of those born with the Moon in Libra can vary quite widely.

It is typical for the Moon-in-Libra individuals to be introduced by the mother, or maybe the whole parents' family, to the world of music, dancing, painting, or some other kind of art. Children with the Moon in Libra learn from their parents to appreciate beautiful things, to pay attention to styles and fashions. They can also learn a lot about the relationships, however those lessons might not necessarily be of a positive nature.

On the other hand, the mother could be somewhat detached, caring more about how the child looks and behaves than what he or she feels. She can give higher priority to the views and opinions of the other people and the society in general than to the emotional needs of the child.

Some of the Moon-in-Libra parents can subconsciously perceive their children as partners rather than kids, and this can result in

---

[284]http://www.astro.com/astro-databank/Child,_Julia

jealousy, competition and other complex negative feelings.

On the positive side however, the Moon in Libra can create a kind of relationships where members of the family understand each other without words and can literally merge together emotionally. This is especially likely when both the parent and the child were born with the Moon in Libra, or one of them has the Moon in Libra while the other's Moon is in either Gemini or Aquarius, the other two Air signs. See a later chapter about the Moon Sign compatibility.

Recovering from a Stress

To recover from a significant stress, a Moon-in-Libra person needs someone else, someone to whom he or she could complain about their problems, who can give an emotional support or even simply listen to them attentively.

Good music can also be very helpful for restoring the energy of the Moon in Libra, especially if there is an opportunity to listen to the music in a beautiful, pleasant, comfortable environment.

Health and Diet

It is very important for the Moon-in-Libra people to keep a healthy balance in everything they do. By nature, they can easily get excited and carried away by something. They can spend the whole day playing a new piece of music or reading an incredibly interesting book, and then they will have some problem with their body, typically manifesting itself as a headache.

The Moon-in-Libra type of physiology is very sensitive to the lack of balance in life, and so it is important for those born with the Moon in Libra to keep a reasonable balance between work and rest, physical and mental activity, to have a balanced diet and lifestyle. If this rule is systematically violated, headaches will come as forewarnings, but then some serious conditions can develop - diabetes, high blood pressure, kidney problems.

The Moon-in-Libra diet should be in every respect somewhere in the middle, without excesses. Not too heavy, not too "healthy", not too spicy, not too hot, not too cold... And a little bit of everything, to form a good balance. Of course, the Moon in Libra will always appreciate if the food looks great and is served in style.

Same as for the other Air signs, breathing exercises can be very helpful for maintaining and restoring health of the Moon-in-Libra people, and living in a place with a clean atmosphere is very much desirable for them.

A Surprise Moment

So far we have predominantly seen the Moon-in-Libra people who either help to make our world more beautiful, like artists, dancers or authors, or contemplate its harmony, like scientists and philosophers.

However, there is a significant number of the Moon-in-Libra individuals who were, or still are, the powerful leaders of the world. Definitely, an innate understanding of the laws of the society helps them in achieving their position. Not only they can play the game by its rules, they can create those rules too.

I was especially interested to see that both US Presidents with the surname Bush, the father and the son, have their Moon in the same sign, Libra.

These are some examples of the powerful and influential Moon-in-Libra people.

- Swami Vivekananda[285], an Indian religious leader, a disciple

---

[285] http://www.astro.com/astro-databank/Vivekananda,_Swami

of Sri Ramakrishna inspired by his teacher to serve men as visible manifestations of God.
- Fidel Castro[286], a Cuban liberator who successfully overthrew President Batista's government in 1959.
- George W. Bush[287], an American politician, a US President for two terms, a Texas oil millionaire and baseball owner, a son of a US President George H. W. Bush.
- George H. W. Bush[288], an American politician who served as the President of the United States from 1989-1993.
- Benazir Bhutto[289], a Pakistani politician, the first woman leader of the Islamic world. She was the daughter of Ali Bhutto who ruled Pakistan in the '70s.
- François Mitterrand[290], a French politician whose career spanned half a century and culminated in the presidency of France when he replaced Valery Giscard de'Estaing in May 1981.
- Dwight D. Eisenhower[291], an American military general in World War II, Commander in Chief of the Allied Forces in North Africa who led the invasion of Sicily and Italy. As a politician, he served as a US President in 1953-1961. He was the first Republican in the White House in 20 years and one of the most popular and influential statesmen to serve.

After the nice Libra, the intense Scorpio follows in the order of the zodiac, and so the next chapter will discuss the talents of people born with the Moon in Scorpio.

[286]http://www.astro.com/astro-databank/Castro,_Fidel
[287]http://www.astro.com/astro-databank/Bush,_George_W.
[288]http://www.astro.com/astro-databank/Bush,_George_H._W.
[289]http://www.astro.com/astro-databank/Bhutto,_Benazir
[290]http://www.astro.com/astro-databank/Mitterrand,_Francois
[291]http://www.astro.com/astro-databank/Eisenhower,_Dwight

The Moon in Scorpio

Scorpio is a fixed Water sign ruled by hot and powerful Mars. You might remember from our discussion of another Water sign, Cancer, that Water signs are mysterious, they are like a pond: the surface is calm and unimpressive but there is a rich life underneath it. The Moon in Scorpio is somewhat similar, except that an image of a pond isn't really appropriate in this case. A volcano, with overheated lava bubbling inside, until the next eruption, could be a much better image. Or at least a geyser, for the more subtle types.

The Moon in Fall

The Moon is in fall in Scorpio - that's an astrological term meaning that it is not comfortable in this sign and has a problem with showing its best sides. A fall is a bit like a hole in the ground where the Moon-in-Scorpio individuals tend to hide their feelings and emotions. Or it might resemble a fallen angel, as the Moon in Scorpio easily attracts dark, negative feelings: jealousy, envy, greed, suspicion, shame, guilt, resentment...

Intense

With powerful Mars ruling Scorpio, and also because of the fixed nature of the sign, the Moon-in-Scorpio people are intense, concentrated, persistent, deep and tenacious in everything they do. They want to get to the bottom of everything, to find out what is hidden beneath the surface. They are never satisfied by shallow or superficial. They are very good with secrets - both with hiding their own and uncovering those of other people. They also have a very good memory, especially for any bad things that happened to them, and they find it very difficult to either forgive or forget those things.

Many of the Moon-in-Scorpio individuals are interested in topics and activities that most other people would consider as tabu, or too frightening, or too dangerous, or too dark. They might be attracted to anything related to death, sex, crime, corruption and could choose a profession like a detective, a policeman, or a surgeon. Or a politician.

Sexy

Sexual life is very important for the Moon-in-Scorpio people. It can provide a great outlet for their difficult and powerful energy, and they usually possess some mysterious magnetism that sexually attracts to them other people.

They desire strong and stable relationships, but they also want to control their partner, and to be sure that he or she is 100% devoted and trustworthy. This can be a difficult requirement, and so many of the Moon-in-Scorpio individuals surround themselves with a wall that prevents non-trustworthy people from coming close.

Extreme

The Moon-in-Scorpio people are attracted to everything which is extreme, and they might feel some special enjoyment when putting their soul and body through a trial, be it a crazy sexual adventure, or an extreme sport, or an extreme fast. The Moon in Scorpio can create macho types, like King of Jordan Abdullah II[292], who was an accomplished marksman, a helicopter and jet-fighter pilot, a deep-sea scuba diver and an avid collector of antique weaponry, as well as Jordan's top counter terrorism specialist and troop leader.

---

[292]http://www.astro.com/astro-databank/Abdullah_II,_King_of_Jordan

However, there are also many extremely gifted Moon-in-Scorpio individuals of other types too, here is a brief collection of them:

- David Livingstone[293], a Scottish physician, author, missionary and explorer of Africa. He was the first white man to cross the dark continent.
- Roald Amundsen[294], a Norwegian scientific polar explorer, the first person to sail through the northwest passage.
- Uri Geller[295], an Israeli psychic and telekinetic with an international reputation. "His ability to read minds, bend metals and 'see' through objects has been tested with odds at a trillion to one that his feats could be reproduced".

Secrets

As it was already mentioned, the Moon-in-Scorpio people have a special penchant with secrets. They can be very secretive themselves, but they are also very interested in finding out some hidden information, revealing the truth, penetrating the veil of mystery. To demonstrate this, I have only a few but very interesting examples:

- Julian Assange[296], an Australian whistleblower, with a background in physics, mathematics and computer programming, best known for his work with WikiLeaks, an investigative journalism Internet-based organization whose mission is to make public otherwise secret information.
- Michel de Nostradamus[297], a French physician and astrologer, famed for his prophecies written in the form of quatrain verse

---

[293]http://www.astro.com/astro-databank/Livingstone,_David
[294]http://www.astro.com/astro-databank/Amundsen,_Roald
[295]http://www.astro.com/astro-databank/Geller,_Uri
[296]http://www.astro.com/astro-databank/Assange,_Julian
[297]http://www.astro.com/astro-databank/Nostradamus,_Michel_de

entitled "Centuries". Nostradamus was the most widely read seer of the Renaissance, and is sometimes referred to as the "prophet of doom", because many of his visions involve war and death.

Actors and Directors

People born with the Moon in Scorpio are very good with influencing the others, and making the other people do what they want. They definitely have loads of sexual magnetism, but their ability to influence, as if to hypnotize, goes far beyond just sexuality. Such people can become excellent actors, and even better directors. Very often, the theme of Scorpio can be visible in their talents or achievements in one or another way.

- Alfred Abel[298], a German film producer and actor. He worked as a forest warden, businessman, bank clerk and designer before being discovered by Asta Nielsen in 1913. An interesting detail here is that business and finances are strongly associated with Scorpio.
- Ben Affleck[299], an American actor, an Academy Award winner for the Best Original Screenplay of the film "Good Will Hunting". Behind this brief fact, there is an amazing story how two students did the movie script as their Harvard assignment, and then insisted they will play the main roles. "When Hollywood snapped up the script, 1997 was an incredible year for the two life-long friends, taking them on a rollicking ride from struggling actors, upstarts on a short list of hot new talent, to winners of the most prestigious award in the field". This could be an example of an ability of a Moon-in-Scorpio personality to influence people and events, I'd say.

---

[298]http://www.astro.com/astro-databank/Abel,_Alfred
[299]http://www.astro.com/astro-databank/Affleck,_Ben

- Alfred Hitchcock[300], a British-American filmmaker, the most famous suspense, humor and horror director of all times. His work strongly resonates with the nature of the sign of Scorpio, in my opinion.
- Steven Spielberg[301], an American film producer and director, the winner of an Academy Award for his direction of the Best Picture of the year, "Schindler's List" (a movie about saving lives of Jewish refugees during World War II). He won the Oscar as Best Director for his "Saving Private Ryan" (a movie about rescuing a last-surviving brother during World War II). You might notice that the movies that made Steven Spielberg famous are full of Scorpio symbolism: death, destruction and survival.
- Whoopi Goldberg[302], an American actress and comedienne who went from welfare to movie star in a few short years. Here we have an example of the theme of rebirth, which is typical for Scorpio. Many individuals with strong Scorpio, like those born with the Moon in Scorpio, somehow manage to completely and totally change themselves and their lives, as if starting a new life, as if being born again.
- Elizabeth Taylor[303], a British-American actress. "She learned ballet shortly after learning to walk and once performed before the Queen".
- Gérard Depardieu[304], a French actor with a rough, heavy face, great charisma and a gift for comedy.

---

[300]http://www.astro.com/astro-databank/Hitchcock,_Alfred
[301]http://www.astro.com/astro-databank/Spielberg,_Steven
[302]http://www.astro.com/astro-databank/Goldberg,_Whoopi
[303]http://www.astro.com/astro-databank/Taylor,_Elizabeth
[304]http://www.astro.com/astro-databank/Depardieu,_Gerard

Scientists

The Moon-in-Scorpio people's desire to penetrate the mysteries and to uncover the truth can move many of them to become scientists, and there are quite a few scientists born with the Moon in Scorpio. Note the strong presence of the Curie family here, with its association with mysterious, invisible and dangerous radioactivity:

- Pierre Curie[305], a French scientist, a physicist and chemist and the co-discoverer of radium with his wife, Marie, for which they won the Nobel Prize in 1903, shared with Henri Becquerel.
- Frederic Joliot-Curie[306], a French chemist. Frédéric Joliot-Curie and his wife Irène Joliot-Curie, daughter of Marie curie, researched production of energy from nuclear fission, and shared the 1935 Nobel Prize for Chemistry for their production of synthesized radioactive elements.
- Antoine Lavoisier[307], a French author, scientist, chemist and tax collector. Isn't it a little bit strange to see a "tax collector" in this list? However, Scorpio is strongly associated with finances, other people's money and taxes, and we can see here an interesting example of how the nature of a person can find different ways to manifest itself.
- Georg Ohm[308], a German physicist who discovered a law named after him.

Singers and Other Musicians

It is interesting how many of the prominent singers were born with the Moon in Scorpio. Many astrologers have noticed that opposite

---
[305]http://www.astro.com/astro-databank/Curie,_Pierre
[306]http://www.astro.com/astro-databank/Joliot-Curie,_Frederic
[307]http://www.astro.com/astro-databank/Lavoisier,_Antoine
[308]http://www.astro.com/astro-databank/Ohm,_Georg

signs of the zodiac can be similar in some ways. The opposite sign of Scorpio is Taurus, and it is another Moon Sign that gave the world many great vocalists. I'd think that the sexual magnetism of Scorpio is an important success factor for the Moon-in-Scorpio singers. Here is a list of them from my collection.

- Eric Clapton[309], a British musician, a strong lead vocalist who has played blues guitar in various bands.
- Lady Gaga[310], an American singer and songwriter.
- Johnny Hallyday[311], a French singing superstar, known as the French Elvis, a major rock star from the '60s.
- Plácido Domingo[312], a Spanish operatic tenor, international music celebrity, conductor, music director and humanitarian.
- Mario Lanza[313], an Italian-American singer and actor, a great vocal phenomenon, the first recording artist to ever sell more than two million albums.

With Scorpio's emotional intensity and depth, there is no surprise that many other great musicians were born with the Moon in this sign, not only singers. Here are a few of them:

- Ennio Morricone[314], an Italian musician, a composer and arranger who has written scores for more than 400 movies and TV series.
- Arturo Toscanini[315], an Italian conductor, revered by many as the greatest conductor of his time during a career that spanned 70 years.

---

[309] http://www.astro.com/astro-databank/Clapton,_Eric
[310] http://www.astro.com/astro-databank/Lady_Gaga
[311] http://www.astro.com/astro-databank/Hallyday,_Johnny
[312] http://www.astro.com/astro-databank/Domingo,_Placido
[313] http://www.astro.com/astro-databank/Lanza,_Mario
[314] http://www.astro.com/astro-databank/Morricone,_Ennio
[315] http://www.astro.com/astro-databank/Toscanini,_Arturo

- Alexander Scriabin[316], a Russian composer who achieved fame in Europe by age 20 as a virtuoso, winning a Gold Medal in 1892.
- Hector Berlioz[317], a French composer, conductor, critic and writer of books on music. Known for his orchestrating genius with program music, his works included symphonies, voice and choral numbers, oratorios and operas.
- Alexander Borodin[318], a Russian chemist, teacher and administrator of the St. Petersburg School of Medicine. Though he insisted on remaining a musical amateur, he achieved high standing as a composer and was known for his works.
- Carl Maria von Weber[319], a German composer who is chiefly remembered for his operas.

Authors

Similar to the other fixed signs, Scorpio possesses a lot of patience and persistence. It is also considered to be prolific, same as the other Water signs, and, ruled by Mars, it has in its depths unlimited resources of energy. Taking all this into account, we can understand why many of those born with the Moon in Scorpio can write *a lot*. In addition, some of the themes of Scorpio can often be noticed in their books.

- Herbert Spencer[320], a British writer and philosopher who was credited with the phrase "survival of the fittest", which is quite a scorpionic concept. According to Wikipedia[321],

---

[316]http://www.astro.com/astro-databank/Scriabin,_Alexander
[317]http://www.astro.com/astro-databank/Berlioz,_Hector
[318]http://www.astro.com/astro-databank/Borodin,_Alexander
[319]http://www.astro.com/astro-databank/Weber,_Carl_Maria_von
[320]http://www.astro.com/astro-databank/Spencer,_Herbert
[321]http://en.wikipedia.org/wiki/Herbert_Spencer

Spencer was "the single most famous intellectual in the closing decades of the nineteenth century".
- John Steinbeck[322], an American famed writer of best-selling novels that were made into films. He wrote in total twenty-seven books, including sixteen novels, six non-fiction books, and five collections of short stories.
- A.J. Cronin[323], a British writer, a noted and inspirational novelist who was a physician and surgeon during World War I. "It was during an illness in 1931 that he wrote his first novel. When the work became an immediate success, he gave up his medical practice to write full time". We can see here a few different themes of Scorpio: he was a surgeon during a war, and then we see another example of a rebirth, when a person left behind one life and started another, a totally different one.
- Cyrano de Bergerac[324], a French poet, philosopher, dramatist and soldier on whose life Edmond Rostand based his famous play of the same name. Yet another Moon-in-Scorpio author who also was a soldier. "A reckless adventurer, he lived dangerously and made many enemies through his travels. His career in the army resulted in serious wounds but little advancement so he turned to science and literature".

Power

Power and influence are very important for the Moon-in-Scorpio individuals, and many of them have made their way to the top of the society in the search of power. There are a few of them in the list below, as an example, but I suspect that the majority of the most influential Moon-in-Scorpio power brokers prefer to stay in the shadow and are not widely known.

[322]http://www.astro.com/astro-databank/Steinbeck,_John
[323]http://www.astro.com/astro-databank/Cronin,_A.J.
[324]http://www.astro.com/astro-databank/Cyrano_de_Bergerac

- August Bebel[325], a German Socialist, writer, and orator. "Bebel was cofounder of the Social Democratic Party (SPD) of Germany and its most influential and popular leader for more than 40 years. He is one of the leading figures in the history of western European socialism".
- Georges Pompidou[326], a French politician, the Premier in 1962-1968 under President De Gaulle. He was a prominent negotiator during the 1968 strikes and riots. From 1969-1974, he served as the 28th President of the Fifth French Republic, during which time he ended France's opposition of Britain's entry into the common market.
- Alfred Krupp[327], a German industrialist, the eldest son of Friedrich Krupp who founded the Krupp works the year before Alfred was born. In 1826, when he was just 14, both of his parents died, leaving him with the secret of making high quality cast steel and the small family workshop. Again, we can see more than one Moon-in-Scorpio theme here: the parents who died, and a secret that made Alfred Krupp rich and influential.
- Nelson Rockefeller[328], an American politician and noted family, the son and heir of John D. Rockefeller Jr., billionaire Governor of New York.
- Nelson Mandela[329], a South African President, a civil rights hero and martyr who claimed victory in his lifetime crusade to establish a non-racial democracy for South Africa.

[325] http://www.astro.com/astro-databank/Bebel,_August
[326] http://www.astro.com/astro-databank/Pompidou,_Georges
[327] http://www.astro.com/astro-databank/Krupp,_Alfred
[328] http://www.astro.com/astro-databank/Rockefeller,_Nelson
[329] http://www.astro.com/astro-databank/Mandela,_Nelson

The Moon in Scorpio in the Family

The Moon in Scorpio shows quite reliably that a person had some emotional trouble as a child. Often the reason for the trouble could be a powerful, controlling mother who doesn't allow other family members to live their lives, or there can be an atmosphere of suspicion or jealousy in the family.

Quite often, you will find that those people who lost one of their parents prematurely were born with the Moon in Scorpio. A somewhat extreme example here is Alfred Krupp mentioned above in the Power section: he lost both of his parents.

Or, the child could have been born to a life if obscurity where nobody ever nurtured it or cared about its emotions. The challenge for this person could be to transform his or her life, and Whoopi Goldberg is a great example of how this can be done.

A parent with the Moon in Scorpio can be somewhat obsessed about his or her children, trying to control their lives. This might work well with some children but not with the others.

It is also quite typical for a Moon-in-Scorpio individual to live in a somewhat unusual environment. This might be, for example, a house which needs a repair, or which is in the permanent state of repair, or which was destroyed in some way. There are many other possibilities here, of course. I remember watching a Grand Design show one day, and there was a couple who dug a hole in the earth and built their house there. I believe that at least one of them was born with the Moon in Scorpio.

Recovering from a Stress

Stresses are abundant in a typical Moon-in-Scorpio person's life, just because these people tend to involve themselves in all sorts of extreme situations and activities. So how do they recover from those stresses then?

Hot water is a great remedy for everyone who was born with the Moon in Scorpio. They adore hot water, so hot that most other people would be probably scalded by it. A nice steaming shower or bath would restore a Moon-in-Scorpio person's energy very quickly.

I used to ask everyone whom I knew had their Moon in Scorpio whether they like hot water, and nobody ever gave me a negative answer, while the most frequent of the answers was: oh yes!

A good sex can also be very helpful for those born with the Moon in Scorpio; it will nicely help to settle down their powerful energy after it was stirred up by a stressful experience.

In fact, anything that is strong and concentrated can be helpful, be it a drink or a dish. I still remember my surprise when many years ago, speaking about astrology with a young and delicate 17 years old girl, who, I knew, had Scorpio for her Moon Sign, I asked what's her preferred way of recovering from a stress. The answer was: well, a nice shot of brandy is always helpful!

Health and Diet

A healthy sexual life is of utmost importance for those who were born with the Moon in Scorpio. Healthy means quite intense in this context. If it is present then many different problems, including problems with health, will simply disappear, or at the very least become less severe.

On the contrary, when the difficult-to-control energy of a Moon-in-Scorpio individual doesn't have a sexual outlet, it can easily become destructive. On the emotional plane, the negative emotions of Scorpio will become stronger and can poison both personal relationships and career, while on the physical plane various chronic inflammatory processes might emerge, especially in the reproductive system area.

As for any Water sign, it would be great for the Moon-in-Scorpio people to live not far from a body of water, be it an ocean or a swamp. It would be even better to bathe in thermal springs regularly, and maybe live in an area where such springs are abundant.

As for the diet, one cannot really expect from a Moon-in-Scorpio to be moderate. They don't live like that, they tend to go to extremes in everything they do. An advice that can be given to them is to be aware of their limits. Not to starve themselves to death, not to overeat to a health-damaging level, not to eat something which can kill. Then they'll be fine.

A Surprise Moment

Have you noticed that most of the Moon-in-Scorpio scientists in my list are strongly associated with chemistry? Believe me, I didn't have an intention to only pick the chemists. Also, Alexander Borodin, who is better known as a Russian composer, was also a devoted chemist!

This looks to me very interesting. Just consider the stereotypical image of a chemical lab: a mysterious space where various liquids are heated by flames - isn't this very much like the Moon in Scorpio? One can also think of the deeper, almost mythological associations with scorpions and poisons.

The next sign in the sequence of the zodiac is optimistic and philosophical Sagittarius, and the next chapter will be all about people born with the Moon in that sign.

The Moon in Sagittarius

Sagittarius is a mutable Fire sign ruled by Jupiter. Those who were born with the Moon in Sagittarius are full of ideas, and they are eager to spread their ideas around the world.

Enthusiastic and Philosophical

These people are enthusiastic, optimistic, outspoken and honest, or at least they can easily make an impression of honesty, so that everyone will trust them, due to their ability to share their enthusiasm with the others.

The Moon-in-Sagittarius people are also philosophical, and many of them spend at least a part of their life searching for an ideal, or for some kind of wisdom. They can make great students, as they are able to quickly assimilate any number of ideas, and manipulate and combine those ideas with great confidence.

They also very naturally assume the role of a wise advisor or a guru. They are generous, benevolent, and tend to patronize.

A relatively weak side of those who have Sagittarius for their Moon Sign is that they don't like to take on responsibility, and they can be very changeable. Oh, come on, there are so many great ideas out there, you can't really expect them to devote the whole of their life to just one little thing!

Another peculiarity of the Moon Sagittarians that can be negative in some cases is that they usually don't want to go into the nitty-gritty; they'd rather prefer to make their decisions at a higher level, to paint with wide strokes. Also, given their tendency to freely spend money to impress someone, these people can make great strategists and marketers, but might be not as good in practical implementation of their own strategy.

Discoverers and Adventurers

Those who were born with the Moon in Sagittarius love freedom and open spaces. They are interested in everything which is faraway - the further it is away, the more they are interested. They like to travel, to visit other countries and experience other cultures. They are adventurous, risk-taking, and are eager to enjoy as much of life as possible.

All these qualities make the Moon-in-Sagittarius individuals natural discoverers and adventurers, and I have a number of examples to illustrate the point:

- Neil Armstrong[330], an American astronaut, the first man to set foot on the Moon, with the quote, "That's one small step for man, one giant leap for mankind".
- Charles Lindbergh[331], an American pilot and author, the most famous hero of his day for his flight from New York to Paris, which earned him the Congressional Medal of Honor.
- Giacomo Casanova[332], an Italian adventurer who is considered the greatest of historic lovers.

Sports People

Being a Fire sign, Sagittarius gives people plenty of energy, and mutable signs are very good in transforming their energy into movement. That's why many of those born with the Moon in

---
[330] http://www.astro.com/astro-databank/Armstrong,_Neil
[331] http://www.astro.com/astro-databank/Lindbergh,_Charles
[332] http://www.astro.com/astro-databank/Casanova,_Giacomo

Sagittarius can make great sportsmen. You will often notice that they excel in a sport which allows them to either spend plenty of time outdoors or to travel a lot. Also, most of the Moon Sagittarians adore horses.

Here are a few examples of sportsmen who were born with the Moon in Sagittarius:

- Agostino Abbagnale[333], an Italian sports champion, the winner of an Olympic Gold Medal for rowing.
- Tiger Woods[334], an American golfer who is perhaps the best young golfer in history.
- Garry Kasparov[335], a Soviet chess player and world champion.

Actors

The Moon-in-Sagittarius people typically have a great sense of humor and a strong charisma, which might be a little bit on the rough side, in some cases. People feel warmer and happier around them. You can notice this Sagittarian charisma in many of the actors born with the Moon in Sagittarius. These are some examples.

- Jim S. Abrahams[336], an American actor, screenwriter, producer, and director. I believe that the following little story, borrowed from Astro-Databank with permission, is very descriptive for Jim's Sagittarian nature: *He was 26 and a private investigator in his hometown when a chance meeting with childhood pals, David and Jerry Zucker, led to their founding of the Kentucky Fried Theatre in Madison, WI, a multimedia presentation that combined live improv skits with*

---

[333]http://www.astro.com/astro-databank/Abbagnale,_Agostino
[334]http://www.astro.com/astro-databank/Woods,_Tiger
[335]http://www.astro.com/astro-databank/Kasparov,_Garry
[336]http://www.astro.com/astro-databank/Abrahams,_Jim_S.

film and video satire. They moved the show to Los Angeles providing the core for "The Kentucky Fried Movie", 1977. Three years later the three scored a surprise box-office hit as co-writers and directors of the film "Airplane!" 1980, a loony spoof of "Airport". Their continued comedies included the "Naked Gun" series.

Here is another interesting detail I found: Abrahams lost his home in a Malibu, CA fire. This is interesting because home is one of the symbolic projections of the Moon, while Sagittarius is a Fire sign. This doesn't mean, of course, that everyone with the Moon in a Fire will sooner or later lose their home in a fire. As you will see in a later section if this chapter, the Moon in Sagittarius can have numerous less dramatic, and more typical, manifestations.

- Dirk Bogarde[337], a British actor, "a total craftsman and one of the leading box-office stars throughout the 1960s".
- Douglas Fairbanks Sr.[338], an American actor "known as a swashbuckling film hero in the '20s to '40s".
- Al Pacino[339], an American actor, "one of the most accomplished stars of his generation who remains a private, enigmatic figure".
- Chuck Norris[340], an American actor who built a substantial career on his skill in martial arts.

Authors

The Moon-in-Sagittarius individuals are great storytellers, and of course you will find many authors among them. They are very

---
[337] http://www.astro.com/astro-databank/Bogarde,_Dirk
[338] http://www.astro.com/astro-databank/Fairbanks_Sr.,_Douglas
[339] http://www.astro.com/astro-databank/Pacino,_Al
[340] http://www.astro.com/astro-databank/Norris,_Chuck

versatile and can write many things in many different ways. However, the most successful of their writings are typically about an adventure, or a foreign country, or they are full of humor, or they carry and disseminate some bright idea. Here are a number of examples which, I believe, are quite typical, especially some of them:

- Lewis Carroll[341], an English logician, mathematician, clergyman, photographer and novelist, considered a master in the genre of nonsense literature. He is particularly remembered for his children's books, "Alice's Adventures in Wonderland" and its sequel, "Through the Looking Glass".
- Art Buchwald[342], an American Pulitzer-Prize winning journalist, columnist, raconteur and bon vivant. "Looking like a genial bulldog dressed in a brightly-colored sports jacket and slacks and puffing a cigar, he begins an anecdote. His eyes light up, his face crinkles and he transforms into an impish boy hoping the world will like him".
- Paulo Coelho[343], a Brazilian esoteric writer whose books are extremely popular and sell internationally. Perhaps the most well known of his books, and definitely one of my most loved books, is "The Alchemist". At a simplest level, it's a story of a Spanish shepherd who made a long and full of adventures journey in order to find a treasure, and you can already see that the book is overfilled with the symbolism of Sagittarius.
- Honoré de Balzac[344], a French novelist and playwright famed from 1829. "A dynamo of activity, he covered a vast enterprise of writing a series, 'The Human Comedy', with 2,000 characters".

---

[341] http://www.astro.com/astro-databank/Carroll,_Lewis
[342] http://www.astro.com/astro-databank/Buchwald,_Art
[343] http://www.astro.com/astro-databank/Coelho,_Paulo
[344] http://www.astro.com/astro-databank/Balzac,_Honore_de

- Federico Garcia Lorca[345], a Spanish writer, a poet and playwright.
- Victor Hugo[346], a French writer, poet, dramatist, novelist, essayist, gifted painter, architect and critic "who, as an eclectic genius, was hard-working, politically active and a humanitarian".

Musicians

Every Moon Sign has its talented people, and of course there are many singers, composers, songwriters, and other musicians who were born with the Moon in Sagittarius. As it is usual with Sagittarius, you will typically find in creativity of this people something of its nature: their music can be sparkling optimistic, like that of Mozart, or they might defy culture and language barriers, or perhaps they created an unimaginable wealth of masterpieces in every imaginable genre. Here are some examples from my collection:

- Wolfgang Amadeus Mozart[347], an Austrian composer who was a prolific child prodigy and who wrote masterpieces in every branch of classical music; he is regarded as one of the world's great geniuses. "His sense of humor was bawdy bordering on scatological and he was inordinately fond of practical jokes". Well, he was a true Moon-in-Sagittarius person after all!
- Salvatore Adamo[348], a popular Belgian composer and singer of Italian ancestry, who, according to Wikipedia[349], "mainly

---
[345]http://www.astro.com/astro-databank/Lorca,_Federico_Garcia
[346]http://www.astro.com/astro-databank/Hugo,_Victor
[347]http://www.astro.com/astro-databank/Mozart
[348]http://www.astro.com/astro-databank/Adamo,_Salvatore
[349]http://en.wikipedia.org/wiki/Salvatore_Adamo

performs in French but has also sung in German, Italian and Spanish".
- Charles Gounod[350], a French composer of operas, choral works, orchestral pieces and piano and chamber music. His mother (the Moon) was his first piano teacher. At some point in his life he gave serious consideration to joining the priesthood (Sagittarius is strongly associated with religion).
- Barry Manilow[351], an American musician, singer, author and songwriter who achieved mega-pop stardom in the 1970s.
- Johannes Brahms[352], a German musician, a composer, pianist and conductor.

Artists

While the works of the artists born with the Moon in a Fire sign are typically bright and colorful, and often symbolic, the Moon in Sagittarius can rise painting to a still higher level, where it becomes more like a message from a faraway realm. A good example is Henri Matisse[353], a French painter, sculptor and lithographer, noted for being one of the foremost decorative French painters of his time and one of the most influential of the 1900s. While his superbly simple line drawings rank among the greatest works of graphic art, he is best known for his abstract, intellectual use of color.

Two other good examples are:

- Pablo Picasso[354], a Spanish artist who lived most of his life in France, Picasso is world-renowned as one of the inventors of the Cubist movement.

---
[350]http://www.astro.com/astro-databank/Gounod,_Charles
[351]http://www.astro.com/astro-databank/Manilow,_Barry
[352]http://www.astro.com/astro-databank/Brahms,_Johannes
[353]http://www.astro.com/astro-databank/Matisse,_Henri
[354]http://www.astro.com/astro-databank/Picasso,_Pablo

- Vincent Van Gogh[355], a Dutch artist, a legend for his brilliant work, lived his brief life in misery and poverty. In the beginning of his life, he was a preacher (yet again, we can see the religious aspect of Sagittarius).

Scientists and Philosophers

Jupiter, the ruler of Sagittarius, is associated with higher education, opening new horizons, vast knowledge, and wisdom. It is very natural then that many of the Moon-in-Sagittarius individuals achieved a significant success in science or philosophy. Some of them, like Copernicus and Einstein, have radically changed the way people see the world.

- Nicolaus Copernicus[356], a Polish astronomer and author, considered the founder of modern astronomy. He established the theory that the Earth rotates daily on its axis and that planets revolve in orbits around the Sun.
- Friedrich Nietzsche[357], a German philosopher who is considered the most influential voice since Kant and Hegel. Nietzsche came from a long line of Lutheran pastors and was destined to follow in the footsteps of his clergyman dad. However, he eventually dropped his theological studies to take up classical philology, and later philosophy.
- Albert Einstein[358], a German-Swiss-American scientist, a physicist who developed the theory of relativity in 1905, and the general theory in 1916, laying the groundwork for 20th century physics and providing the essential structure of the cosmos.

---
[355]http://www.astro.com/astro-databank/Van_Gogh,_Vincent
[356]http://www.astro.com/astro-databank/Copernicus,_Nicolaus
[357]http://www.astro.com/astro-databank/Nietzsche,_Friedrich
[358]http://www.astro.com/astro-databank/Einstein,_Albert

- Alexander Fleming[359], a Scottish researcher in bacteriology. His best known discovery is the antibiotic penicillin.
- Thomas Alva Edison[360], an American inventor who patented over a thousand inventions that included an electric voice recorder, a phonograph, an incandescent electric lamp, a movie projector, and a talking motion picture - an incredible creative genius.
- Erich Fromm[361], a German-American psychoanalyst, professor, author and social philosopher.

Outworldly

The ruling planet of Sagittarius, Jupiter, is responsible for everything that is far away, both literally and metaphorically. Therefore, Sagittarius is associated with religion, spirituality, esoteric knowledge, and mysticism. I found quite a few people who were born with the Moon in Sagittarius and chose in their life to pursue higher knowledge, exotic religions, metaphysics, or Eastern philosophies. Here are some of them:

- Rev. Joy Adams[362], an American psychic who has channeled since pre-school, talking regularly to a dead grandmother. Joy previously lectured at the Metaphysical Center in San Francisco for many years.
- Ram Dass (Richard Alpert)[363], an American educator and author, fired as a Harvard professor for early experiments with LSD and other hallucinogenic drugs, who became a follower of the path of Eastern philosophy.

---

[359] http://www.astro.com/astro-databank/Fleming,_Alexander
[360] http://www.astro.com/astro-databank/Edison,_Thomas_Alva
[361] http://www.astro.com/astro-databank/Fromm,_Erich
[362] http://www.astro.com/astro-databank/Adams,_Rev._Joy
[363] http://www.astro.com/astro-databank/Ram_Dass

- Jiddu Krishnamurti[364], an East Indian teacher and religious leader. A philosopher and metaphysician from his youth, Krishnamurti obtained world recognition as a spiritual teacher and lectured to groups as diverse as the U.N. delegates, diplomats, scientists at Los Alamos National Laboratory and to people all over the world.
- Sri Aurobindo[365], an Indian religious leader and writer, a guru.

Spicing Up

When I think about what some of the notable Moon Sagittarians did for the humanity, the best definition that comes to my mind is that they've added some spice to the typically rather boring life of human beings. Here is a couple of examples:

- Alexandre Legrand[366], a wine merchant and industrialist of the 19th century who in 1863 invented the liqueur known as Bénédictine from a mixture of native herbs and exotic spices. He is (in French) named like Alexander the Great, but this is his real name. You will read about another person who was called The Great in a later section of this chapter.
- Carlo Benetton[367], an Italian industrialist, a fashion producer of sporting goods.

The Moon in Sagittarius in the Family

Those who were born with the Moon in Sagittarius usually have some of the symbolic meanings of this sign associated with their

---
[364] http://www.astro.com/astro-databank/Krishnamurti,_Jeddu
[365] http://www.astro.com/astro-databank/Aurobindo,_Sri
[366] http://www.astro.com/astro-databank/Legrand,_Alexandre
[367] http://www.astro.com/astro-databank/Benetton,_Carlo

mother, the whole parents' family, or sometimes with the father. The parents could be immigrants, and so the child was treated as a foreigner from the early age and had to be multilingual, or the parents' family could be religious, and that could influence the choice of the life path and profession, or perhaps the mother was interested in esoteric knowledge and was happy to share her knowledge with the child.

Alternatively, the parents' family could move often from place to place or from country to country. The mother could be like a guru, teaching her child to understand and explore the world.

A typical Moon-in-Sagittarius person can feel at home pretty much everywhere and will be only happy to have a life full of movement. Being a parent, a Moon Sagittarian might be not that great in terms of caring and nurturing the child, but instead will help the child to develop an optimistic worldview and to see life as an exiting adventure full of wonderful opportunities.

Recovering From Stress

For a typical Moon-in-Sagittarius individual to recover from a significant stress, it would be great to leave the hustle and bustle of the city, where he or she might feel claustrophobic, to go to the countryside and have a good walk in the fields or in a forest.

Sitting at a camp fire, a fireplace, or at least a wood-burning-stove, making a barbecue, or just reading a sci-fi book can restore a Moon Sagittarian's energy very quickly.

Or, if you have more funds, a trip to an exotic country can make a miracle with you. Just forget your worries and spend all the time visiting mysterious temples or exotic bazaars, and in a few days you will be like new.

Health and Diet

To live a healthy life, a person born with the Moon in Sagittarius should have as much contact with Nature as possible. It would be great to live in the suburbs rather than in the city, or at least have a garden, and an opportunity to see live fire from time to time, like in a fireplace, would be great.

Regular traveling is a must. The further and the more exotic the destination, the better.

But also, a true Moon Sagittarian will not be satisfied with just the physical circumstances of life. To be happy, and healthy, he or she needs a higher purpose, something that will fill their life with sense, be it a science, a religion, or some alternative kind of spirituality.

From the diet point of view, the Moon in Sagittarius will always want to try as many different cuisines and kinds of food as possible, and that's fine. It is essential to remember however that the liver of the Moon-in-Sagittarius people can be very sensitive, and some extremely and persistently foreign food can be harmful for it. Also, the Moon in a Fire sign like Sagittarius is already "on fire", so an overly spicy food can cause problems with the digestive system.

A Surprise Moment

Yet again, I find that common stereotypes can be quite misleading. We can easily imagine a Moon Sagittarian who is an exotic, or highly adventurous, philosophically minded person, who spends most of his or her time either traveling around the world or writing books about imaginary travels. A typical Sagittarian shuns responsibility and prefers freedom.

Can we imagine a Moon-in-Sagittarius individual becoming a powerful and influential world leader? Well, if we can't, then we need to work a little bit on our imagination, because there are some striking examples of exactly this kind of individuals born with the Moon in Sagittarius. What's more interesting, we can notice that the qualities of Sagittarius were at the core of their success. We could say that they've achieved what they've achieved not despite but thanks to the fact that they were born with the Moon in Sagittarius.

Have a look:

- Peter I, Czar of Russia[368] aka Peter the Great, a Russian royalty, Czar from age ten until his death. "At a seminal time in their history, Peter the Great took the Russian people from the Middle Ages into the modern world. He raised his country to a world power, becoming well-noted for gaining access to the sea for Russia and Westernizing Russian customs and institutions". Speaking of his plans, he used to say that he is going to "cut through a window to Europe".
- Gerald Ford[369], an American politician, a lawyer, congressman and Vice-President under Richard Nixon in 1969 and the 38th President of the United States. He was the first president in history to succeed to the nation's highest office due to the resignation of a president.
- Rupert Murdoch[370], an Australian-American entrepreneur who, after journalistic experience in London in 1962, "took over the family's small newspaper and parlayed a barely profitable enterprise into several successful papers within two years".

---

[368]http://www.astro.com/astro-databank/Peter_I,_Czar_of_Russia
[369]http://www.astro.com/astro-databank/Ford,_Gerald
[370]http://www.astro.com/astro-databank/Murdoch,_Rupert

The Moon in Capricorn

Capricorn is a cardinal Earth sign ruled by Saturn. The Moon is in detriment here - which is an astrological term meaning that it is in a part of the zodiac exactly opposite to her home in Cancer.

Moon-in-Capricorn people are somewhat dissimilar to the other people with the Moon in a cardinal sign. They are not so quick to start something new, because they are very careful, but on the other hand, once something was started, they won't abandon it easily, as they feel themselves responsible for whatever they've done.

They are ambitious, patient, conservative, and very systematic in their approach. They have a great instinct for everything that can elevate a person in the society.

The Detriment

Here, in the house of cold and rigid Saturn, the Moon finds itself in a hostile environment, so resources are scarce, and it needs to be careful, cautious and tenacious in order to survive there. The Moon's qualities are manifested in this sign in a way that is opposite to the nature of the Moon.

The Moon is naturally emotional and irrational, moved by a mood rather than logic, but the Moon-in-Capricorn people tend to control their emotions, hide their feelings, to be rational, organized and dispassionate. The Moon is changeable and moves quickly; however those who were born with the Moon in Capricorn take a long time to make a decision but then stick to it. The Moon would love to merge emotionally with everyone, but the Moon-in-Capricorn folks have an in-born tendency to create an emotional barrier around them, to distance them from the others.

Old When Young, Young When Old

Saturn rules the old age, and the Moon-in-Capricorn individuals often look older than their peers in childhood and youth. Or they might just feel older because they are more cautious, serious, self-controlling, or unusually responsible. Men of this Moon Sign can grow a beard in order to look older.

However, these people age well, and as they grow older, at some point they start looking younger than their peers. They will also probably stay efficient and keep working until a later age than an average person, especially if they are successful in their career.

Traditional

Those people who have Capricorn for their Moon Sign adore everything traditional, ancient, or simply old. They might be not very keen on innovations since they believe that a truly good thing should pass the test of time. After all, if people used something for centuries, it should be really trustworthy, even if it looks a little bit shabby!

Moon-in-Capricorn people love everything that reminds them of the good old times. A friend of mine, born with the Moon in Capricorn, enjoys his iPad, but he has constructed for it a special harness with a keyboard which makes the iPad looking like a typewriter from the beginning of the 20th century.

Politicians and Career People

You will definitely find many career people among those born with the Moon in Capricorn.

A Moon-in-Capricorn person is a little bit like a rock climber: he or she moves slowly, thoroughly contemplating every step, but eventually emerges at the top of the mountain, high above everyone else.

These people have a strong drive to be the best, to get to the very top. And with their cool efficiency, tenaciousness, self-respect, and sometime ruthlessness, they are very well suited to achieving their goal. Order and discipline are important for them, and they can make an efficient use of limited resources. They can find the social ladder pretty much everywhere, and they immediately make an effort to climb up that ladder, if only one step.

I have quite a few politicians and world leaders with the Moon-in-Capricorn in my collection; these are some of the most prominent of them:

- John Quincy Adams[371], an American President in 1825-1899. He had four public careers: diplomat, law-maker, Secretary of State and President.
- Al Gore[372], an American politician, "an attractive member for the Democratic Party with a famous political name, a solid family life, and strong religious conviction".
- Sun Yat-Sen[373], a Chinese politician, elected as the first President of the Republican Government of China in 1911, and founder of the Kuomintang Dynasty.
- Otto von Bismarck[374], a Prussian statesman who united the German people under the government of one empire.
- Moshe Dayan[375], an Israeli general and political leader who became a crusader for peace. "Skilled in both battle and diplomacy, he played a key role in four wars, but also helped negotiate the historic Israeli-Egyptian peace treaty". Indeed, many of the Moon-in-Capricorn individuals find the Army

---
[371] http://www.astro.com/astro-databank/Adams,_John_Quincy
[372] http://www.astro.com/astro-databank/Gore,_Al
[373] http://www.astro.com/astro-databank/Sun_Yat-Sen
[374] http://www.astro.com/astro-databank/Bismarck,_Otto_von
[375] http://www.astro.com/astro-databank/Dayan,_Moshe

an appropriate environment for their career aspirations. This might be because Mars is exalted in Capricorn.
- Archbishop Makarios III[376], a Greek ecclesiastic who served as an Archbishop as well as the President of Cyprus. In 1948, he was elected bishop and in 1950 rose to the position of Archbishop. He was elected to the office of President of Cyprus three times.
- George Washington[377], an American politician, the first president of the US in 1789-1797.
- Napoleon I Bonaparte[378], a French general and emperor, a giant figure in European history and known as one of the greatest military strategists in history.
- Indira Gandhi[379], an Indian politician, the Prime Minister of India in 1966-1977. "The daughter of Jawaharlal Nehru, she grew up with the impassioned politics of India's struggle for independence". Her father was a Prime Minister, and she became a Prime Minister. Quite appropriate for the Moon in Capricorn.
- Robert F. Kennedy[380], an American author, attorney, politician and noted family. He was a politician but people treated him like a pop star. See A Surprise Moment section below for an interesting parallel.

Engineers and Industrialists

People who were born with the Moon in Capricorn usually have a great understanding of various structures, schemes and constructs, while their patience and disciplined mind allow them to understand and create even the most complex of systems. Many of them can use

---
[376]http://www.astro.com/astro-databank/Makarios_III,_Archbishop
[377]http://www.astro.com/astro-databank/Washington,_George
[378]http://www.astro.com/astro-databank/Bonaparte,_Napoleon_I
[379]http://www.astro.com/astro-databank/Gandhi,_Indira
[380]http://www.astro.com/astro-databank/Kennedy,_Robert_F.

their talents in the industry or engineering, and here is a couple of examples of people who achieved a top position in their profession:

- Enzo Ferrari[381], an Italian industrialist and car racing enthusiast, "considered the world's most famous auto maker after Henry Ford, whose blood-red racing cars became a symbol of wealth and sportiness for those who could afford their six-figure cost".
- Ferdinand Graf von Zeppelin[382], a German engineer, inventor and military member in 1858-1891. "He is most noted for inventing the dirigible that carries his name, the first airship of a rigid type, in 1900. The ship crashed on landing on its maiden voyage, but he continued to successfully build and fly airships for his lifetime".

Musicians

Interestingly, music might be the next most popular occupation for the Moon-in-Capricorn individuals after making a career. This is probably because Saturn, the ruler of Capricorn, is strongly associated with rhythm, and rhythm is very important in music.

Interestingly, the Moon in Capricorn is definitely associated with choreography. This is easy to understand if you think of the hard labor, patience and discipline required to become, for example, a ballet dancer. The same can be actually said about any music performer - to be at the top of their profession, they need to spend their whole life honing their skills.

Here are some Moon-in-Capricorn musicians from my collection:

---

[381]http://www.astro.com/astro-databank/Ferrari,_Enzo
[382]http://www.astro.com/astro-databank/Zeppelin,_Ferdinand_Graf_von

- Paula Abdul[383], an American singer, songwriter, dancer, choreographer, actress and television personality.
- Luigi Boccherini[384], an Italian virtuoso, an eminent cellist and one of the leading composers of the latter 18th century.
- Dmitri Shostakovich[385], a Russian composer noted for his daring and experimental style.
- Yehudi Menuhin[386], an American musician known as one of the most exquisite violinists in history.
- Ozzy Osbourne[387], a British rock star known for extravagant if crude showmanship.
- Charles Aznavour[388], "a French singing rage for many years, retaining a loyal following".
- Frédéric Chopin[389], a Polish classical pianist/composer, recognized as a musical prodigy at age eight and hailed as the next Mozart.
- Billie Holiday[390], an American blues and jazz singer nicknamed "Lady Day", whose incomparable voice was the essence of jazz.
- Anton Bruckner[391], an Austrian composer and organist best known for his nine splendidly constructed and lengthy symphonies.
- Jon Bon Jovi[392], an American musician, the superstar leader of "Bon Jovi".

---

[383] http://www.astro.com/astro-databank/Abdul,_Paula
[384] http://www.astro.com/astro-databank/Boccherini,_Luigi
[385] http://www.astro.com/astro-databank/Shostakovich,_Dmitri
[386] http://www.astro.com/astro-databank/Menuhin,_Yehudi
[387] http://www.astro.com/astro-databank/Osbourne,_Ozzy
[388] http://www.astro.com/astro-databank/Aznavour,_Charles
[389] http://www.astro.com/astro-databank/Chopin,_Frederick
[390] http://www.astro.com/astro-databank/Holiday,_Billie
[391] http://www.astro.com/astro-databank/Bruckner,_Anton
[392] http://www.astro.com/astro-databank/Bon_Jovi,_Jon

Scientists

The Moon-in-Capricorn people are naturally attracted to science because of their desire to find order in chaos, to establish rules and laws and give them to the other people to use. They also possess an intellectual discipline and patience that allow them to devote long hours to their studies. Here are some of the famous scientists born with the Moon in Capricorn:

- Karl Abraham[393], a German psychoanalyst, a student of Freud. He founded the International Institute of Psychology in Berlin. You might remember that Roberto Assagioli had his Moon in Virgo, while Sigmund Freud's Moon was in Gemini, and Carl Gustav Jung's Moon was in Taurus. I find that the Moon's position in either an Earth sign or a sign of Mercury can give an interest in the area of psychology, psychiatry or psychoanalysis. That's because the soul, the Moon, is studied practically and analytically in those disciplines.
- William Herschel[394], a German astronomer, who was also a technical expert, a musician and a composer. It's quite amazing how different talents of the Moon in Capricorn came together in one person.
- Fridtjof Nansen[395], a Norwegian scientist and politician. Again, two different talents of the Moon in Capricorn came together. For his exploration of the North Pole, Nansen was awarded the Nobel Peace Prize in 1922. Saturn is a cold planet, and the North Pole can be seen as the top of our planet. A Capricorn will always find where to climb.
- Percival Lowell[396], an American author, scientist and astronomer. "He is known for his belief of the possibility of life

---

[393] http://www.astro.com/astro-databank/Abraham,_Karl
[394] http://www.astro.com/astro-databank/Herschel,_William
[395] http://www.astro.com/astro-databank/Nansen,_Fridtjof
[396] http://www.astro.com/astro-databank/Lowell,_Percival

on Mars and for building the Lowell Observatory at Flagstaff, AZ. In 1905 he predicted the discovery of the planet Pluto, and has authored several books". In fact, one of the symbols for Pluto in use between astrologers is made of the initials of Percival Lowell.

Designers

People born with the Moon in Capricorn can be very strict and demanding when it comes to other people's appearance and outfit. Some of them have developed their understanding of beauty to such a degree that they became the world's trend-setters. Here are a few of them:

- Prue Acton[397], an Australian fashion designer, a major figure in the Australian industry of style and design. With the financial help of her parents, she founded Prue Acton Pty Ltd in 1964, describing her early work as "fabric sculpture". This sounds very appropriate for the Moon in the rocky Capricorn.
- Yves Saint Laurent[398], a French-Algerian designer; in the world of fashion, a once-in-a-generation designer and pace-setter.
- Paloma Picasso[399], a French designer and noted family. "One of Pablo Picasso's three children, she emerged from her father's shadow as a trend-setter in style. She created a jewelry and perfume line from her own original and bold brand of chic".

---
[397]http://www.astro.com/astro-databank/Acton,_Prue
[398]http://www.astro.com/astro-databank/Saint_Laurent,_Yves
[399]http://www.astro.com/astro-databank/Picasso,_Paloma

The Moon in Capricorn in the Family

The Moon-in-Capricorn parents have a very serious and responsible attitude towards parenthood and family life. Their tendency to control their emotions and hide their feelings, which helps them so much in their work, can create problems in close relationships in the family; but nevertheless, they are trying hard to do everything properly since their family is a part of their social status. So at those times when they are not overloaded with their career, the Moon-in-Capricorn parents can be very attentive and efficient in their family role.

Somehow, it might still feel like they are a bit formal in their attitude to kids and other family members, and it might be very difficult for them to create at home a warm and cozy environment.

Children with the Moon in Capricorn usually don't have many happy memories about their childhood. Their parents might be very busy with their career, like for example the Prime Minister father of Indira Gandhi, or maybe they paid a lot of attention to order, responsibility and discipline in the family, those things that do not usually make kids very happy. In one or another way, there was something about the parent's home that made it a bit cold and uncomfortable. Kids were not free to express their emotions there. The parent's family could be at the very top of society, and so there were many necessary formalities in the family life, or it could be at the very bottom, so that every vital resource was scarce.

Quite often, the Moon-in-Capricorn individuals find a permanent partner later in their life, and that partner can be significantly older. That's because the romantic side of relationships isn't really that important for them. What *is* important is the social status and security that the relationship can give them.

Recovering From a Stress

A Moon-in-Capricorn individual can become quite a nuisance when he or she is recovering from a significant stress. That's because in order to feel better, they'll want to see themselves at the top of the mountain, and they can do things or say words that will put other people, even if they are beloved family members, somewhere below their feet.

It might be better for such a person to recover somewhere in solitude, in a place where they can forget about their numerous plans and responsibilities.

Health and Diet

The physiology of those born with the Moon in Capricorn can often be not very efficient, in one or another way. They might be sensitive to cold, and so they need to be careful and dress warmly enough; or their digestion might be not very efficient, or there might be some problems with the protective systems of the body, or with the bones. These people should pay enough attention to their health and try not to allow little problems to become chronic diseases, even if they are very busy with their career.

Similar to the other Earth signs, Moon Capricorns will benefit from a regular massage, so that to activate the circulation of fluids and energies in the body.

Many of the Moon-in-Capricorn individuals will be happier if they will have an opportunity to live in a hilly or mountainous area, and skiing in the mountains in winter can be the best kind of sport for them. They might also like to live in an elevated location, like a top of the hill, an upper floor of a skyscraper, or at the very least have their attic converted into a study.

Digestion of the Moon in Capricorn might be not very efficient, so it is important for these people to not overeat, and at the same time make sure that their food is easily digestible and has a high nutritional value.

Artists

To be honest, I didn't find many artists with the Moon in Capricorn, but I did find one, and a very prominent one: Peter Paul Rubens[400], a Flemish-German artist, a baroque painter widely recognized as one of the foremost painters in the history of Western art.

Tell me that I am stupid about art, but for me those magnificent ladies in Rubens's paintings could easily compete with Arnold Schwarzenegger! And you'll find out soon that Schwarzenegger was born with the Moon in Capricorn.

Authors

I find that authors born with the Moon in Capricorn often reflect the themes of Capricorn or Saturn in their writings in one or another way. Alternatively, their creations can be somewhat quirky, similar to those of the authors with the Moon in Cancer.

Here is a couple of examples:

- Ernest Hemingway[401], an American writer, novelist and adventurer who was awarded the Pulitzer Prize in 1953 for "The Old Man and the Sea", and in 1954 the Nobel Prize for Literature. Note that perhaps the most famous of Hemingway's books is about an old man - that's one of the typical symbolic images of Saturn.

---

[400]http://www.astro.com/astro-databank/Rubens,_Peter_Paul
[401]http://www.astro.com/astro-databank/Hemingway,_Ernest

- Federico Fellini[402], an Italian film maker, a screenwriter and director of top Italian films, known by many as the master of cinema. "He thrived on chaos and confusion, and his films are noted for being weird, strange and exaggerated".

A Surprise Moment

I was surprised by the number of prominent male actors who were born with the Moon in Capricorn. Interestingly, these are some of the sexiest actors, or those who are considered to be like an etalon of a cool man. My attempt of explanation for this is that the Moon is the symbol of the feminine, but when it is in Capricorn, in the sign of its detriment, those who were born with such a Moon have the least amount of femininity in their image, and so they are very successful when playing strongly masculine characters.

I won't insist that my theory is great, I am not sure how it will work for ladies, but have a look at the following selection of the Moon-in-Capricorn actors:

- Arnold Schwarzenegger[403], an Austrian-born actor and politician, "began his career as a body-builder, ultimately winning several titles for his strength and magnificently sculpted body". Note that he is also a politician!
- Matt Damon[404], an American actor, the author of a movie script that he and his buddy, actor Ben Affleck, wrote for themselves, called "Good Will Hunting". They sold the script to Miramax for over $1 million, and played the key roles themselves.

[402]http://www.astro.com/astro-databank/Fellini,_Federico
[403]http://www.astro.com/astro-databank/Schwarzenegger,_Arnold
[404]http://www.astro.com/astro-databank/Damon,_Matt

- Brad Pitt[405], an American actor and sex symbol. According to Wikipedia[406], "he has been described as one of the world's most attractive men, a label for which he has received substantial media attention".
- George Clooney[407], an American actor with several appointments to annual Best-dressed, Most Stylish, Most Eligible and Sexiest Man Alive lists.

The next sign of the zodiac, Aquarius, is also ruled by Saturn - at least from the point of view of the Traditional Astrology. However, it is very different in many ways, and the next chapter will be devoted to the people born with the Moon in Aquarius.

[405]http://www.astro.com/astro-databank/Pitt,_Brad
[406]http://en.wikipedia.org/wiki/Brad_Pitt
[407]http://www.astro.com/astro-databank/Clooney,_George

The Moon in Aquarius

Aquarius is a fixed Air sign. Its traditional ruler is Saturn, while its modern ruler is Uranus. Uranus is an interesting planet, very different from the others: every other planet is standing upright while rotating around the Sun, but Uranus is lying on its side. That's an astronomical fact. Not surprisingly, Uranus is associated with rebels and revolutionaries.

People born with the Moon in Aquarius love freedom, and they usually have some strong ideal that they follow and promote no matter what. As Aquarius is a fixed sign, they can be very persistent, adamantly true to their ideal and, as some would put it, extremely stubborn.

Rebels

Another interesting fact is that Aquarius is opposite to Leo in the zodiac. Leo is associated with the central power, traditionally - royal power, while Aquarius opposes that power. It might believe that it has an alternative idea about how the society should be built and how the country should be ruled.

This is why many of the people born with the Moon in Aquarius openly oppose the established rules and customs and go their own way. A striking example here is Diana, Princess of Wales[408]. Donna Cunningham in her book *Moon Signs. The Key to Your Inner Life* calls Princess Di "the most rebellious and shocking member of the royal family".

There are other examples too. All these are the Moon-in-Aquarius individuals:

---
[408] http://www.astro.com/astro-databank/Diana,_Princess_of_Wales

- Timothy Leary[409], an American professor, guru of the 1960's drug culture who coined the phrase, "Turn on, tune in, drop out". "Well ahead of his time, he was fired from Harvard for his controlled experiments with psychedelic drugs. Arrested 29 times, he was imprisoned in 1970 for two years and was eventually paroled in 1976. President Richard Nixon once called him 'the most dangerous man in America'".
- Voltaire[410], a French writer of philosophy, poetry and history. As an encyclopedist, satirist, novelist and dramatist, he gained lasting fame, despite the fact that he served several stints in prison for political offenses.
- Alexandra David-Néel[411], a Belgian-French explorer, scholar, author, mystic, spiritualist, Buddhist, and anarchist, who became famous worldwide for her wanderings through central Asia. According to Wikipedia[412], "during her childhood she had a very strong desire for freedom and spirituality". That was the Moon in Aquarius calling!
- Muhammad Ali[413], an American light-heavyweight gold medalist, the only man to win the heavyweight championship of the world three times. According to Wikipedia[414], "A controversial and even polarizing figure during his early career, Ali is today widely regarded not only for the skills he displayed in the ring but for the values he exemplified outside of it: religious freedom, racial justice and the triumph of principle over expedience". At some point in his life, Muhammad Ali refused to be conscripted into the US military. He was arrested, found guilty and stripped of his boxing title.

---

[409]http://www.astro.com/astro-databank/Leary,_Timothy
[410]http://www.astro.com/astro-databank/Voltaire
[411]http://www.astro.com/astro-databank/David-N%C3%A9el,_Alexandra
[412]http://en.wikipedia.org/wiki/Alexandra_David-N%C3%A9el
[413]http://www.astro.com/astro-databank/Ali,_Muhammad
[414]http://en.wikipedia.org/wiki/Muhammad_Ali

Social Reformers

Even if they are not rebels, the Moon-in-Aquarius people are strongly interested in the life of society, and often come up with ideas on how to make it better, or how to solve the society's problems. They can achieve a very high position in the society. Do you remember that idea about Aquarius opposing royal Leo? Moon Aquarians are **also** kings or queens - but alternative!

Here is a number of examples to demonstrate the point:

- Ralph Abernathy[415], an American Civil Rights Activist and founder of the Southern Christian Leadership Conference with Dr. Martin Luther King, Jr. In his life, he organized quite a number of demonstrations and boycotts to protest against various things.
- Niccolo Machiavelli[416], an Italian statesman, politician, philosopher and theorist who advocated in his book, "The Prince", that the end justifies the means. According to Wikipedia[417], "He was for many years an official in the Florentine Republic, with responsibilities in diplomatic and military affairs. He was a founder of modern political science, and more specifically political ethics".
- Tony Blair[418], a British Labour Party politician, elected Prime Minister in 1997, the youngest person to fill the post in 185 years, and ending a generation of Conservative rule. The Labour Party then went on to win two more elections under his leadership. Under his leadership, the party used the phrase "New Labour" to distance it from previous Labour policies.

---

[415]http://www.astro.com/astro-databank/Abernathy,_Ralph
[416]http://www.astro.com/astro-databank/Machiavelli,_Niccolo
[417]http://en.wikipedia.org/wiki/Niccol%C3%B2_Machiavelli
[418]http://www.astro.com/astro-databank/Blair,_Tony

Scientists and Inventors

All the Air signs - Gemini, Libra, and Aquarius - are interested in communication and information. Gemini is curious and will eagerly consume just any source of information. Libra is more selective and prefers the information coming from selected, trusted people or a specific section of society. Aquarius is even more focused and concentrated. A typical Aquarius person (and I include the Moon-in-Aquarius people here) is very knowledgeable - but in a specific, quite narrow area of knowledge.

He or she might be an expert, even a genius, in his or her realm, but totally ignorant in many other things, even those which are common knowledge for most people. They can be very much like a mad scientist from a movie!

Quite naturally, many of the Moon-in-Aquarius individuals do become scientists, mad or not. Here is a selection of them:

- George Abell[419], an American educator and astronomer. He was a member of Ciscop, a group of scientists who were adamantly anti-astrology. This is a great example in a few different ways. First, a typical astronomer just doesn't know enough of astrology to give an opinion on it, but a Moon-in-Aquarius individual can easily become "adamantly anti" anything which isn't within his area of expertise. Second, Moon Aquarians are rational thinkers. Very few of them can grasp anything that is outside of the Procrustean bed of the contemporary science, no matter how innovative or eccentric they are. Third, the Moon-in-Aquarius people are eager to form or join a group of similarly-minded individuals (like Ciscop) in order to promote or attack a specific idea.
- Antoine Becquerel[420], a French physicist, a pioneer in the

---

[419]http://www.astro.com/astro-databank/Abell,_George
[420]http://www.astro.com/astro-databank/Becquerel,_Antoine

study of electric and luminescent phenomena. In the beginning of the 19th century, when he worked, electricity was quite a new and exciting thing.

- Carolus Linnaeus[421], a Swedish botanist, also known as Carol von Linne. He was the first to organize the principles for defining genera and species of organisms as well as to create a uniform system for naming them. I'd say he manifested very well the systematic nature of the traditional ruler of Aquarius, Saturn.

Authors

The Moon Aquarians love books! Many of them surround themselves with books at home, or they might work in a place where there is plenty of books. This is probably because a book is a concentrated and fixed form of knowledge or information - exactly the kind of information Aquarians are keen on. Or maybe a book reminds them a trusty friend who can tell a long and interesting story.

They can also be quite good in writing books as they possess the depth of understanding, and persistence required to write hundreds and hundreds of pages. You will often find something unusual, typically Aquarian, either in life or in the books of the Moon-in-Aquarius authors.

- Rafael Sabatini[422], an Italian writer, one of the most widely read novelists of the 20th century. An article in Wikipedia about him[423] provides the following unusual detail: "At a young age, Rafael was exposed to many languages, living with his grandfather in England, attending school in Portugal

---

[421]http://www.astro.com/astro-databank/Linnaeus,_Carolus
[422]http://www.astro.com/astro-databank/Sabatini,_Rafael
[423]http://en.wikipedia.org/wiki/Rafael_Sabatini

and, as a teenager, in Switzerland. By the time he was seventeen, when he returned to England to live permanently, he was the master of five languages. He quickly added a sixth language – English – to his linguistic collection".
- Dane Rudhyar[424], a French-American astrologer, one of most noted and respected astrologers of the 20th century who was the proponent of humanistic, or "free will" astrology.
- Rex Stout[425], an American novelist best known for his mystery stories of "Nero Wolfe", the detective who generally solves crimes without leaving home. And who loves reading good books.
- Charlotte Bronte[426], a British writer, one of three sisters who became published authors. A Wikipedia article[427] tells an interesting story about her. After the death of their mother, Charlotte acted as "the motherly friend and guardian of her younger sisters". She and her siblings "created their own literary fictional worlds and began chronicling the lives and struggles of the inhabitants of their imaginary kingdoms". So we can see here a community of writers that emerged from a family. I find this very appropriate for the Moon in Aquarius.
- Juan Ramon Jimenez[428], a Spanish poet who won the Nobel prize for literature in 1956. His numerous romantic adventures gave plenty of material for his erotic poems.
- Albert Camus[429], a French writer, an essayist, novelist and dramatist. "With great technical skill, he stressed man's need to carry out responsibilities in a fight against social evils".

---

[424]http://www.astro.com/astro-databank/Rudhyar,_Dane
[425]http://www.astro.com/astro-databank/Stout,_Rex
[426]http://www.astro.com/astro-databank/Bronte,_Charlotte
[427]https://en.wikipedia.org/wiki/Charlotte_Bront%C3%AB
[428]http://www.astro.com/astro-databank/Jimenez,_Juan_Ramon
[429]http://www.astro.com/astro-databank/Camus,_Albert

Industrialists and Entrepreneurs

People born with the Moon in Aquarius are knowledgeable, inventive, and very persistent, which gives them an ability not only to come up with an innovative idea but also to make sure that their idea is implemented in the world, and on a large scale. In addition, both Saturn and Uranus, the rulers of Aquarius, are very good with technical, technological and other specific kinds of knowledge, which puts them high above the largely ignorant mass of common people.

Here are a few examples of how Moon-in-Aquarius individuals were able to achieve a great success with large-scale projects.

- Henry Ford[430], an American auto entrepreneur, father of the Model T and initiator of mass production with his automobiles. "He was the man who put America on wheels with the production and sale of a car that the average person could afford, selling more than 15 million cars".
- Ernest Gallo[431], an American vintner, entrepreneur and multimillionaire, credited with bringing wine to American tables and putting California on the world's winemaking map.
- Mayer Amschel Rothschild[432], a German entrepreneur-financier who established the Rothschild family fortune by opening a money exchange and investment house. At his death in 1812 he left a huge fortune to his five sons.

Actors and Directors

Many of the Moon-in-Aquarius individuals possess a powerful charisma. This might be because of the high intensity of their

---
[430] http://www.astro.com/astro-databank/Ford,_Henry
[431] http://www.astro.com/astro-databank/Gallo,_Ernest
[432] http://www.astro.com/astro-databank/Rothschild,_Mayer_Amschel

character or thanks to their ability to very efficiently control their emotions and manipulate their public image. Some turn this image-manipulation talent into profession and become prominent actors, directors, or showmen. Here are a few examples from my collection:

- Bruce Willis[433], an American actor, "a relatively unknown talent when cast in the TV series "Moonlighting" as a suave, wisecracking detective. He became an instant celebrity in 1985".
- George Lucas[434], an American director, writer, producer, and film genius.
- David Copperfield[435], an American magician, "a natural-born showman world famous with his outstanding productions of some 500 live performances a year plus TV spectaculars".
- Marilyn Monroe[436], an American actress, outstandingly famous as a sex symbol.
- Woody Allen[437], an American comedian, writer, actor and film director, screenwriter, playwright and musician, gifted and appealing.

Chefs

I checked the dates of birth of a number of world-famous chefs, and I do believe that Aquarius is one of a few signs of the zodiac where most of them have their Moons (the other often encountered signs are Virgo, Capricorn and, somewhat less often, Aries). I explain this to myself like so: the Moon Aquarians are inventive and innovative with food, and this is what makes them famous. You don't expect them to make fish and chips - unless this is a very unusual fish and

---

[433]http://www.astro.com/astro-databank/Willis,_Bruce
[434]http://www.astro.com/astro-databank/Lucas,_George
[435]http://www.astro.com/astro-databank/Copperfield,_David
[436]http://www.astro.com/astro-databank/Monroe,_Marilyn
[437]http://www.astro.com/astro-databank/Allen,_Woody

chips in one or another way, right? They can also be great showmen, which is also very helpful.

Unfortunately, the exact birth time isn't known for most of those famous chefs I looked at, so I can't include them into my collection. Still, I have one person to show as an example:

- Jody Adams[438], an American celebrity chef and cookbook author. She is the daughter of librarians - this is interesting for us because Aquarius is strongly associated with books.

Aviators

Uranus, the ruler of Aquarius, is associated with new technologies, high altitude, space exploration, while the sign of Aquarius is an Air sign. It is understandable then that in astrology Aquarius has a strong symbolic connection with aviation. I was pleased to find that indeed, some prominent aviators were born with the Moon in Aquarius. Here is a couple of examples:

- Otto Lilienthal[439], a German pioneer of aviation who became known as the Glider King. He was the first person to make well-documented, repeated, successful gliding flights.
- Auguste Piccard[440], a Swiss scientist, inventor and physicist who, as a man of many talents, was the originator of an airtight, airborne gondola in which he ascended to about 53,000 feet in 1932. In 1953, Piccard manned a bathyscaph that descended some 10,330 feet into the sea. This is an especially interesting example. Although not purely about aviation, but reaching both extreme depths and heights is so truly Aquarian!

---

[438]http://www.astro.com/astro-databank/Adams,_Jody
[439]http://www.astro.com/astro-databank/Lilienthal,_Otto
[440]http://www.astro.com/astro-databank/Piccard,_Auguste

Musicians

Many of the Moon-in-Aquarius people have music abilities - first, because the ruler of Aquarius Saturn gives them a great sense of rhythm, an second, they have the intellectual stamina and persistence required to become a good musician.

It is interesting that in the life and creativity of many prominent Moon-in-Aquarius musicians one can often see the features of Uranus and Aquarius: they can be inventive and innovative, or socially conscious and active, or eccentric, or rebellious. Have a look at this list:

- John Lennon[441], a famous British musician. "An icon in popular culture, Lennon became a megastar in the internationally renowned rock'n roll group, The Beatles, followed by a solo career that reflected the angst of the times". According to his Wikipedia article[442], "Lennon revealed a rebellious nature and acerbic wit in his music, writing, drawings, on film and in interviews. Controversial through his political and peace activism, he moved to New York City in 1971, where his criticism of the Vietnam War resulted in a lengthy attempt by Richard Nixon's administration to deport him, while some of his songs were adopted as anthems by the anti-war movement". So you can see that he was a true Moon Aquarian!
- Richard Wagner[443], a German composer and poet who was "a controversial and fascinating genius of the European artistic scene. He was known for writing dramatic operas with a revolutionary technique and did his first symphony at the age of 19. Largely self-educated, he became the music director at theatres in Magdeburg".

---

[441]http://www.astro.com/astro-databank/Lennon,_John
[442]https://en.wikipedia.org/wiki/John_Lennon
[443]http://www.astro.com/astro-databank/Wagner,_Richard

- George Gershwin[444], an American composer, "famous for show tunes, swing rhythms and his unique style of blending commercial pop, jazz and blues music with classical structure".
- Béla Bartók[445], a Hungarian-American musician, "a leading composer and pianist who was a leading composer of modern times and one of the all-time greats".

The Moon in Aquarius in the Family

Many times, reading the life stories of people born with the Moon in Aquarius, I found that one of their parents had died when they were still very young. I don't think this should be considered as a rule, but still the Moon isn't really comfortable in cold and often detached Aquarius. Its rulers Uranus and Saturn might be the least child-friendly of the planets, after all.

The Moon-in-Aquarius people often have an unusual childhood, in one or another way. Their parents might have been highly educated, and they could have grown up surrounded with books, or maybe their parents were very active socially, or eccentric in one or another way. The parents of a Moon-in-Aquarius child might also have been driven by some strong idea, and the child might have inherited that idea from them.

Whatever is the case, chances are that the child felt emotionally detached from the parents, and not properly cared for.

Becoming a parent, such a person might find it difficult to nurture his or her kids. They tend to view them more like friends rather than children, and can be very demanding at times. However, if the child has the Moon in the same sign, or at least in one of the other Air signs, Libra or Gemini, they might develop a long and lasting

---

[444]http://www.astro.com/astro-databank/Gershwin,_George
[445]http://www.astro.com/astro-databank/Bart%C3%B3k,_B%C3%A9la

friendship. They will play the same computer games and enjoy the same gadgets very happily.

Recovering From a Stress

To recover from a significant stress, a Moon-in-Aquarius person needs to switch to something very interesting, whatever they find interesting. It can be a good book, or an especially tricky programming problem, or a spaceship design.

Another approach which might be fruitful is to defeat one stress with the help of another one - but this other stress should be a healthy, exciting one, like a parachute or bungee jump, or maybe just a flight on a hot air balloon.

Health and Diet

Blood circulation and nerves are the sensitive parts of the system of those who were born with the Moon in Aquarius. They need to make sure that every liquid circulates well in their body, so a regular and extended but not very strainful session in a gym can be very helpful, as well as other regular but not too taxing physical activities. Massage can be very good too.

The dietary advice is similar to that given to the Moon-in-Capricorn people: food should be nutritious and not overloading. Specifically for the Moon Aquarians I will add an advice to not read when eating. Concentrate on your food, not on your book.

A Surprise Moment

We already know that the Moon-in-Aquarius people can be quite innovative in terms of social life, and they have powerful influence and charisma that make other people believe in their ideals. Still, it was a surprise for me when I read in Donna Cunningham's *Moon Signs* book the following abstract:

You may recall that the Mormons believed in polygamy. Joseph Smith, founder of the Mormons, and his follower, Brigham Young, both had Moon in Aquarius.

This was especially stunning for me because I already had an example of polygamy in my collection, and this person was also born with the Moon in Aquarius. Here he is:

- David Koresh[446], an American religious fanatic and psychopath. He was a high school dropout and rock musician before becoming the polygamist preacher of the Davidian Sect. He built his church on a simple message: "If the Bible is true, then I'm Christ".

Of course I don't mean that every Moon Sagittarian is potentially a polygamist. It's just one of the numerous possible manifestations of this unusual, eccentric sign.

The last in the sequence of the signs of the zodiac is the mysterious Pisces, and the next chapter will tell you how this sign manifests itself in the lives of people born with the Moon in Pisces.

[446]http://www.astro.com/astro-databank/Koresh,_David

The Moon in Pisces

Pisces is a mutable Water sign. Its traditional ruler is philosophical and religious Jupiter while its modern ruler is mysterious and hazy Neptune. In practice, both rulers are important and meaningful in understanding the life and character of those who were born with the Moon in Pisces.

If Water signs were compared to different bodies of water then Pisces would be undoubtedly an ocean. This sign is wide open to the collective unconscious with its whales of archetypes and sharks of ideas. If someone is born with the Moon in Pisces, his or her personal subconscious (the Moon) gets directly connected to the collective unconscious (Pisces). As a result, such people get a deep and natural intuitive understanding of other people's joys and troubles, and they also get a direct access to an endless source of creativity.

Venus, the planet of love and beauty, has its exaltation in Pisces, and therefore love, sympathy, beauty and harmony are very important for the Moon Pisceans. They can also be very romantic, charming and entertaining. Many of them possess a powerful charisma, and some of them can even become an etalon of beauty. Here is an example:

- Cindy Crawford[447], an American model. "During the 1980s and 1990s, Cindy Crawford was among the most popular supermodels, and a ubiquitous presence on magazine covers. Her success at modeling made her an international celebrity that has led to roles in television and film, and to work as a spokesperson".

[447]http://www.astro.com/astro-databank/Crawford,_Cindy

On the other hand, due to the nature of Pisces, they can also be easily carried away by the sea of emotions. They can be unreliable and unpredictable even for themselves, as they really don't know which emotional current they will come across in the next five minutes.

Due to the influence of Neptune, the Moon-in-Pisces people can be idealistic, somewhat unreal or otherworldly, imaginative and dreamy. They can also be selfless and devoted to a high idea but at the same time quite helpless when it comes to practical matters.

Politicians

People born with the Moon in Pisces aren't usually that much interested in career or social position - much less than Moon Capricorns anyway. However, the world of big politics is all about secrets, hidden influences and subtle nuances. This is where Moon Pisces feel themselves like fish in the sea, so many of them can achieve a prominent position pursuing a political career.

I find that the Piscean themes can be clearly seen, in one or another way, in the life of such politicians and society leaders, just have a look at the examples below.

- Otto Friedrich Abetz[448], a German politician, an Ambassador to Vichy France. "He was formerly an art teacher in a girl's school. He was anti-Semitic and played an active role in sending French Jews to the gas chamber. Sentenced as a war criminal in July 1949 to 20 years prison". What a strange life, one might say! I am giving it here as an example because the whole life story of this man is saturated with the symbolism of Pisces. The main themes are art and beauty (an art teacher in a girl's school) - this is a clear association

---

[448]http://www.astro.com/astro-databank/Abetz,_Otto_Friedrich

with Venus exalted in Pisces; through its rulers Neptune and Jupiter, Pisces is strongly associated with religion, especially Christianity, and therefore religious intolerance, like anti-Semitism; through Neptune, it is connected to chemistry and poisoning (gas chambers); through its similarity with the 12th house, Pisces is associated with the places of isolation, like prisons.

- J. Edgar Hoover[449], an American Director of the Federal Bureau of Investigation from 1924, "famous for his dramatic campaigns against public enemies and organized crime. As the FBI's leader, he made the Bureau into one of the world's most efficient law-enforcement agencies". Pisces is strongly associated with everything which is hidden, including secrets, covert operations, and organized crime.
- Che Guevara[450], an Argentinean revolutionary who led guerrilla groups with the aid of Fidel Castro in their attempt to spread communism in South America and Africa. Again we can see the theme of secret activities, and any ideology, but especially Communist ideology, is strongly associated with Neptune, the ruler of Pisces.
- Cardinal Richelieu[451], a French ecclesiastic and politician. "With ability, energy and extreme ambition, he became a member of the Royal Council, a Cardinal in 1622, and as chief minister to King Louis XIII, he was the virtual ruler of France from 1624-42".

Healers and Mystics

Whether they realize it or not, many of the Moon-in-Pisces individuals possess some kind of a psychic gift, or at least just a

---

[449]http://www.astro.com/astro-databank/Hoover,_J._Edgar
[450]http://www.astro.com/astro-databank/Guevara,_Che
[451]http://www.astro.com/astro-databank/Richelieu,_Cardinal

strong intuition. If such a gift gets developed, they can tap into the collective unconscious and virtually create miracles. They are also very much spiritually inclined and can be interested in any kind of religion or mysticism.

Here are a few examples from my collection:

- Barbara Brennan[452], an American holistic healer, author of several books, and founder of the Barbara Brennan School of Healing.
- Ramakrishna[453], an Indian saint and mystic, renowned as the founder of the Ramakrishna Mission, better know in the West as the Vedanta Society. "An assistant in the temple of the goddess Kali from 1855, he devoted his life to his religious ideals. He was a pantheist, believing that all religious paths lead to God-consciousness. To many Hindus he represented a 'supremely realized self' and an incarnation of the divine".
- Fredrick Davies[454], a British psychic, astrologer and clairvoyant who claimed a 80% accuracy. "Formerly an actor, director and producer, he began a newspaper column and radio show in London that started his road to fame. He had a noted clientele for 20 years of show business and public personalities".

Movie People

The illusory life of the movies, if you look at it from the astrological point of view, is strongly associated with Neptune, the ruler of Pisces. A typical Moon-in-Pisces person spends a significant part of his or her life watching movies, and if the circumstances allow, they will never miss a chance to become a part of that mysterious

---

[452]http://www.astro.com/astro-databank/Brennan,_Barbara
[453]http://www.astro.com/astro-databank/Ramakrishna
[454]http://www.astro.com/astro-databank/Davies,_Fredrick

world. Here are a few examples of people who succeeded in making their dream a reality:

- Robert De Niro[455], an American actor, director and businessman, the winner of two Oscar awards for Best Supporting Actor.
- William Berke[456], an American film maker, a cameraman until cataracts on both eyes forced him to change his venue to producing and directing.
- Georges Melies[457], a French illusionist, a pioneer of special effects for cinematography.

Artists

Venus is an exalted planet in Pisces. It gives those who were born with the Moon in Pisces an ability to appreciate beauty and, at least to some of them, to create beauty. Add to this an unlimited imagination of Neptune, as well as the Moon's deep connection with the subconsciousness, full of images, and you will understand why some of the world's greatest artists have their Moon in Pisces.

- Michelangelo[458], an Italian Renaissance artist, sculptor, poet and architect, considered even today as the greatest figure in the history of art.
- Paul Cézanne[459], a French artist who "did not have his first one-man show until he was age 56. In the following decade, he was acknowledged as one of the brilliant contributors to the world of art, becoming an important influence on the 20th

---

[455] http://www.astro.com/astro-databank/De_Niro,_Robert
[456] http://www.astro.com/astro-databank/Berke,_William
[457] http://www.astro.com/astro-databank/Melies,_Georges
[458] http://www.astro.com/astro-databank/Michelangelo
[459] http://www.astro.com/astro-databank/C%C3%A9zanne,_Paul

century creative process. He is considered the spiritual father of Impressionism".
- Raoul Dufy[460], a French artist, a painter who was one of the major artists of the Fauve group and considered a master draftsman.

Musicians, Dancers and Singers

Given everything which was already said about the Moon in Pisces, it isn't a big surprise that most of my examples of the Moon-in-Pisces individuals became famous for their input into the world of music. Just have a look at this list of glorious names:

- Elvis Presley[461], an American pop singer, one of the most famous entertainers in history whose notoriety became worldwide.
- Frank Sinatra[462], an American legendary superstar of a singing career as well as TV and movies.
- Enrico Caruso[463], an Italian opera singer with a brilliant voice, world known as one of the greatest tenors in history. Noted for his strong, romantic voice, he captivated audiences with his musical range and depth of feeling.
- Christoph Wilibald Gluck[464], a German musician and one of the finest reformers of opera. He tried to make all parts of the opera serve the drama as in "Orfeo ed Euridice".
- Michael Jackson[465], an American singer, dancer and exceptionally talented entertainer.

---
[460]http://www.astro.com/astro-databank/Dufy,_Raoul
[461]http://www.astro.com/astro-databank/Presley,_Elvis
[462]http://www.astro.com/astro-databank/Sinatra,_Frank
[463]http://www.astro.com/astro-databank/Caruso,_Enrico
[464]http://www.astro.com/astro-databank/Gluck,_Christoph_Wilibald
[465]http://www.astro.com/astro-databank/Jackson,_Michael_(1958)

- Vaslav Nijinski[466], a Russian dancer, noted for being one of the greatest male ballet dancers of all time, his style being one of spectacular high leaps. His supreme virtuosity and a combination of featherweight lightness with steel-like strength made Nijinski a genius of the ballet.
- George Friedrich Handel[467], a German composer of oratorios, operas, concertos, cantatas, anthems and sonatas. He is known universally for his "Messiah", which he wrote in 25 days.
- Maurice Ravel[468], a French composer, a leader in the French musical impressionist movement, considered to be one of the modern masters of orchestration, known for the vigor and beauty of his orchestral and ballet studies.
- Franz Schubert[469], an Austrian composer, who left a colossal lifework of nearly 1,000 compositions, more remarkable considering that he died at age 31.
- George Balanchine[470], a Russian-American dancer, known as one of the most famous choreographers in the field of ballet.
- Andres Segovia[471], a Spanish guitarist, one of the world's foremost classical guitarists with his remarkable virtuosity and musicianship.
- Charles Valentin Alkan[472], a French composer and pianist. He spent his life as a piano teacher in Paris. His compositions require extreme virtuosity.
- Mikhail Glinka[473], a Russian composer who called attention to Russian folk music that influenced the musical development in the 1800s.

---

[466] http://www.astro.com/astro-databank/Nijinski,_Vaslav
[467] http://www.astro.com/astro-databank/Handel,_George_Friedrich
[468] http://www.astro.com/astro-databank/Ravel,_Maurice
[469] http://www.astro.com/astro-databank/Schubert,_Franz
[470] http://www.astro.com/astro-databank/Balanchine,_George
[471] http://www.astro.com/astro-databank/Segovia,_Andres
[472] http://www.astro.com/astro-databank/Alkan,_Charles_Valentin
[473] http://www.astro.com/astro-databank/Glinka,_Mikhail

- Adriano Celentano[474], an Italian pop singer, actor, director, producer.

Scientists

The Moon-in-Pisces people typically have an irrational mind that works very efficiently with multidimensional images, abstract concepts, subtle hints, but not so well with hard facts. Thanks to their deep intuition, they can discover solutions that more pragmatic people would simply have never imagined.

The sphere of interests of these people is vast, and they can be famous in more than one activity, as the examples below demonstrate:

- Leonardo da Vinci[475], an Italian renaissance artist, inventor, engineer, sculptor and painter, he was truly a universal genius.
- Benjamin Franklin[476], an American printer, author, publisher, inventor, scientist, public servant and diplomat, a renaissance man, extraordinarily gifted.
- Samuel F.B. Morse[477], an American inventor of the first successful electric telegraph and of Morse code. He was also an excellent portrait painter.

Authors

With their rich imagination, powerful fantasy and ability to create whole imaginary worlds in their mind, the Moon-in-Pisces people can definitely become outstanding writers, and the examples below confirm this:

[474]http://www.astro.com/astro-databank/Celentano,_Adriano
[475]http://www.astro.com/astro-databank/Da_Vinci,_Leonardo
[476]http://www.astro.com/astro-databank/Franklin,_Benjamin
[477]http://www.astro.com/astro-databank/Morse,_Samuel_F.B.

- Petrarch[478], an Italian poet and scholar, whose works marked the beginning of the Renaissance.
- Robert Louis Stevenson[479], a Scottish writer, novelist and poet whose stories are noted for adventure and imagination. One of his most famous works is "Treasure Island".
- Johann Wolfgang von Goethe[480], Germany's most famous writer, a great literary genius of imagination and versatility who was unsurpassed as a poet and whose name is entered in the pages of history as one of the world's great thinkers.
- Percy Bysshe Shelley[481], a British writer known as one of the greatest lyric poets of the English Romantic age, a writer of delicate beauty.
- Gene Roddenberry[482], an American writer best known for creating the TV series "Star Trek" which ran on NBC for three years and had 78 episodes.
- Leonard Cohen[483], a Canadian novelist and songwriter-folksinger who became a Buddhist monk, "shaving his head and living part-time in a monastery on Mount Baldy, outside of Los Angeles, CA". This person is so versatile and multi-talented that it would be hardly possible to classify him into just one single category, but the symbolism of Pisces, Jupiter and Neptune is clearly visible in all the different aspects of his life.

The Moon in Pisces in the Family

Those who were born with the Moon in Pisces might experience their parents' family as a sea of selfless love. Their parents could

---

[478]http://www.astro.com/astro-databank/Petrarch
[479]http://www.astro.com/astro-databank/Stevenson,_Robert_Louis
[480]http://www.astro.com/astro-databank/Goethe,_Johann_Wolfgang_von
[481]http://www.astro.com/astro-databank/Shelley,_Percy_Bysshe
[482]http://www.astro.com/astro-databank/Roddenberry,_Gene
[483]http://www.astro.com/astro-databank/Cohen,_Leonard

have been not very good in handling social responsibilities and might have been not able to teach discipline to their child, but they would have certainly made sure that the child had the best emotional atmosphere possible and could freely express his or her creativity. This is also how Moon-in-Pisces parents tend to treat their own kids.

However, this was an ideal scenario. In fact, mysterious Neptune, the ruler of Pisces, can have very different manifestations. Other possible scenarios can be parents who are so fascinated with a spiritual or creative journey that they hardly remember that they have any kids, and so their children feel abandoned. It is also not unusual to see a child born into the family of alcoholics to have the Moon in Pisces.

And of course, there are numerous variations in between the good and the bad extremes. Quite often one can see that difficult emotional conditions in the childhood only help the Moon-in-Pisces individuals to develop and bring out their best talents and abilities.

Recovering From a Stress

To recover from a significant stress, a Moon-in-Pisces individual would need to forget about the world of harsh reality and find him or herself in the world of fantasy and imagination. The easiest way to do this would be to watch a movie or to read an interesting book.

Contact with water is very important for the Moon Pisceans. Even a simple shower can wash away many of their troubles. A visit to a swimming pool or a spa would be even better, but if they can afford to spend a couple of weeks on a tiny island in the middle of a huge ocean, that can heal their soul from many of its wounds.

It would be difficult to overestimate the importance of a clean emotional atmosphere for those who were born with the Moon in Pisces. They are very much aware of the moods and sometimes even thoughts of the surrounding people, and if those moods and thoughts are negative, they will suffer and try to find a more suitable environment.

Alcohol can be quite helpful as an anti-stress remedy, but it is important to remember that the Moon in Pisces makes people more sensitive to alcohol than an average person. They should be very careful both with the quality of alcohol and the quantity of it. Also, if they develop a dependence on alcohol or drugs, which again is more likely for a Moon-in-Pisces person than for an average person, that will eventually weaken them and make them more stress-prone.

Health and Diet

First of all, it would be very good for a Moon-in-Pisces individual to live by the sea. A river or a lake might be a suitable option too, but nothing can really be compared to a proper sea or ocean. A walk by the sea, a sea-smelling breeze will help to relieve or even carry away all the troubles and stresses, making one's life healthier and happier.

Any treatment involving water, especially seawater, such as a spa treatment, will be highly effective for people born with the Moon in Pisces.

One thing is very important to remember: the Moon in Pisces is very sensitive to various chemicals, drugs and artificial stimulants. This includes alcohol and narcosis used in surgery. A Moon-in-Pisces person can easily get an overdose - the sad story of Michael Jackson can be an example here - or develop an addiction.

As for the diet, it is very important to make sure that the food is very fresh and is of a high quality. The Moon-in-Pisces people should never try any food that looks suspicious, or maybe just stayed in the fridge for too long. Their digestion is acutely sensitive to any poisons and can react violently to a food that most other people would consider perfectly acceptable.

A Surprise Moment

Now, this was really a surprise for me. Given everything I know about Pisces, Neptune and Jupiter, can I understand why most of the leaders of the automobile industry in my collection were born with the Moon in Pisces? Perhaps not. But I will keep thinking about this.

- Ernesto Maserati[484], an Italian industrialist, the builder and designer of the high performance Maserati automobile. He built and raced his own cars before devoting full time to manufacturing; he had planned and overseen every step of the creation of his prize-winning race cars. Interestingly, the emblem of the Maserati cars is very similar to the symbol of Neptune.
- André Citroën[485], a French industrialist, the creator and manufacturer of a front wheel drive car, the Citroen.
- Ferruccio Lamborghini[486], an Italian industrialist, the builder of the Lamborghini automobiles.

Now that we've covered all the twelve signs of the zodiac and how the Moon manifests itself in them, I want to use this knowledge as a foundation and go a little bit further. The first topic to discuss is how different Moon Signs relate to each other, what kind of energy background they create in a relationship.

[484]http://www.astro.com/astro-databank/Maserati,_Ernesto
[485]http://www.astro.com/astro-databank/Citro%C3%ABn,_Andr%C3%A9
[486]http://www.astro.com/astro-databank/Lamborghini,_Ferruccio

The Moon Sign Compatibility

You have definitely read in newspapers, magazines and other sources of popular astrological information that different people can be more or less compatible depending on their "star signs" - which means, as you already know, depending on their Sun Signs.

While the Sun Sign compatibility is certainly important (at least when it is analysed by a competent astrologer), I believe that **the Moon Sign compatibility** is *a lot more important*, especially in long-term relationships like marriage. Let me explain why.

Why the Moon Sign Compatibility is Very Important

The Sun is associated in astrology with consciousness, and so the Sun Sign compatibility is important when you want to understand how successfully the two people can do something consciously together - for example, work, or play, or solve a problem.

On the other hand, the Moon rules the unconscious part of life - instincts, habits, automatic reactions, what kind of environment the person prefers, what makes him or her feel comfortable and happy; also what annoys them, perhaps without any particular logical reason. The Moon Sign helps to understand how people relax, recover from stress, how they prefer to spend time when they don't have to do anything specific - like in those precious few hours after work.

If you think about it, the activities ruled by the Moon take the greatest majority of the day - and of life in general. And if two people live together but have different jobs, it's the Moon Sign compatibility which will define how successfully, and for how long, they will be happy to coexist under one roof.

A Note For Astrologers

If you are familiar with the technical side of astrology - all the different planets, aspects and houses - you might believe that to estimate compatibility properly, you need to take into account all those different details, and that a simplified approach, like the Moon Sign compatibility, is too simplistic.

For this, I will remind you the ancient principle *as above so below*. The luminaries, the Sun and the Moon, are the most obvious and clearly visible objects of the surrounding Cosmos, so I believe that in astrological interpretation they should form a foundation for everything else. The Sun and the Moon define the main theme of life, with all the other factors adding to that main theme numerous details.

Speaking of compatibility, if we'll estimate it using simply the Moon Sign and the Sun Sign, we'll know what makes the foundation of the relationship, with all other factors building on top of this foundation.

What this means in practice is that if, for example, two people have the same Moon Sign, and especially if their Moons are close by degree, they will unconsciously feel so comfortable together that they will be able to live together for many years even if all the other factors say that they are not compatible. And vice versa, if two people have a strong compatibility at the level of, say, Venus and Mars, but no support at the level of the Moon, they will be powerfully attracted to each other sexually but might find it difficult to live together for any significant amount of time.

Levels of Compatibility

I believe that the unconscious connection between two people, which will help them to live together for many years and to overcome many troubles, exists when they share the same Moon Sign. I will elaborate on this in the next section.

The next strongest combination is when the Moon Sign of one partner coincides with the Sun Sign of the other partner. Occasionally, you will find partners with a mutual match: the Moon Sign of the partner A is the same as the Sun Sign of the partner B, while the Sun Sign of the partner A is the same as the Moon Sign of the partner B. This kind of match, especially the mutual one, can provide a very strong foundation for the relationship, but still not as strong as the same Moon Sign - I will try to explain below why I believe so.

Next comes the match where the Moons of the partners are in the signs of the same element - for example, both are in the Air signs (like one partner's Moon is in Gemini while the other's is in Libra). A similar but somewhat less potent combination is when the Moon of one partner is in the same element as the Sun of the other partner.

The last level of compatibility which will be discussed here is when the Moon Signs of the two partners belong to friendly elements, like Air and Fire, or Earth and Water.

Please understand that one chapter of a single book is totally insufficient to cover all possible kinds of relationships. For example, there will be a strong emotional link if the Moon of the one partner is in the same sign as Venus of the other partner, especially if there is a mutual match of this kind, but I don't have space to discuss all the possible important combinations here.

Also, I won't discuss a purely Sun Sign compatibility - firstly because I believe it is most meaningful for a work or business relationship, not for a long-term compatibility I am concentrating on here; but also, you can read about the Sun Sign match in pretty much every other popular astrology book discussing compatibility.

What I am trying to do here is to attract your attention to a very important aspect of compatibility which remains mostly neglected in the contemporary popular astrology.

The Same Moon Sign

Partners who share the same Moon Sign are very strongly connected at some deep level, although this connection can be unconscious. They have the same, or very similar, automatic reaction to different situations. They might try to say the same words at the same moment, or get the same desire simultaneously.

More importantly, their ideas of how to relax and be themselves are very similar, so when they are both at home and are not busy with anything particular, they feel very comfortable with each other.

They can have similar preferences in food; they like to live in the same kind of environment. They both prefer one kind of people and situations, and both will try to avoid some other kind.

People with the same Moon Sign usually have similar childhood experience, similar relationships with their parents and, when the time comes to become parents themselves, they will have similar ideas about raising kids.

An important point to understand here is that the deep connection at the level of the Moon Sign is unconscious, so it might not be obvious or easy to understand. Partners can look very different, they can be different in many ways, but somehow they just manage to be comfortable with each other.

The Moon Sign of One Partner is the Sun Sign of Another Partner

For example, one person has the Moon in Libra and the other person has the Sun in Libra.

Since the Sun is associated with the consciousness, this kind of compatibility is usually easily noticeable and can often be perceived as a good match. It can really show a strong compatibility which in addition has an attraction of polarities to it: the Sun is the symbol of the male while the Moon is the symbol of the female; so I believe this kind of match can be even more important between partners of different genders.

Still, since the Sun Sign manifestations are conscious, my understanding is that this kind of compatibility is not as deep and reliable as a pure Moon Sign match.

What happens here is that the partner whose Sun Sign makes the match usually does something in his or her life which feels very natural, or comfortable, and therefore very pleasing, for the other partner. The Sun Sign partner's manifestation in the outside world touches some deep strings in the soul of the Moon Sign partner.

All the above will become the order of magnitude more significant if there is a mutual match, like when one partner has the Moon in Libra and the Sun in Aries while the other partner has the Sun in Libra and the Moon in Aries. This match can show a very strong compatibility, but I still believe it won't be as good as the Moon Sign match, at least for partners who live together.

Imagine that they both came home after a difficult day of work. All they want is to relax and do pretty much nothing for the rest of the day. So they switch off their Suns, so to say, and allow their Moons to do the restorative work in the body and the soul. If their Moons are not in harmony, what will remain from their compatibility then?

The Same Element

From now on, I will be only writing about the Moon Signs match, but keep in mind that the same will be true for the Moon Sign - Sun Sign match too. The general rule is that when the Sun is involved, the match is easier to notice and understand, but it is not as deep and reliable in the long run.

Let's consider the case when the Moons of the two partners are in different signs but those signs belong to the same Element.

Just to remind you, the Fire signs are Aries, Leo and Sagittarius. If both partners have a Fire Moon, they are both full of energy and ideas. They have an active and creative life, and they enjoy their ride. Occasionally, they can become too temperamental and their emotions can flare up, but after the period of overheating is over, they will feel still closer and better together.

If both partners' Moons are in the signs of Air (Gemini, Libra, Aquarius), they both live in the world of information and have a great reliable channel of communication between them. Even if they are interested in different things, they enjoy telling stories to each other, and if there is a problem between them, they can speak it through and find a solution. The partner with the Moon in Aquarius will probably have more fixed opinions, but then the other partner should be able to make a compromise and be flexible.

Earth Moons (and the Earth Signs, if you remember, are Taurus, Virgo and Capricorn) are practical and pragmatic. Both partners like to do something tangible, something that makes sense and has a practical value. For example, they might both like gardening, or cooking, and a reference to practicability and common sense will help them to steer out of conflicts.

If both Moons are in the Water Signs (Cancer, Scorpio, Pisces), the partners are deeply emotional and can communicate without words. This kind of match is probably the closest to the case of the same Moon Sign because the partners are strongly connected at the subconscious level, although of course the fixed powerful emotions of Scorpio are very different from currents and tides of Pisces.

Friendly Elements

There are two pairs of the Elements that work with each other very well. Just think about it: fire won't burn without Air, and Water makes Earth fertile.

Similarly, those people who have their Moon Signs in friendly elements usually need each other for something and can help each other in one or another way.

A partner with an Air Moon will provide the partner with a Fire Moon with information which will help to make sense of his or her ideas, while the latter will give the former plenty of energy, and desire to go and find more information.

A partner with an Earth Moon will add practical sense to the fantasies and inspirations of the partner with a Water Moon, while the latter will add to the logical plans of the Earth emotional depth and attractiveness.

I want to complete this chapter with a quotation from Donna Cunninghum's "Moon Signs: The Key to Your Inner Life", an excellent book which I recommend wholeheartedly to everyone.

> Carl Jung, famous analyst of a mystical bent, studied astrology very seriously and used it in his practice. At one point, he became curious about what made marriages work, so he designed a research study with the charts of 483 married couples. He found that those

who got married and stayed married had one of three major chart contacts. The Moon of one may have been standing next to the Sun of the other, in the same sign and close together by degree. In other cases, the Moons of the couple were standing together, and in others, the Moon was standing on the other person's Ascendant. His results would have happened by chance in only one in ten thousand tries - in other words, the results were of great statistical significance.

Although, for simplicity's sake, we didn't pay attention to the exact degree of the Moon and the Sun, the Moon Sign match and the Moon/Sun Sign match discussed in this chapter are quite close to the first two important compatibility factors discovered by Jung. As for the Ascendant, it would introduce a whole new realm of information that would deserve at the very least a separate book, so I am not even touching the Ascendant here.

Now that you know both your Moon Sign and your Sun Sign (if you still don't know any of them, please check the Appendix A for the Moon Sign and the Appendix B for the Sun Sign), the natural question is: how do these two work together? This is exactly what we are going to discuss in the next chapter.

The Moon Sign and the Sun Sign - How They Work Together

I want to remind you the idea which I introduced in the beginning of the book: the Sun symbolizes in astrology our eternal Self, a sparkle of the Divine, which travels from life to life to learn different lessons, to gain valuable experience, to enrich the World with a new understanding.

The Moon, on the other hand, is the current incarnation, one specific lesson to learn, and all the different circumstances associated with this lesson.

Once we know both the Moon Sign and the Sun Sign for someone, we can try to figure out what his or her grand journey is about, and what is the specific lesson they are dealing with in the current incarnation. There is no guarantee that we'll come to some clear and meaningful answer in each and every case but we can definitely try. Even if we only get some glimpses of understanding, they might become invaluable at some stage of life, and they can gradually develop into a deeper knowledge.

To write my interpretations, I am going to use the traditional astrological concept of "the houses". However, you won't need any additional knowledge to understand them, I'll try to make everything as clear and simple as possible.

Technically, we are going to count in which sign, starting from the Sun Sign, one's Moon is located. For example, if someone has Aries for his or her Sun Sign and Gemini for the Moon Sign then this person's Moon is in the third sign from the Sun. You can use the zodiacal diagrams offered in the first chapter to verify this; however, for your convenience, I will offer tables with every possible combination of the Sun Sign and the Moon Sign that is appropriate for the given interpretation.

This approach, looking from the Sun to the Moon, allows us to see the role of our current incarnation from the point of view of the eternal journey. However, we can view the same situation differently, from the Moon's point of view. In that case, from the circumstances of the daily life, we might try to figure out where we came from, where we'll go afterwards, and maybe guess what the whole journey is about. Looking this way, in the example given above, we'll find that the Sun in Aries is in the eleventh sign from the Moon in Gemini.

I will try to combine both points of view in a single interpretation; let's see how I will manage to do that.

For some additional clues, you might want to have a look at the lists of celebrities in the Appendix C. I made sure that all of them have both their Moon Sign and the Sun Sign listed.

Now, let's start our quest from the simplest case which doesn't actually require any tables for understanding.

The Moon and the Sun are in the Same Sign

Both the consciousness and the subconsciousness are powered by the same kind of energy, and there is an inherent integrity in the character and life of such a person. He or she is good at concentrating on one particular thing or activity, and can achieve very significant results because of their concentration. They also manifest the qualities of their sign of the zodiac very strongly, and are sometimes called the "double" representatives of that sign, like "double Aries", "double Taurus", and so on.

From the grand journey's point of view, the lesson of the current life is to learn about yourself, your own abilities, to try and fully develop everything the body and the soul have to offer. Some egotism and self-centeredness are only natural for this combination of signs; they are a part of the challenge. There can be a strong interest in one's own body and its health, as well as in self-development.

From the Moon's point of view, this combination of signs can hint that the source of all knowledge and possibilities is actually inside, somewhere deep in your soul, and if you are looking for the God, then the best place to look is within yourself.

Astronomically, if someone was born with the Sun and the Moon in the same sign, this means that the moment of his or her birth was close to a New Moon. The Moon is not visible in the sky at this time of the lunar month, and speaking the language of astrology we might say that the feminine principle in nature is at its low ebb. I have noticed that women who were born near a New Moon often have a more extravert and active life than it is typical for a woman in the given society. A typical scenario is when in the absence of husband they need to be a father and a mother for their children at the same time.

The Moon is in the Second Sign From The Sun

The Moon Sign	The Sun Sign
Aries	Pisces
Taurus	Aries
Gemini	Taurus
Cancer	Gemini
Leo	Cancer
Virgo	Leo
Libra	Virgo
Scorpio	Libra
Sagittarius	Scorpio
Capricorn	Sagittarius
Aquarius	Capricorn
Pisces	Aquarius

The main lesson of the current life is to learn how to deal with resources. This of course means money and various material possessions, but not only them. The second house is also responsible for the accumulated skills, knowledge and other immaterial resources that we might have. The challenge is to both accumulate your resources in significant amounts *and* spend them with benefit, not just hold on to them.

In Hindu astrology, this house is strongly associated with speech, both oral and written, so your ability to express yourself in speaking and writing can play an important role.

Looking from the Moon, the Sun will be in the twelfth house, which means that the long-term spiritual goal is well hidden from people with this combination of signs. Alternatively, if they do realize that there is a bigger journey, they might feel that it is too limiting or frightening, they don't want to lose all the goodness given to them in the current incarnation.

The Moon is in the Third Sign From The Sun

The Moon Sign	The Sun Sign
Aries	Aquarius
Taurus	Pisces
Gemini	Aries
Cancer	Taurus
Leo	Gemini
Virgo	Cancer
Libra	Leo
Scorpio	Virgo
Sagittarius	Libra
Capricorn	Scorpio
Aquarius	Sagittarius
Pisces	Capricorn

The key lesson here is to learn how to communicate with people. You need to learn how to approach them, how to understand what they are up to, how to make them understand what you have to say, and also how to listen to their answer.

To learn this lesson properly, you will need to move a lot, so it also includes various means of transportation, and understanding of how to use them efficiently. Also everything that helps to establish communication, like phones or computers, can play an important role in this life.

Looking from the Moon, we'll find the Sun in the eleventh house. This means that the current lesson is only a part of a major study whose purpose is to create communities of people grouped around an important goal or idea. This combination of signs can be very good for a politician, or someone for whom people's opinions and an ability to influence them are very important.

The Moon is in the Fourth Sign From The Sun

The Moon Sign	The Sun Sign
Aries	Capricorn
Taurus	Aquarius
Gemini	Pisces
Cancer	Aries
Leo	Taurus
Virgo	Gemini
Libra	Cancer
Scorpio	Leo
Sagittarius	Virgo
Capricorn	Libra
Aquarius	Scorpio
Pisces	Sagittarius

Home, family and ancestors are important for people who were born with this combination of signs. The lesson is to build upon the foundation created by your parents, grandparents and other ancestors, and to create a possibility of a good start for your own children. This can involve continuing or establishing a tradition, or a family business, or perhaps building a house where the whole family can live securely and comfortably.

This combination of signs belongs to people who were born close to the First Quarter of the Moon, the phase that offers plenty of energy and a strong desire to do something by all means. This is why they usually take an active position in their life. They don't sit and wait, they act, they want to move and achieve.

Looking from the Moon Sign, the Sun is in the tenth house of high social achievements. It is thanks to those who build houses that cities and states emerge, and the foundation you are creating in this life will make some very important achievement possible in the larger scheme of things.

The Moon is in the Fifth Sign From The Sun

The Moon Sign	The Sun Sign
Aries	Sagittarius
Taurus	Capricorn
Gemini	Aquarius
Cancer	Pisces
Leo	Aries
Virgo	Taurus
Libra	Gemini
Scorpio	Cancer
Sagittarius	Leo
Capricorn	Virgo
Aquarius	Libra
Pisces	Scorpio

In this combination, the Moon Sign and the Sun Sign belong to the same Element, and you might want to read again about that Element in the first chapter to better understand the character and life of this person. As a general rule, this is a very beneficial combination as the consciousness and the subconsciousness speak the same language; this gives an ability to achieve great results without applying too much of an effort.

Sometimes you will notice that people with the Moon and the Sun in the same Element are a little bit spoilt by their destiny. They might have many beneficial opportunities in their life but not enough desire to pursue them, so some external stimulus might be needed to make them moving.

Returning to the position of the Moon in the fifth sign from the Sun, the keynote of this lesson is creativity. You are expected to play with life, to enjoy it, to be like a child. Try to forget about needs and duties, follow the path which leads to joy. This lesson involves love, and children as the fruit of love, so if you'll manage to forget what your lesson is about, just look at your children and play with them. They will remind you what happiness and creativity are about.

Looking from the Moon Sign, the Sun is in the ninth house of spiritual wisdom. This explains for me very well the joyful nature of the fifth sign experience: the God is Love, and to know the God we need to be like children. The true happiness and creativity of even a single individual brings everyone closer to the God.

The Moon is in the Sixth Sign From The Sun

The Moon Sign	The Sun Sign
Aries	Scorpio
Taurus	Sagittarius
Gemini	Capricorn
Cancer	Aquarius
Leo	Pisces
Virgo	Aries
Libra	Taurus
Scorpio	Gemini
Sagittarius	Cancer
Capricorn	Leo
Aquarius	Virgo
Pisces	Libra

This lesson is about work, efficiency, and making things functioning properly. The person might be interested in medicine, both official and alternative, and health in general. He or she might find themselves in a position when they quietly do the bulk of work behind the scenes while it is always someone else who gets credited for the final achievement.

Looking in the grand scale of things, this life is an episode of an important process of gaining influence, significance and control over the other people. It is important to learn the nitty-gritty of things now so that you didn't miss something important as your power will grow.

You will notice that in this combination the Sun Sign and the Moon Sign belong to the Elements that do not mix together well, like Fire and Water, or Air and Earth. This might bring into life many situations where some sort of adjustment is needed, or a requirement to make working together things that do not naturally match.

The Moon is in the Seventh Sign From The Sun

The Moon Sign	The Sun Sign
Aries	Libra
Taurus	Scorpio
Gemini	Sagittarius
Cancer	Capricorn
Leo	Aquarius
Virgo	Pisces
Libra	Aries
Scorpio	Taurus
Sagittarius	Gemini
Capricorn	Cancer
Aquarius	Leo
Pisces	Virgo

This is a very strongly partnership oriented combination of signs as the Sun and the Moon are in the seventh sign from each other. The lesson is how to establish relationships with the other people, and how to make them work. The keyword here is *balance*: you need to learn how to both strongly rely on your partner and at the same time remain independent, wholesome and self-sufficient.

People with the Sun and the Moon in the opposite signs were born close to a Full Moon. The Moon is at its brightest at this time of the lunar month, we can say that the feminine principle in Nature is at its peak, and I've noticed that men who were born close to a Full Moon are often much better aware of the invisible side of things, of the subconscious, and are much more sensitive than a typical male would be.

Also, the Full Moon gives a very high, sometimes overwhelming amount of energy. People born around this time often have some very important idea or purpose in their life, and they are moving towards their goal full steam ahead.

The Moon is in the Eighth Sign From The Sun

The Moon Sign	The Sun Sign
Aries	Virgo
Taurus	Libra
Gemini	Scorpio
Cancer	Sagittarius
Leo	Capricorn
Virgo	Aquarius
Libra	Pisces
Scorpio	Aries
Sagittarius	Taurus
Capricorn	Gemini
Aquarius	Cancer
Pisces	Leo

The important lesson of this life is to learn how to influence other people and how to control them - mostly invisibly, at the energy and emotions level rather than giving orders or commands. Also, proficiency in financial matters can be an important factor in making the most from the combination of energies offered by these signs.

Such people might tend to break things and relationships in order to find out what's inside them or to test how well they were built. As a result, they can have more than an average number of critical situations and extreme experiences in their life.

Looking from the Moon, the Sun is in the sixth sign. This means that the whole program of studies is about making things work efficiently, fixing problems, building complex but reliable systems in order to improve the health of the World in general.

The Moon is in the Ninth Sign From The Sun

The Moon Sign	The Sun Sign
Aries	Leo
Taurus	Virgo
Gemini	Libra
Cancer	Scorpio
Leo	Sagittarius
Virgo	Capricorn
Libra	Aquarius
Scorpio	Pisces
Sagittarius	Aries
Capricorn	Taurus
Aquarius	Gemini
Pisces	Cancer

Everything that is far away, both literally, and intellectually and spiritually, is important for the lesson of this life. It can be full of long journeys, higher studies, or maybe a search for a Guru is an important part of it. People from far away countries and connections with them can play an important role, and a person born with this combination of signs can be a little bit like a foreigner in his or her own land due to his or her unusual experience or understanding.

From the Moon Sign point of view, the Sun is in the third house, so the larger scale task is, once all the knowledge and wisdom were accumulated, to put them to a good practical use, to teach other people and to find better ways of communicating with them.

The Moon and the Sun here are in the signs of the same Element, so this combination of signs is often associated with high level of harmony and integrity in one's life since the consciousness and the subconsciousness can speak the same language and work together quite well.

The Moon is in the Tenth Sign From The Sun

The Moon Sign	The Sun Sign
Aries	Cancer
Taurus	Leo
Gemini	Virgo
Cancer	Libra
Leo	Scorpio
Virgo	Sagittarius
Libra	Capricorn
Scorpio	Aquarius
Sagittarius	Pisces
Capricorn	Aries
Aquarius	Taurus
Pisces	Gemini

The focus of this life's lesson is career, or achieving a prominent position in the society. At the very least, the person should raise noticeably above the level of society into which he or she were born. They need to learn how to properly establish relationships with all sorts of important people, and how to find those little opportunities that lead upwards in life.

Looking at this combination from the other side, we can think that the bigger plan is to find one's most appropriate place under the Sun, to build his or her own castle, to create a strong family which will be well known for generations to come, to establish a tradition.

This combination of signs belongs to people who were born close to the Last Quarter of the Moon, the time of the lunar month that fills people with desire to do something, to move, to achieve. As a result, such people move energetically through their life, actively pursuing any opportunities they manage to find and trying not to waste any of their time.

The Moon is in the Eleventh Sign From The Sun

The Moon Sign	The Sun Sign
Aries	Gemini
Taurus	Cancer
Gemini	Leo
Cancer	Virgo
Leo	Libra
Virgo	Scorpio
Libra	Sagittarius
Scorpio	Capricorn
Sagittarius	Aquarius
Capricorn	Pisces
Aquarius	Aries
Pisces	Taurus

The main lesson here is about finding good friends and allies, in order to be able to take on the plans that would be too big or too complex to approach without a good support. One needs to learn how to establish a cooperation in which every member's unique individuality would be respected, so that a group of people could multiply its creative potential by allowing each member to express his or her own creativity.

Looking from the Moon Sign, the Sun is in the third sign from it, so the grand plan is to surround yourself with people who are like brothers and sisters for you, who can understand you easily and will support all your initiatives.

The Moon is in the Twelfth Sign From The Sun

The Moon Sign	The Sun Sign
Aries	Taurus
Taurus	Gemini
Gemini	Cancer
Cancer	Leo
Leo	Virgo
Virgo	Libra
Libra	Scorpio
Scorpio	Sagittarius
Sagittarius	Capricorn
Capricorn	Aquarius
Aquarius	Pisces
Pisces	Aries

These people were born not long before a New Moon, the time of the lunar month when the energy level approaches its lowest point in preparation for the beginning of the next lunar month. This is the time for completing those things that can be completed, letting go everything else and preparing for new opportunities that might come after a while.

Such a combination of signs can be quite challenging as its lesson is about humility in face of limitations, ability to sacrifice and understand that not everything in life can be acquired or conquered; many things should be accepted as they are.

On the bigger scale, the plan is to understand that the true and eternal values are not of the material nature, and from that point of view someone with lots of money can be actually quite poor while those with very little material possessions can be in fact rich and happy.

More About the Natal Phase

You've probably noticed that different combinations of the Moon Sign and the Sun Sign correspond to particular phases of the lunar month: the New Moon, the Full Moon, and so on. In fact, every such combination has its phase, in the sense of distance between the luminaries.

The interesting point here is that the day when the luminaries in the sky repeat the phase at which you were born has a special significance for you. For example, if you were born at the Full Moon then each Full Moon will be a special day for you, but if you were born when the Moon was in the fifth sign from the Sun then your special day will be each time when the Moon is in the fifth sign from the Sun.

To fully understand this idea, you need to know about the daily motion of the Moon, and that's the topic for the next chapter. Just bear in mind for now that there is a very special day for you in every lunar month, and it is defined by the positions of the Sun and the Moon; I will return to this topic later.

The Moon Signs in Daily Life

The Moon makes a complete circle around the starry sky in about 27.3 days - it's a so-called sidereal lunar month. If you divide this by 12, you'll understand that it spends a little bit over two days in each of the signs of the zodiac.

While the Moon is in a particular sign, it's like the whole world has its Moon in that sign, and since we are all an inseparable part of the world, we all temporarily adopt that sign as our collective Moon Sign. We still each have our individual Moon Sign that we acquired at birth, as it was described in the previous chapters, but at the same time we temporarily adopt to some degree the qualities of the sign the Moon is traveling through at the moment.

The important point here is that all the people on the Earth adopt temporarily the transiting Moon's sign, whether they realize it or not, so the knowledge of where the Moon is at the moment can be used to understand the emotional atmosphere of the day, the subconscious wavelength on which people tend to communicate on this particular day.

Each sign of the zodiac makes certain activities easier while some other activities more difficult, and if we'll take this into account when planning our activities, we'll be able to achieve more with less efforts, and ultimately live our life happier and healthier. Isn't it a good reason for making that little effort required to figure out which sign of the zodiac the transiting Moon is in during an important day?

When the Transiting Moon is in Your Own Moon Sign

You now know what is your Moon Sign is, and you will soon know how to find out through which sign of the zodiac the Moon is traveling on each particular day. In each month, there is a couple of days when the Moon is transiting through your Moon Sign, and these days are important in at least three different ways.

First, the whole world is a little bit like you on these days. We might say you are better compatible with everyone around you because everyone adopts your Moon Sign temporarily, to some degree. They start to feel and subconsciously react a little bit like yourself, and if you understand this, you can achieve more in whatever you do when the Moon is passing through your Moon Sign.

Second, there is an astrological technique named *lunar return* that uses the precise moment when the Moon crosses over the location where it was at the moment of your birth. We can somewhat relax the rules of this traditional technique and say that the days when the transiting Moon is in your Moon Sign are very important for the whole month ahead. Things happening to you on these days might give you a hint at what's coming, and by reacting to the events wisely you can actually have an influence on your future. For example, by resolving peacefully a minor conflict on one of the days when the Moon is in your Moon Sign, you might avoid a major conflict during the next lunar month.

Third, the probability is high that your Moon Sign is pointing at some vulnerabilities in your body. You will learn a little bit about the vulnerable areas later in this chapter, and a lot more in the next chapter. You should understand that when the transiting Moon s in your Moon Sign, those vulnerabilities will increase, but at the same time your body will be very sensitive to a good natural treatment (but not surgery! - see the next chapter).

Now you are probably impatient to know how to find out where the transiting Moon is on a particular day. I am very happy to explain that.

How to Find Out the Transiting Moon's Sign

From the astronomical point of view, the movement of the Moon along its orbit is highly irregular; its speed keeps changing all the time. As a result, there are no easy to use simplified calculations that would tell us where the Moon is in the sky at the moment. If you want to figure that out, you need to use like a page of astronomical formulae and a calculator that can do trigonometric functions... Which obviously isn't an attractive option for most of us.

In pre-computer era the publishers of the popular lunar calendars and astrological books about the Moon had to offer to their readers lengthy tables listing the dates and times of the Moon's entry into each of the signs. Those tables used to take a substantial part of the book, they were only good for a few years, and they were a pain to use. Let's say such a table in a particular book was calculated for New York, and it says that the Moon will be in Aries from 7:23pm on the 1st of August. In San Francisco, the time will differ by a few hours, and the readers would be supposed to figure out the difference themselves. In Tokyo, even the day might be different, and again the readers would be expected to make a correction on their own.

Even worse, I saw lunar tables where the publisher, in an attempt to reduce the number of pages taken by the tables and offer tables for more years, assigned whole days to particular signs, like saying that the Moon is in Pisces on the 1st of August and in Aries on the 2nd of August. Those tables are totally useless as the Moon can enter a sign at any moment during a day and, to repeat myself, the time will be different for different places on the Earth.

We are fortunate to live in the computer era when we can trust all those tedious calculations to one of the computers that surround us in our lives. I myself have developed a range of tools that make the Moon-related calculations as easy and as precise as possible. Let me tell you about some of them.

The Universal Lunar Calendar at Lunarium

Universal Lunar Calendar

The Universal Lunar Calendar is a part of my Lunarium project. It calculates and displays many different factors for many years ahead, and for many past years too. It is completely free, you can use it from any computer connected to the Internet, but I do recommend you to use a more or less up-to-date web browser to make sure that everything works properly.

Let me offer you a whirlwind tour of the Universal Lunar Calendar[487]. By default, it is set to London (just because this is the closest major city to where I live, and I am quite egoistical!), and to the current month.

You can easily change the month, but most important of course is to set the calendar to your location. You should be able to do this only once; the calendar will then remember your location and do all the calculations for it on the consecutive visits. Click on the *Edit* link at the top right of the calendar and you will see the Lunarium Preferences[488] page.

Lunarium Preferences

Date/Time Format
- ⦿ 29/07/13 20:01 ○ 7/29/13 8:01 PM ○ 29/07/13 8:01 PM

Location
Country: Argentina   City: Buenos Aires
Current Time in this Location: 29/07/13 17:01
Latitude: -34.36 (Southern is negative)   Longitude: -58.27 (Western is negative)

Save Preferences

Lunarium Preferences

You can select a country and one of the predefined locations in that country. You can also select your preferred date format, and Lunarium will remember it. However, there are always not enough of predefined locations, and I never have time for adding all those locations requested by the users, so I created an Interactive Location Selector[489]. The idea is that you can click on your location in the

---

[487]http://www.lunarium.co.uk/calendar/universal.jsp
[488]http://www.lunarium.co.uk/settings.jsp
[489]http://www.lunarium.co.uk/location.jsp

map, select a time zone for it, and Lunarium will use the specified information in its calculations.

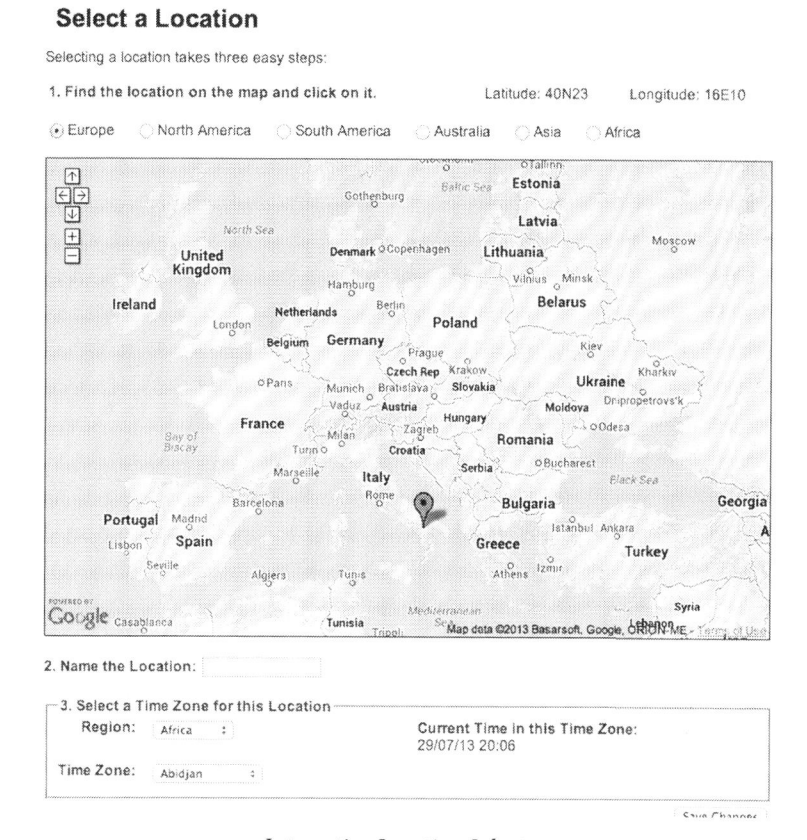

Select a Location

Selecting a location takes three easy steps:

1. Find the location on the map and click on it.   Latitude: 40N23   Longitude: 16E10

( ) Europe   ( ) North America   ( ) South America   ( ) Australia   ( ) Asia   ( ) Africa

[map image]

2. Name the Location:

3. Select a Time Zone for this Location
Region: Africa
Current Time in this Time Zone: 29/07/13 20:06
Time Zone: Abidjan

Interactive Location Selector

Let's say you've selected your location successfully, and calculated the calendar for the month of interest. Now how do you understand what the calendar tells you? Here is a few days range from the calendar:

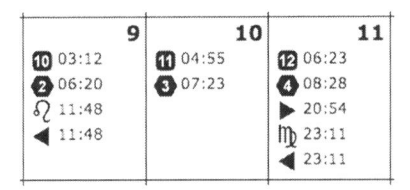

9	10	11
🔟 03:12	⑪ 04:55	⑫ 06:23
❷ 06:20	❸ 07:23	❹ 08:28
♌ 11:48		▶ 20:54
◀ 11:48		♍ 23:11
		◀ 23:11

A few days from the Universal Lunar Calendar

Please find the symbol of Leo on the 9th day with 11:48 written next to it. That's in the 24-hour format. If you selected another format, it should be used in the calendar. You might be unfamiliar with the symbols of the signs of the zodiac but there is a table at the bottom which will help you:

♈ Aries	♎ Libra
♉ Taurus	♏ Scorpio
♊ Gemini	♐ Sagittarius
♋ Cancer	♑ Capricorn
♌ Leo	♒ Aquarius
♍ Virgo	♓ Pisces

The symbols of the Signs of the Zodiac

Can you now figure out where is the symbol of Leo with 11:48 written next to it? Very well! That's exactly the day and the time of the displayed month for the selected location (in this example, July 2013 for London) when the Moon enters the sign of Leo. Can you now figure out when the Moon enters the next sign, Virgo? A hint: you need to find the symbol of Virgo, approximately two and a half days later, and see what time is shown next to it.

The answer is: 23:11 on the 11th of July.

This is how you can figure out when the Moon enters some sign of the zodiac in the Universal Lunar Calendar. There are many other symbols in this calendar, but if you are not familiar with them, stick to the Moon Signs for now. Everything else will become clearer with time, and some of these symbols will be explained in the coming chapters.

iLuna

I've also created a mobile app named iLuna that offers the most essential information from the Universal Lunar Calendar. iLuna isn't free, but its price is comparable to that of a cup of coffee (or maybe it might be much cheaper than a cup of coffee, depending on where you buy your coffee!), so it shouldn't be a problem for any budget.

The benefit of having iLuna is that you don't need any Internet connection in order to find out what's going on with the Moon at the moment. The app is completely self-sufficient; it contains data for 20 years ahead, so you can have your lunar calendar in your pocket no matter where you are. In addition, iLuna uses the time zone selected on your device, so you don't need to worry whether the time settings are correct. If your smartphone displays local time correctly then the information displayed by iLuna is also correct for your location.

Currently, iLuna exists for the two most popular smartphone platforms, iOS and Android, and I am working on an update that should come to both platforms before Christmas 2013 with a range of new features. After the update is ready, I am planning to start working on Windows 8 and Windows Phone 8 versions of the app.

Since the current versions of the app for iOS and Android are substantially different, let me show them separately.

iLuna for iOS

This is how *iLuna for iOS* looks when you just start the app. It's an iPhone app, i.e. it wasn't designed specifically for iPad. The next version is going to be a universal iPhone/iPad app, but for now let me show you what you can use right now. First of all, you will see the *Now* view.

The *Now* view of iLuna for iPhone

Right in the middle, you can see the current Moon Sign, Gemini, and if you press the **i** button, you'll see a brief interpretation for it. You can also see until when the Moon will be in Gemini. Press the **NEXT** button, and you will see the next sign of the zodiac the Moon will be in. This way, pressing NEXT, you can go 20 years ahead; iLuna has enough information for that, but of course navigating through the time like that would be inconvenient. The **Month** view is much more appropriate for a long journey in time.

The *Month* view of iLuna for iPhone

You can see the narrow bands of four colors: red, green, yellow and blue. People keep asking me again and again what do these colors mean. Well, I had to show somehow where one sign ends and the next one begins, and it seemed natural to use the traditional colors of the Elements: Fire is red, Earth is green, Air is yellow and Water is blue. The symbols of the signs, which I advise you wholeheartedly to learn by heart, are also colored according to their element. The wider gray bands show the Void-of-Course periods, described in the last chapter of the book. You can see that they can be of different lengths. There are also symbols of the phases of the Moon that will be discussed later in this chapter.

You can tap on a day you are interested in, and you'll see the lunar situation during that day displayed in the *Day* view.

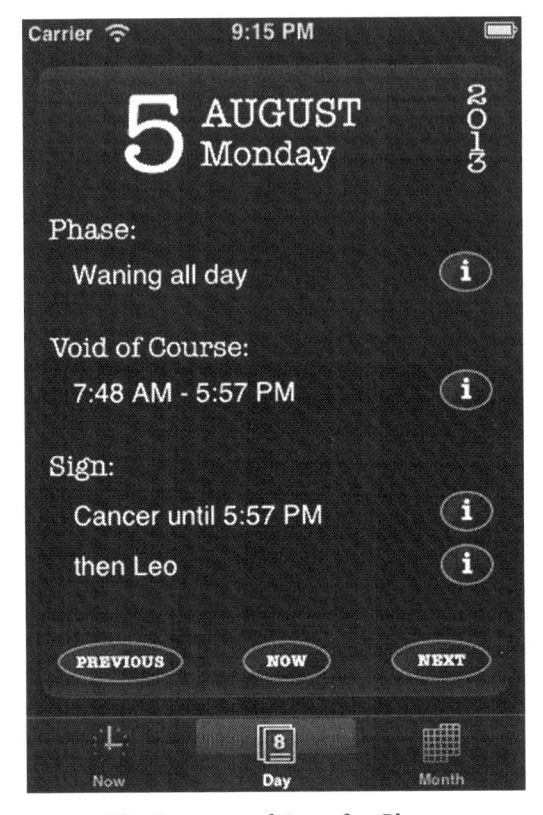

The *Day* view of iLuna for iPhone

Here the most interesting for now information is under the Sign. Sometimes the Moon will stay in the same sign for the whole day but sometimes it will change signs, like this screenshot demonstrates. Press the **i** button to read a brief description of each of the signs (you will find more detailed descriptions below).

Now let's have a brief look at the iLuna for Android.

iLuna for Android

The initial view of *iLuna for Android* is similar to the iOS version.

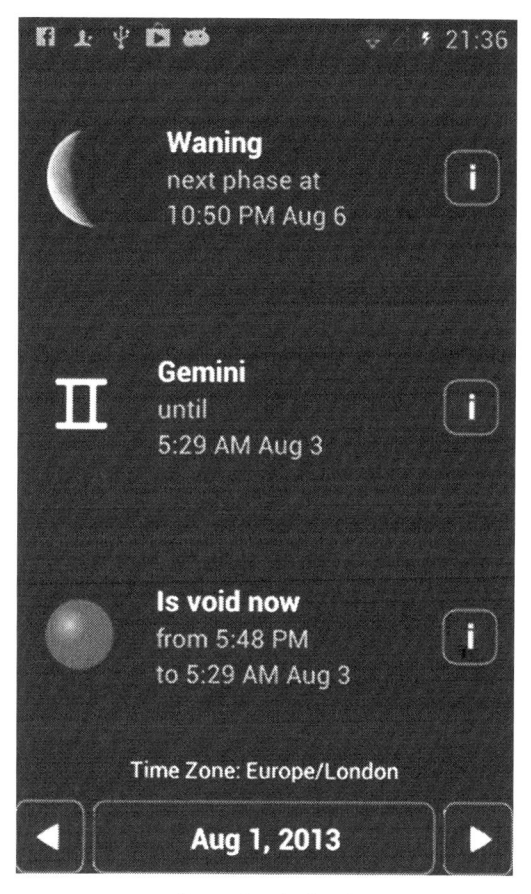

iLuna for Android

You can press the arrow buttons to go to the next or the previous day, you can press the large button with the date to select any other date in the calendar that appears. In general, iLuna for Android offers all the same information as iLuna for iOS but in a more compact way. Although I would agree that the month view with colored bands would be useful here, and I am planning to add it in the next version of the app, which will also offer an appropriately designed interface for Android tablets.

Now that you know how to find out when the Moon is located in each of the signs, it's the time to learn what meaning such a transit of the Moon has for the World in general and for each of us in particular.

The Transiting Moon in Aries

Speed, energy and impulsiveness. The world accelerates when the Moon enters Aries, and many things that seemed inconceivable a day before can now become possible. Initiative and courage are on the rise, as well as a desire to achieve and to win. People are open to new experience, and are keen to make the first step in some new direction.

At the same time, there can be an increase in impatience and aggressiveness. It should be also noted that the Moon in Aries does not favor any collective work. People tend to be more self-centered and self-sufficient than on the other days, they prefer to fight for their own cause.

It would be good to use the excess of energy available on the days when the Moon is in Aries for something constructive, or perhaps just to go to gym. Otherwise this extra energy will be splashed around in conflicts and irritation.

If you are prone to headaches, they can become worse when the Moon is in Aries. Also beware burns and scalds.

Good for: starting something new, being proactive, showing initiative, brainstorming, pushing ahead something that got stuck in the past. Also for competing, fighting, doing anything that requires bravery and decisiveness, for sports and workouts.

Not good for: doing anything that requires patience, diplomacy, prolonged effort, and cautiousness.

The Transiting Moon in Taurus

Persistence, patience, practicality. These days favour a prolonged effort and concentration, especially in occupations that are related to something valuable, or pleasant, or tasty, or are in connection with the Nature, like gardening. People appreciate value and quality of things when the Moon is in Taurus, so these days are good for important purchases, as well as for selling premium goods.

When the Moon is in Taurus, people don't like to be distracted or hurried, and if the conditions are right, they can do an enormous amount of work. Alternatively, they might decide not to do any work at all and instead enjoy life, indulge themselves in good food and wine.

Throat can become very sensitive on these days, so be cautious with cold drinks and ice cream when enjoying the Moon in Taurus on a hot summer day!

Good for: occupations that require patience, persistence, prolonged effort; enjoying Nature and good food.

Not good for: new beginnings; anything that requires speed, initiative, or ability to do several things simultaneously.

The Transiting Moon in Gemini

Communication, versatility, curiosity. These days activate all sorts of communication channels and help information to flow smoothly. There is more understanding between people, at least at the level of words, and this can be very useful for any discussion.

Intellectual abilities also get enhanced when the Moon is traveling through Gemini, and there is an interest in everything happening around. One one hand, people are able to grasp any knowledge or information quicker than usual, this is good for learning. On the other hand, they can easily get distracted by some news or events, which can interfere with a work or study requiring concentration.

Lungs and air passages of the body are sensitive when the Moon is in Gemini, so make sure you are dressed warm enough on a cold windy day.

Good for: any kind of communication but especially verbal communication: meetings, interviews, discussions; any kind of study, but especially lectures, seminars and workshops; occupations that require doing several things at once.

Not good for: occupations that require concentration, persistence, doing just one single thing; anything that prevents people from communicating to each other.

The Transiting Moon in Cancer

Emotionality, security, care. People can be more vulnerable than usual on these days; they value their privacy highly and protect their space. Everything related to home and family gains more importance; people appreciate emotional closeness and like being cared for. This is a good time to spend with small children, making sure all their needs are satisfied, or to visit one's parents.

Bear in mind that if they feel threatened, people tend to act more emotionally than it would seem reasonable when the Moon is in Cancer. They might even look aggressive, whereas in reality they are just trying to protect either themselves or those who are dear to them.

Stomach and breasts are sensitive when the Moon is in Cancer, so avoid anything that can hurt them, such as overly hot and spicy food that can be irritating for your stomach.

Good for: spending time with kids and family, staying home, cooking, and taking care of people.

Not good for: active communication, anything that can expose one's feelings and increase vulnerability.

The Transiting Moon in Leo

Brightness, creativity, leadership. On these days, people want to be seen, noticed and appreciated. Creativity is on he rise, as well as desire to be loved and praised. People tend to show-off, to get on a stage, to demonstrate how good they are, and they tend to be a bit more egocentric than on the other days. You can get lots of favor from your superiors if you'll let them know how much you enjoy being led by them, even if that will be an obvious flattery.

Days when the Moon is traveling through Leo are usually very good for presentations and shows, as well as for celebrations, entertainment, all kinds of games and gambling. Although speaking of gambling, you might feel on these days more lucky than you really are, so be reasonable.

The heart is especially sensitive when the Moon is in Leo, so be careful not to overload it, especially if you know that you have some problems with your heart. The back is also associated with Leo, so don't hurt it when exercising or lifting heavy items.

Good for: Performing, being creative, getting noticed. Gaming, gambling, entertaining. Playing with children. Praising and rewarding people. Presenting and showing off.

Not good for: Criticism. People can react very negatively to critics because they expect to be praised instead. Also activities that require subtle emotional sensitivity might not go very well.

The Transiting Moon in Virgo

Attention to detail, perfectionism, making it right. On these days, people tend to notice faults everywhere, even where they'd usually think everything is fine. So if you want to present the results of your work, better avoid doing that when the Moon is traveling through Virgo. On the other hand, if you want to do something complex, tedious, requiring a lot of attention and tenacity, this is the best time for it.

People in general tend to be more efficient on these days, and more interested in health-related topics. Any kind of practical, hands-on study will go well, as also repairs, clean-ups and critical reviews.

The body is more sensitive to imperfections in food, so anything which isn't very fresh or natural or familiar enough can cause problems with digestion. Also, the body might try to attract your attention to the areas where something wrong is happening by creating various pains or aches in those areas.

Good for: finding faults and rectifying them, improving health, cleaning and tidying up, criticizing, DIY, any kind of craftsmanship.

Not good for: occupations in which compassion and generosity are important. People might have a problem with seeing forest behind the trees when the Moon is in Virgo as they are very much focused on details.

Transiting Moon in Libra

Diplomacy, partnership, being nice. People tend to pay more attention to their partner when the Moon is traveling through Libra, and they want to find their second half, or to please him or her if they already found one. These days favor discussions that require diplomacy, objectivity and balanced approach. However, they might be difficult for formulating the final difficult verdict, as there appear to be more and more important factors to consider.

The Moon in Libra increases interest towards arts, music, everything that is beautiful and attractive. People tend to be nice and kind, and they want to enjoy life, especially if they can do that together with their loved ones.

Libra is associated with kidneys and all sorts of balances in the body, so any excess on these days can provoke health problems. Since Libra is opposite to Aries, the days when the Moon is transiting through this sign can be marked with stronger headaches in those who are prone to them.

Good for: dating, meeting people, making compromises. Dealing with beautiful things, enjoying arts, music and nice things of life. Peacefully resolving conflicts.

Not good for: difficult decisions, activities requiring stamina, persistence or aggression, things which are not aesthetically appealing.

The Transiting Moon in Scorpio

Intensity, struggle, secrets. When the Moon is traveling through Scorpio, emotions are deep and strong. These are the days when the animal side of the human nature is activated. Some of the hidden, forbidden or difficult themes come closer to the foreground - struggle for survival, sexuality, envy, jealousy. Sexual desire is stronger than usual, and there is a tendency to extremes, to pushing the reasonable limits.

Power struggle and intrigues are on the increase when the Moon is in Scorpio. There is a strong interest in anything that is hidden or secret, and a desire to investigate and uncover it. People's emotions can get overheated very quickly, the probability of scandals and upheavals is high; everyone is ready to fight to death for their cause.

Anatomically, Scorpio corresponds to sexual organs, and sexual desire can be very strong when the Moon is transiting through Scorpio. It is advised however to avoid going over the top in sex at this time as this can easily prove to be detrimental for your health, both sexual and general.

Good for: defeating enemies, destroying anything that blocks progress, uncovering secrets, investigating mysteries, dealing with the hidden side of life; politics and financial activities.

Not good for: anything that requires balance and harmony, optimism and positive outlook; anything that can further heat up emotions; in a meeting, emotions can be stronger than reason, and so the result can be very far from expected.

The Transiting Moon in Sagittarius

Adventure, optimism, global thinking. This is the time of emotional openness and generosity. People tend to freely share their ideas and opinions, and can be eager to give an advice. An interest to learning and teaching is increased, and if there is a problem of some kind, it is quite common to approach it with a philosophical attitude when the Moon is traveling through Sagittarius.

This sign is associated with foreign travel and vast open spaces, and the Moon in Sagittarius favors exotic holidays, sports, lengthy walks in the countryside and everything that raises spirits and helps to realize that our world is huge and full of adventures.

Liver is sensitive on these days, so overly heavy or exotic food, as well as an excessive consumption of alcohol, might be not good for your health.

Good for: traveling, adventures, philosophical discussions, spiritual studies, religious ceremonies, sports in the open air, anything that benefits from optimism and generosity.

Not good for: occupations that require concentration and responsibility, as people can be easily distracted on these days by any interesting idea.

The Transiting Moon in Capricorn

Seriousness, responsibility, achievement. People become more serious when the Moon is traveling through Capricorn; they are aware of their position in society and might want to erect around them an emotional barrier so that nobody could undermine their dignity. This is an appropriate time for any important work that requires responsibility, perfect timing and understanding of priorities.

Emotionally, these days can be a bit cold as people tend to be formal, distant and pay a lot of attention to various rules and regulations. A holiday or celebration planned on the days when the Moon is in Capricorn can prove to be dull and boring, while a high profile business meeting at this time will definitely become a success.

Your body is more sensitive to cold than usual when the Moon is transiting Capricorn, so it will be wise to dress warmly when going outside. Also all the functions of the body are a bit less efficient, but especially digestion, so don't overexert yourself in any way, and light, easily digestible food would be preferable on these days.

Good for: business meetings, work that requires seriousness and responsibility, career moves, important decisions.

Not good for: anything that requires emotional closeness and sensitivity; holidays, celebrations, having fun.

The Transiting Moon in Aquarius

Group interests, inventiveness, originality. The Moon in Aquarius favors group activities, collaboration of people sharing the same interest or idea. This is the time of the increased interest towards knowledge of all kinds but especially scientific or related to something new, like new technologies. Everything that requires concentration on a specific complex subject, as well as innovation and inventiveness, can be accomplished easier than usual on these days.

These days can be very good for meeting with friends, doing something interesting together or just having fun. The image of Aquarius is a bit of a rebel who doesn't accept the established routine and prefers to live in his or her way, so when the Moon is traveling through Aquarius you might consider doing something unusual, something you didn't dare to try before, or something which will allow you to proudly manifest your unique individuality.

In the body, Aquarius is associated with the lower parts of the legs and with blood circulation, therefore the time when the Moon is in this sign can be good for everything that helps the blood to circulate, like long walks, which are especially good for those who spends a lot of time at the computer or reading books.

Good for: group activities, intense intellectual work, dealing with anything that is new or unusual; also for everything that doesn't fit the established pattern of thinking or behaviour.

Not good for: occupations that require flexibility, adaptability or emotional sensitivity.

The Transiting Moon in Pisces

Compassion, intuition, changeability. When the Moon is traveling through Pisces, emotions and feelings can dominate over the intellect, at least on some occasions. People become dreamy, a little bit out-worldly, interested in legends and fairy tales, sensitive to art and music, and they might be not very successful in expressing their thoughts. This is a good time for charitable activities, music festivals or leaving the hustle and bustle of the world of business for a tiny island in the middle of an ocean.

However, this can be a difficult time for anything that requires concentration, attention to detail or responsibility. There is a high probability of mistakes and confusions. You might think that someone who wrote a document or did a calculation with the Moon in Pisces was drunk! On the other hand, mysterious subjects that require a wide perception and rely on the synthetic abilities of the mind can go very well at this time.

The body is sensitive to any chemicals when the Moon is transiting through Pisces, so please be careful with drugs and alcohol at this time. Even a prescribed medicine can act much stronger than expected, or cause significant side effects. I've also noticed that mass food poisonings often happen when the Moon is in Pisces.

Good for: daydreaming, reading fairy tales, watching movies, being charitable; anything that requires intuition, compassion, subtle emotional sensitivity; enjoying music and arts.

Not good for: work requiring attention to detail, logic, tenacity or responsibility; be very careful with alcohol and drugs.

The Phases of the Moon

Any discussion of the Moon's travel around the sky would be incomplete without at least a brief mention of the phases of the Moon.

While the sign of the zodiac the Moon is traveling through shows the *quality* of energy on a particular day, the phase of the Moon is mostly about the *quantity* of energy. Here we are dealing with the so-called synodic lunar month that continues from one New Moon to the next one and takes approximately 29.5 days. There are four important moments during a synodic month: the New Moon, the First Quarter, the Full Moon and the Last Quarter.

The New Moon

This is a quiet time of the month. The Moon is invisible in the sky since it is turned to the Earth with its non-illuminated side. The energy in Nature is at its lowest point at this time. The day before the moment of the New Moon is good for completing things, for getting rid of something unwanted, like a bad habit, and for paying debts. The day after the moment of the New Moon is good for starting new activities, especially those that can be completed within the month.

Please note that I am writing about the *moment* of the New Moon. Each phase becomes precise on a specific day, hour, minute and second, but it is commonly considered to be in action for some length of time before and after that moment. I'd say, as a rule of thumb, that the influence of the New Moon and the Full Moon is typically noticeable 24 hours before the exact phase and 24 hours after it, while for the First Quarter and the Last Quarter the influence is felt for about 12 hours before and after the exact moment of the phase.

Coming back to the New Moon, everything that is associated with the Moon is at the lowest point in its cycle of development at this time: emotions, physiological processes in the body, memory. This can be a critical day for people suffering from depression, or those with abnormally high or low blood pressure. You can't expect to find plenty of enthusiasm in people close to the New Moon, so it is better not to plan anything that requires plenty of energy at this time.

The First Quarter of the Moon

This phase comes about a week after the New Moon. Exactly a half of the lunar disc is illuminated by the Sun at this time. Symbolically, it's the time of fight between the dark and the light; practically, this phase is characterised by a high amount of energy, high level of stress, desire to do something. It was however noticed that if you do something close to the First Quarter under the influence of an impulse, chances are that you will soon regret about what you've done.

This is also the time when all sorts of polarities are especially noticeable in life: between men and women, the rulers and the population, the wife and the husband. Therefore, the probability of conflicts increases significantly.

The Full Moon

The Moon is gloriously bright when it's full as we see its fully illuminated side at this time of the lunar month. This is the high point in development of all those things associated with the Moon. Emotions are on the rise, various processes in the body and the subconscious mind are very active; there is plenty of energy in Nature. Animals are very active and can be restless around the Full Moon, and not only big animals, microorganisms too. It was noticed that if a fermentation process (like the one used for sauerkraut) was started at the Full Moon, it often goes over the top and the product gets wasted. Also wounds have a higher than normal chance to get infected at this time on the same reason.

This is another critical time for people suffering from too high or too low blood pressure, or from sleep disorders. It was also noticed, and even mentioned in non-astrological books and reports, that the number of psychiatric emergencies and violent crimes increases significantly around the Full Moon.

Quite surprisingly, the problems of the Full Moon are in many ways similar to those of the New Moon. This will be easier to understand if we recollect that the highest tides take place in the ocean at both of these phases.

Here is a quotation from the *Dynamic Astrology* book by John Townley, it will be a good example here:

At the University of Miami psychologist Arnold Lieber and his colleagues decided to test the old belief of full-moon "lunacy", which most scientists had written off as an old wives' tale. The researchers collected data on homicide in Dade County (Miami) over a period of 15 years - 1, 887 murders, to be exact. When they matched the incidence of homicide with the phases of the moon, they found, much to their surprise, that the two rose and fell together, almost infallibly, for the entire 15 years! As the full or the new moon approached, the murder rate rose sharply; it distinctly declined during the first and last quarters of the moon.

To find out whether this was just a statistical fluke, the researchers repeated the experiment using murder data from Cuyahoga County in Ohio (Cleveland). Again, the statistics showed that more murders do indeed occur at the full and new moons.

Dr. Lieber and his colleagues shouldn't have been so surprised. An earlier report by the American Institute of Medical Climatology to the Philadelphia Police Department entitled "The Effect of the Full Moon on Human Behavior" found similar results. That report showed that the full moon marks a monthly peak in various kinds of psychotically oriented crimes such as murder, arson, dangerous driving, and kleptomania. People do seem to get a little bit crazier about that time of the month.

The Last Quarter of the Moon

This phase is similar to the First Quarter as again exactly a half of the Moon is illuminated and therefore visible. In terms of the energy in Nature during this phase, I could just repeat everything that was said for the First Quarter, as they are very similar. There is however some difference: during the Last Quarter the efforts seem to be mostly concentrated on career, profession and the social status, while for the First Quarter the emphasis on personal life is more typical.

The Waxing and the Waning Moon

After the New Moon and until the Full Moon the Moon is waxing, or increasing in light. This time is considered to be appropriate for beginnings or those activities that are in the stage of growth and development. One of the Lunar Gardening traditions considers the Waxing Moon a good time for planting those plants that produce the desirable result (a fruit, or flowers, or leaves, etc) above the earth. You can read about the two main traditions of the Lunar Gardening in my article Lunar Gardening and its Different Traditions[490].

After the Full Moon and until the next New Moon the Moon is waning, or decreasing in light. This time is considered to be appropriate for completing and giving away things, and in the above mentioned gardening tradition this is the time for the plants that give the desired result below the earth.

There is also an interesting idea expressed in *The Art of Harmony with Nature and Lunar Cycles* book by Johanna Paungger and Thomas Poppe:

> *If the moon is waxing as it passes through the sign, then all measures taken to supply nutrient materials and strengthen the region of the body ruled by the sign are more effective than when the moon is on the wane.*

[490]http://www.lunarium.co.uk/articles/lunar-gardening.jsp

If it is waning, then all measures taken to flush out and detoxify the region in question are more successful than when the moon is waxing.

You will find out which regions of the body are ruled by which signs in the next chapter.

More About Your Personal Phase of the Moon

You remember from the previous chapter that the combination of the Sun Sign and the Moon Sign provides information about your personal phase of the Moon. The word "phase" is used here in its more general sense, like the angular distance between the Sun and the Moon, it doesn't necessarily mean just those four special cases, the New Moon, the First Quarter, the Full Moon and the Last Quarter.

The easiest way to measure the phase of the Moon is in the signs of the zodiac, counting from the Sun to the Moon. You can use the pictures from the first chapter to do the counting.

Let's say someone's Sun Sign is Gemini while the Moon Sign is Cancer. In this case, the Moon is in the second sign from the Sun, and the phase of this person's Moon can be defined as "the second sign from the Sun".

Now, can you tell me what is the Moon Sign of the person born with the Sun in Libra if the phase of her Moon is "six signs from the Sun"? The answer is *Pisces*. And if the same person was born at the Last Quarter of the Moon, which corresponds to the phase "the tenth sign from the Sun", what will be her Moon Sign? The answer is Cancer. I hope this kind of logic isn't too difficult for you.

The important point here is that **the time when the transiting**

Moon and the transiting Sun form in the sky the same phase as the one at your birth, that time will be important for you.

If you were born at a Full Moon then every Full Moon will be important for you. If you were born with the Moon eleven signs ahead of the Sun then each time when the transiting Moon is eleven signs ahead of the transiting Sun will be important for you.

You already know how to find out the sign the transiting Moon in on a specific day. If you don't know how to find the Sun Sign for that day, please refer to the Appendix B. Now I want to concentrate on explaining **in which way the time when the Sun and the Moon in the sky repeat the phase they made at your birth is important to you.**

First of all, this time can be good for sportsmen and for other people for whom physical energy is important. I remember reading an interview with a prominent Ukrainian sports coach. He mentioned that he pays a lot of attention to the current phase of the Moon in his work, and that's because he found that sportsmen tend to show the best results when the transiting phase repeats the phase they had at birth. On the other hand, when the current phase is opposite to their birth phase, sportsmen tend to be vulnerable and not as good as usual.

Dr. Eugen Jonas of Slovakia has discovered that women have a high probability of getting pregnant when the current phase of the Moon repeats exactly their birth phase, even if that time falls on an inappropriate part of their hormonal cycle. On the other hand, men seem to have a higher than usual sperm count during such a phase return. You can find out more about this discovery from my article Lunar Conception: a Discovery of Dr. Jonas[491].

In addition, here is another quotation from John Townley's *Dynamic Astrology* that offers a somewhat contradicting but still very interesting confirmation of the importance of the Moon's phase

---
[491] http://www.lunarium.co.uk/articles/jonas.jsp

repetition.

> *An Atomic Energy Commission-funded project at Sandia Laboratories in Albuquerque, New Mexico, came up with a report entitled "Intriguing Accident Patterns Plotted against a Background of Natural Environmental Features", which correlated on-the-job accidents of government employees over a period of 20 years with various natural cycles. This preliminary report (the researchers suggested further study was in order) found that accidents peak with the sunspot cycle and - even more intriguing and "astrological" - that people were more likely to have accidents during the phase of the moon the same as or opposite to that under which they were born.*

You can figure out the approximate days when the phase in the sky is the same as the phase at your birth just using the Moon Sign and Sun Sign approach as explained above. However, if you want to try the method of Dr. Jonas, you'll need an astronomically precise calculation, and I am offering two tools that can do it for you.

One of these tools is the online and free Lunar Conception Calculator[492]. The other one is an iPhone app named Phase Day[493]. It isn't free but isn't expensive either, and you can have it always with you at all times. If there will be any interest, I will create an Android version of this app too.

You have noticed that on a number of occasions I was mentioning the relationship between signs, phases and health. Many

[492] http://www.lunarium.co.uk/calendar/conception.jsp
[493] http://www.lunarium.co.uk/iPhone/PhaseDay/

people know that situation in the sky should be taken into account when something important in respect of health is planned, such as surgery, and I am often asked questions about the best day for this or that kind of surgery. Therefore, I decided to write a separate chapter explaining how to use the knowledge about the Moon when planning a surgery.

The Moon and Surgery

Paracelsus, who is sometimes called "the father of modern medicine", once wrote that a doctor who doesn't know astrology is a "pseudo-medic". That was in the 16th century, and medicine became a lot more powerful since then. It can use a powerful antibiotic to suppress an infection and so it doesn't need to care whether a surgery was made on the Full Moon or not. It has complex machinery that can do miracles, from the 16th century point of view.

But when the surgery is over, it's us who have to live with the result of it, and even if Nature was defeated by medical machinery for a while, it will certainly have a chance to restore the work of its laws over time. And we might find then that in contemporary medicine one department doesn't know what the other department does, and the department responsible for, say, lungs, doesn't care if a successful surgery caused problems somewhere else in the body - that's just more work for some other department. We, however, are those who do care, or who should care, at least. This is why many people are trying to make sure that, when they have an influence on planning, a surgery is made at the time when it won't violate the laws of nature, or at least when it will violate as few of those laws as possible.

When choosing a date for a surgery, you should pay attention to the following:

1. The Moon should not be in the Sign of the Zodiac which is related to the operated part of the body.
2. Any surgery should be avoided close to the New Moon and the Full Moon. This is especially important when these phases form eclipses of the Sun or of the Moon.

3. There is a range of other factors, not related to the Moon, which can be important, especially in complex cases. I will discuss them in a separate section below.

It is always advisable to ask for a consultation of an experienced astrologer, if you have one available to you, as there are individual factors that can be very important but can be discovered only in a precisely calculated personal birth chart.

The Anatomical Correspondences of the Signs of the Zodiac

The main rule was formulated most clearly in *The Art of Harmony with Nature and Lunar Cycles* by Johanna Paungger and Thomas Poppe.

> *Everything that is done for the well-being of those parts of the body and organs ruled by the sign through which the moon is currently passing is doubly useful and beneficial - with the exception of surgical operations involving those regions.*

> *Everything that puts a special burden or strain on those parts of the body and organs ruled by the sign through which the moon is currently moving is doubly unfavourable or even harmful. ... Surgical operations in these areas should be avoided during these days if at all possible.*

Now we need to figure out which areas of the body are ruled by which sign, and since I've already quoted *The Art of Harmony with Nature and Lunar Cycles*, I will extract the necessary information from this book as well.

The Sign of the Zodiac	Body Zone	Organ System
Aries	Head, brain, eyes, nose	Sense-organs
Taurus	Larynx, thyroid, teeth, jaws, tonsils, ears	Blood circulation
Gemini	Shoulders, arms, hands, (lungs)	Glandular system
Cancer	Chest, lungs, stomach, liver, gall bladder	Nervous system
Leo	Heart, back, diaphragm, circulation, artery	Sense-organs
Virgo	Digestive organs, nerves, spleen, pancreas	Blood circulation
Libra	Hips, kidneys, bladder	Glandular system
Scorpio	Sex organs, ureter	Nervous system
Sagittarius	Thighs, veins	Sense-organs
Capricorn	Knees, bones, joints, skin	Blood circulation
Aquarius	Lower leg, veins	Glandular system
Pisces	Feet, toes	Nervous system

You will notice that different astrological sources can put the same organ under two different signs. This often happens to liver as it is so big, and because it has two different functions in the body, or in the above table veins are under both Sagittarius and Aquarius. Regarding teeth, many authors will say that they are under Aries, some will insist that the upper jaw is under Aries while the lower jaw is under Taurus, and Paungger & Poppe believe that teeth belong to Taurus.

In cases like these, I tend to avoid surgery when the Moon is in any of the signs associated with the area in question. For example, I would avoid dental surgery when the Moon is in either Aries or

Taurus, and this is logical because both the head (the Aries area of the body) and the throat (the classical Taurus area) will be affected by such a surgery.

In an attempt to explain why different authors can somewhat contradict each other, I will offer you a quotation from *Encyclopaedia of Medical Astrology* by H.L. Cornell which, I believe, illustrates the problem nicely.

> *Some parts of the head are ruled by the Taurus and Scorpio signs, but the head taken as a whole is ruled by the Aries sign. Also Aries exerts an internal, external, and structural rulership over various parts of the head, and these will be mentioned in this section. The head is a very complicated part of the body, due to its many parts and organs, and all of the planets have a special rule over the different parts and organs of the head.*

Dr. Cornell then gives a lengthy list of different parts and organs and their astrological correspondences which, I believe, wouldn't be appropriate here.

The point is: since human body is very complex, when it comes to the anatomical correspondences of the Signs of the Zodiac, the answer might depend on the context of the question. So when in doubt, ask a qualified astrologer for an advice.

The New Moon, the Full Moon, and the Eclipses

As I've mentioned before, the New Moon and the Full Moon, although visually are very different, can be quite close in their influence on health, so I will not be doing a distinction between them here. Both are the major critical points of the lunar month.

They are associated with bleeding, very high or very low blood pressure, high probability of infection, and if an operation was done during any of these phases, the body might find it more difficult to restore its proper functioning in the following days.

Twice a year, when the Earth, the Sun and the Moon happen to be on the same line in space, a New Moon can turn into an eclipse of the Sun while a Full Moon can become an eclipse of the Moon. Any of the eclipses is a major stress for Nature, and any surgery should be avoided, if possible, at least for a week before and after an eclipse.

Other Factors

Here is a list of various factors that were used by my teacher of astrology Augustina Semenko when choosing an acceptable day for a surgery, and I do believe that they are important, especially in complex cases.

- Any surgery should be avoided during the last month before the person's birthday, as the energy level of the body is very low at that time. Ideally, the sixth month from birthday should be avoided as well as it can be rich in complications and side effects. *An example*: if the person was born on the 25th of August then the last month before birthday will be from the 25th of July to the 25th of August while the sixth month will be from the 25th of January to the 25th of February.
- Any surgery on the female organs should be avoided when Venus is retrograde. I extend this rule to kidneys too.
- Any surgery on the male organs should be avoided when Mars is retrograde. I will also add muscles and adrenal glands to the list.
- By extension, any surgery on nerves and organs of speech should be avoided when Mercury is retrograde.

You can find out when any of these planets are retrograde by looking at the Home page of Lunarium[494]. Here is how the information looks right now:

Recent and Coming Retrograde Motion of Planets

Recent Retrograde Periods	Current or Coming Retrograde Periods
Mercury: 23/02/13 - 17/03/13 20:02	Mercury: 26/06/13 - 20/07/13 19:22
Venus: 15/05/12 - 27/06/12 16:06	Venus: 21/12/13 - 31/01/14 20:48
Mars: 24/01/12 - 14/04/12 04:52	Mars: 01/03/14 - 20/05/14 02:31

Current information about retrograde planets displayed by Lunarium

---

The last chapter will be about the Void-of-Course Moon, an interesting factor borrowed from the toolbox of the Traditional Astrology, that is very popular nowadays but is often misunderstood.

---

[494] http://www.lunarium.co.uk/

The Void-of-Course Moon

I live in the UK, and here most astrologers are very surprised by the popularity of such an astrological factor as the void-of-course Moon in the United States, even between people who know very little about astrology.

We use this factor in our astrological work all the time, but only in one very specific and highly technical branch of astrology, the Horary. There, if we find that the Moon was void-of-course at the moment when a question was asked, we might decide that it is not appropriate to answer such a question. Or, if some of us will still decide to proceed with the answer, they will most probably say that nothing will come out of the matter in question (which, depending on the question, might mean that there is nothing to be afraid of).

For quite a while, I was hesitant about whether it really makes sense to pay attention to the void-of-course status of the Moon in daily life, outside of the technical considerations of the horary work. However, on a few important occasions I've noticed that the outcome of my initiative undertaken when the Moon was void-of-course was very different from my expectations, and quite in line with the meaning of the void-of-course.

I will give some examples, as well as expand on the meaning of this factor, but first of all I want to attempt an explanation of what exactly is the void-of-course Moon. I will try to do this mainly because I believe that the good understanding of the nature of the void period will help to understand its negative and positive sides better. But also, it would be good if the general public had a better idea of how it all works. Right now the common level of understanding is quite low, which is demonstrated by the questions I am getting from the visitors of Lunarium from time to time.

What the Void-of-Course Moon Is

It's a common knowledge that the Moon circles around the Earth, and it completes the circle in about 27 days, the lunar month (there is another lunar month called *synodic* which lasts almost 30 days, but it's of no interest to us here). The Moon moves all the time along the zodiac, and there are 12 signs of the zodiac, each of them is exactly 1/12 part of the circle. It is easy to calculate then that it takes about two and a half days for the Moon to cross one sign of the zodiac.

Each sign is like a chapter in the book of life, and moving through it the Moon is telling a story. When the Moon enters the next sign, it starts a new story. We still remember the old one, but we are not deeply involved into it anymore. Whether we notice it or not, each time the Moon enters the next sign of the zodiac, something substantially changes in our life, some context, or the emotional background of events. Most of the time we aren't aware of this change because the Moon is strongly connected to our subconsciousness, not to our consciousness. It is the subconsciousness that is deeply aware of the change.

So in each of the signs the Moon starts a new story when it enters the sign, but those stories can have different lengths. Some of them continue for almost the whole two-and-a-half-day period, others are much shorter, but *always* there is a pause in the end of the story. It can be short or long, but it is always there. **That pause in the end of the story is the void-of-course period of the Moon.**

We don't know why it happens, this pause. Maybe the storyteller gives us the time to think about the content of the story we've just heard, or maybe it is a chance to prepare to the next story, because it is going to be very important. We just know that the pause is there.

That was a metaphorical description of the void-of-course period; now let me try another one, a little bit more technical.

Moving through each sign, the Moon makes contacts with the planets. It isn't really important what are those contacts and how they are made, but it is exactly those contacts who provide the content of the sign's story. The exact number of the contacts and their distribution in time depends on where all the planets are in the zodiac, and this arrangement changes eternally.

At some point the Moon makes its last contact in the given sign. That's the end of the story, but the new story won't start until the Moon enters the next sign of the zodiac.

So here is a more or less precise definition:

The void-of-course period of the Moon is the period of time from the moment the Moon makes the last contact with any planet in the current sign of the zodiac, and until it enters the next sign.

The void-of-course period can be very short, only a few minutes, but it can also be very long, about two days (although that happens quite rarely).

I was writing these words on the 11th of May 2013, soon after the New Moon in Taurus (which was also a solar eclipse). It so happened that exactly that New Moon was the last contact the Moon made in the sign of Taurus, and it took place on the 10th of May at 0:28 of Universal Time (it was 1:28am in London, UK). That New Moon was the last word in the story the Moon was telling in Taurus.

However, the Moon stayed in Taurus until 21:22 UT of the same day (10:22pm in London), at which time it entered the next sign, Gemini. So most of the 10th of May 2013, from 1:28am to 10:22pm here in the UK, was one lengthy void-of-course period.

Let's see how it was shown in the Universal Lunar Calendar[495]:

---

[495] http://www.lunarium.co.uk/calendar/universal.jsp

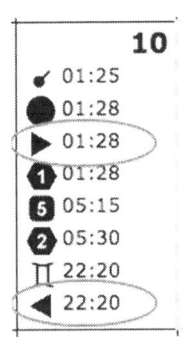

The void-of-course period on the 10th of May 2013 in London

The arrow pointing right above, with 01:28 next to it, is the beginning of the void-of-course period. You can see that it is exactly below the symbol of the New Moon with the same time, 01:28, next to it.

Below you can see an arrow pointing left with 22:20 next to it. That's the end of the void-of-course period. You can see that it is exactly below the symbol of Gemini with the same time, 22:20, next to it. This means that the void-of-course period has ended when the Moon has entered Gemini.

If you have an iPhone or an iPad, your life will be easier as you won't need to decipher any symbols. My app iLuna for iOS[496] will describe for you everything in plain English, see the screenshot below. There you will see that the Moon was void-of-course at the moment the screenshot was made, and it will remain void until 5:29 am on the 3rd of August.

---

[496]http://appstore.com/iluna

The *Now* view of iLuna for iPhone

If you have an Android smartphone, you can get a similar result with iLuna for Android[497]:

---

[497] https://play.google.com/store/apps/details?id=uk.co.lunarium.iluna

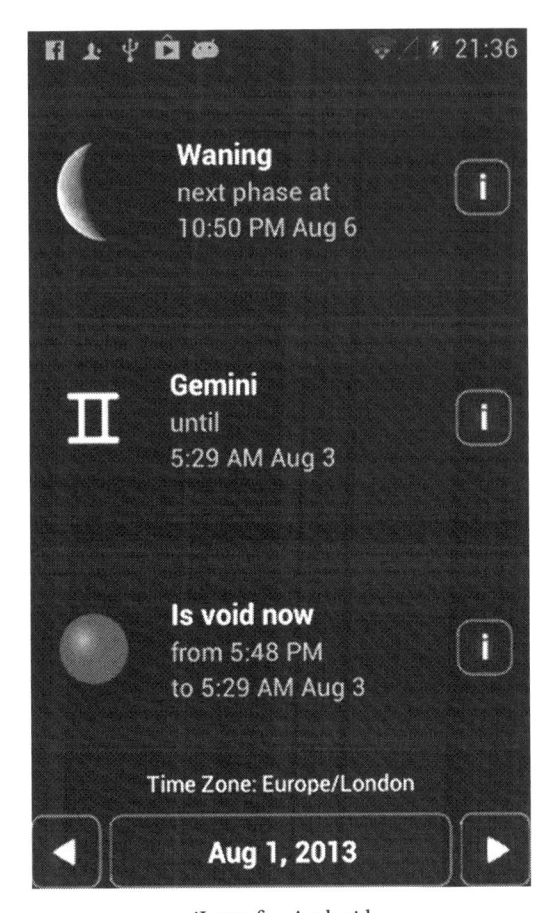

iLuna for Android

Now you should have an idea of what the void-of-course period of the Moon *is*.

What the Void-of-Course Moon Isn't

There is a widespread misunderstanding that when the Moon is void-of-course, it is in no sign of the zodiac but in some kind of a hole, an empty space. This is very wrong.

The signs of the zodiac are the 12 sections of the ecliptic, the imaginary path of the Sun around the sky. The ecliptic is a circle, so there are 360 degrees in it. Each sign is a 30 degrees section, 30 x 12 = 360. There are no holes and no empty spaces in this system.

The Moon is always in one or another Sign of the Zodiac. Please understand this, and if you still don't understand what the void-of-course period is then please re-read attentively the previous section. If you still don't get it after that, please let me know, and I will try to write an even less technical explanation.

The Meaning of the Void-of-Course Moon

In Horary Astrology, we are looking at the contacts with planets (aka aspects) that the Moon is going to make before it leaves the sign it is in. Those aspects will tell us what is going to happen about the situation in question. But if the Moon is void-of-course, i.e. it isn't going to contact any planets before the end of the story, then the only possible answer is that *nothing is going to happen*. So if a person asked "will I get married?", the answer will be perceived as negative, but if someone was worried and asked "will I get fired?" then the answer *nothing will happen* will be perceived as positive.

Similarly, in daily life void-of-course periods aren't necessarily bad. We just need to keep these words in mind: *nothing is going to happen*, and then see if this result desirable for us or not.

One day I had two job interviews, one a few hours after another but both during a void-of-course period. The interviews were both positive, and from my previous experience I would think that I am going to have two job offers by the end of the day. However, before the end of the day the Moon has entered another sign of the zodiac, another story had started, and not only I didn't receive any job offers, I never got any feedback from the job agencies that arranged the interviews, which was quite unusual.

On the other hand, on a few occasions I had to get certain things done in a country where many officials are famous for being corrupt. I was worried that they will challenge me, and since I don't know how to give bribes I'll be in trouble. However, both situations happened during void-of-course periods of the Moon, and everything went unbelievably smoothly, to my huge relief.

Not so long ago, I found an article by Estelle Daniels in an old 1997 Llewellyn's Moon Sign Book. The article is titled *Using the Void-of-Course Moon*, and it offers some great ideas and examples. Quoting from this article,

During a void Moon you should not sign a contract, make plans, close a deal, or start a project. Basically anything which you want to have a concrete real-world result should not be started, signed or sealed. If you do, these things will never get off the ground, never materialize, have to be re-done, or have so many problems and setbacks as to be useless anyhow.

On the other hand,

... if you want to drop a bombshell, and yet have fewer repercussions in the long run, during the void-of-course Moon is the time to do it.

And then goes a brilliant example:

> *Remember President Reagan, the "Teflon® President", who never got blamed for any of the bad stuff? Well he was very careful to schedule those presidential news conferences where he would answer the hard questions about nasty controversial stuff during void Moons. There would be questions and discussions, yet the next day nothing would ever really be said in the paper or on TV. The topic was just dropped, forgotten, or glossed over, and nobody really ever noticed. The void Moon was Reagan's Teflon®. Even in August 1988,*

> when Nancy Reagan admitted at the Republican national convention on live TV with Dan Rather that the Reagans used astrology, it was during a void Moon, and nobody really noticed or cared. ... Of course, when President Reagan had something wonderful to say which would make him look good and he wanted people to notice, he was very careful to make sure the Moon was not void-of-course, so he would receive maximum notice and credit.

So it looks like the void-of-course periods were given to us as a time for those little stories which we don't want to be written into the books of our lives. They are a little bit like little stickers with a few words which you can stick somewhere in a book - they are there, and not there at the same time.

How to Find Out When the Next Void-of-Course Period Is

We do agree that void-of-course periods are important, don't we?

Now, the bad news is that it can be difficult to figure out when exactly those periods take place. That's not a kind of information you can find in a typical calendar or a newspaper (at least not in those calendars and newspapers I am aware of), and you can't just calculate them on a piece of paper. It takes a few pages of astronomical formulas to do all the necessary calculations.

The good news however is that these days pretty much everyone has some sort of computer at hand, be it a desktop, a notebook or a smartphone. And those computers are more than happy to do for us all the tedious calculations in a split of a second. For more than a decade I am working on various software programs that make basic astrology available for everyone, and here are the solutions I can offer right now for those who want to keep track of the void-of-course Moon:

1. The Universal Lunar Calendar[498]. Its benefit is that it is available to everyone for free, and you can calculate a calendar for pretty much every year, and for more or less any location on the Earth. The downside is that it might require a little bit of effort to figure out what all those symbols mean, and the information in the calendar is somewhat dense. Another downside is the platform on which the Calendar is built, which is Google AppEngine, is a bit flaky. You might need to reload the page a few times until it will stop reporting a weird error and start showing the real stuff.
2. iLuna app, which currently exists in two versions: iLuna for iOS[499] and iLuna for Android[500].

I also have plans to create iLuna for Windows 8 - both tablets and phones - and to upgrade the existing apps and add a number of important new features, like the ability to export void-of-course periods to a calendar of choice. However, I can only work on my own projects after a full time job, and that means that I am chronically overloaded with plans while moving forward very slowly.

Do You Like Happy Ends?

The void-of-course Moon has another very interesting side to it, which I never saw being used or even mentioned. Do you still remember that metaphor where the Moon is telling a story by making contacts with planets? The very last contact within the

---

[498] http://www.lunarium.co.uk/calendar/universal.jsp
[499] http://appstore.com/iluna
[500] https://play.google.com/store/apps/details?id=uk.co.lunarium.iluna

current sign should then be the end of the story, the very last word of it, right?

Those contacts are called in astrology *aspects*, and come of them are nice and easy, sometimes they are called *harmonic*, while others are difficult and problematic, sometimes called *stressful*.

The last contact can be with any of the planets, and some of those planets are so called *benefics*, which means they are good and kind, like Venus and Jupiter, but there are also *malefics*, like Mars and Saturn, who are much less pleasant to deal with.

Now imagine that a story ends with the Moon making a harmonic aspect to Venus, while another story ends with a stressful aspect to Mars. Would it be appropriate to think that the void-of-course period after the end of the first story will be much milder than the one after the one after the second story?

I do believe that the nature of the last contact the Moon makes in the given sign does have a substantial influence on the void-of-course period which follows, and therefore some of these void periods can be a lot more beneficial than the others. I am now doing a research in this direction, and I will share my findings with you when they'll be ready.

One of my latest observations is about job interviews again. On the 16th of July, I had two of them, and both were scheduled by an employment agency right in the middle of a lengthy void Moon period. The first interview seemed to be okay but the second looked very, very positive, I was actually expecting to have the job offered in a few hours. the interview started at 1pm and continued for about half an hour, and at 3:25pm the Moon has entered the next sign. I haven't heard any feedback for a while, and only much later I was told that although the last company liked me so much, they've eventually offered the job to another candidate. The last contact of the Moon before that void-of-course period was a square to the Sun, a stressful aspect.

Now I have in development an opportunity which appeared again during a void Moon (on some reason, I have all these opportunities scheduled on void periods, maybe just to give me more material for my research!) but this time the last aspect was a harmonic sextile with Mercury. The next week should show whether there was any difference.

(I am updating this text a couple of weeks later. I did get that job.)

The problem with considering the nature of the last contact before a void-of-course period is that it is quite difficult to figure out for a non-astrologer what exactly that aspect is. There are tables of the ephemeris that would give you all the necessary information, and some of them are even available online for free, but you would have to be well versed in various astrological symbols to be able to read them.

What I can offer you right now is more like a workaround, and you will still need to know a few symbols, but if you really want to learn something new about void-of-course periods, you'll definitely manage that. With time, I promise to add the information about the last aspect to iLuna, and maybe to the Universal Lunar Calendar too, but right now the solution is to use together the Universal Lunar Calendar[501] **and** the Lunar Gardening Calendar[502].

I won't tell you anything about the Lunar Gardening Calendar in this book. Let's just say it's an experimental feature of Lunarium. Why it will be useful for us is because it displays all the aspects during each day.

Now, I want to find out what was the last aspect before the void-of-course period that started in London on the 14th of August 2013. Here you can see a couple of days displayed by the Universal Lunar Calendar:

---

[501] http://www.lunarium.co.uk/calendar/universal.jsp
[502] http://www.lunarium.co.uk/calendar/gardening.jsp

14	15
⑲ 11:15	♐ 02:04
◐ 11:56	◀ 02:04
⑨ 14:27	⑳ 09:24
▶ 22:29	⑩ 15:36

A void-of-course period displayed by the Universal Lunar Calendar

You can see that the void-of-course period starts at 22:29. From the previous discussion, you should realise that some aspect was formed by the Moon at that moment, and that was the last aspect before the void period. Now let's have a look at the same day displayed by the Lunar Gardening Calendar:

14	15
☽△♂ 10:47	☿△♄ 03:10
◐ 11:56	☽□♆ 09:24
☽↑ 14:27	☽↑ 15:36
♏ 15:48	☽△♄ 22:47
☽✶♀ 22:29	
☽↓ 23:33	

The aspects displayed by the Lunar Gardening Calendar

What we are looking for is an event that took place exactly at 22:29, and we can clearly see that event. If you don't know what the symbols mean, you will find them listed under the calendar. For now, I will save your time and tell you that the aspect was a sextile to Venus, and it is one of the most positive.

My expectation is that if the activity you are planning resonates well with the nature of the last aspect, then you have high chances of success during the following void period. After a harmonic contact to Venus anything related to romance, beauty and amusements should go quite well, with no trouble.

It would be great if you joined my research and emailed me about your experience.

To properly learn about the planets and aspects, I would advise you to read my free astrology lessons at What-is-Astrology.com[503], but for now here is a quick key:

The good aspects are trine, sextile and conjunction, but conjunction is only positive when it is with one of the good planets, which are Jupiter, Venus and Mercury.

You should be able to figure out the rest on your own.

This completes the Moon Sign book. I have a few other ideas in development but they are not ready to be published yet, so I will leave them for the later editions of the book.

If you are interested in the topics discussed here, I would advise you to visit my website, Lunarium[504], to subscribe for the newsletter, to send a feedback.

---

[503] http://what-is-astrology.com
[504] http://www.lunarium.co.uk/

Appendix A. How to Find Out Your Moon Sign

You probably already know that the tools I recommend for calculating your Moon Sign are:

- The free online Moon Sign Calculator[505].
- Moon Sign iOS app[506].
- Moon Sign Android app[507]. Or you might prefer to get it from the Amazon App Store[508].

However, one important requirement for calculating the Moon Sign is that you need to know the birth time, and the more precisely you know it the better. Unfortunately, there are many people in the world who don't know their time of birth at all. They still have a good chance to find their Moon Sign nevertheless, let me explain how.

If No Birth Time Is Available

On the average, the Moon's daily journey is 13 degrees long. This means that it needs a little bit over two days to cross one sign. This also means that for at least one day the Moon will be entirely within the same sign, and so for people born on that day there is no need to know their birth time, they will have the same Moon Sign no matter when they were born.

---

[505] http://www.lunarium.co.uk/moonsign/calculator.jsp
[506] http://appstore.com/moonsign
[507] https://play.google.com/store/apps/details?id=com.siriuslab.moonsign
[508] http://www.amazon.com/Alexander-Kolesnikov-Moon-Sign/dp/B00DPSXLS2/

On the other days, the Moon will be in one sign for the first part of the day and in the next sign for the last part of the day. Still you only need to figure out between two signs, and you can very often guess successfully from the descriptions of the signs which one is yours.

It would be even easier for you to decide if you knew that the Moon was in the first sign for only a couple of hours and then in the second sign for the rest of the day. The probability of you having the second Moon Sign would be much higher then. Or maybe you have some vague idea of the time of the day when you were born, like in the afternoon, or in the evening. That will make your task even easier.

Let me show you a few examples of how one could find out his or her Moon Sign when the time of birth is unknown.

Using the Universal Lunar Calendar

The Universal Lunar Calendar is probably the best tool for the job as it can be generated for any month of any year in the range 1900 - 2020, and it shows the time when the Moon has entered or will enter each of the signs. Let's take an example.

Let's say some person was born in London on the 11th of June 1970, and she doesn't know her birth time. We then go to the Universal Lunar Calendar[509] and generate a calendar for London, for June 1970. Here is a screenshot of the range of three days from the resulting calendar:

---

[509] http://www.lunarium.co.uk/calendar/universal.jsp?calendarYear=1970&calendarMonth=5

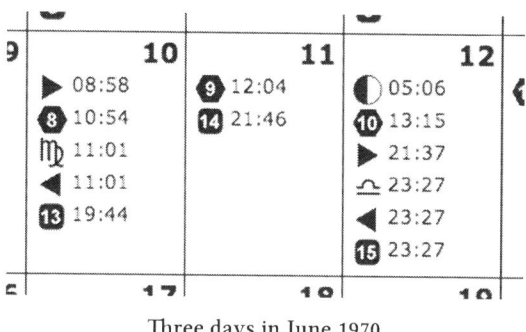

```
   9        10              11             12
       ▶ 08:58      ⑨ 12:04       ◐ 05:06        ◀
       ⑧ 10:54      ⑭ 21:46       ⑩ 13:15
       ♍ 11:01                     ▶ 21:37
       ◀ 11:01                     ♎ 23:27
       ⑬ 19:44                     ◀ 23:27
                                   ⑮ 23:27
   c        17              10             10
```

Three days in June 1970

I'll assume that you've read *The Moon Signs In Daily Life* chapter, and so you know how to find out from this calendar when the Moon enters the next sign, and which sign is that.

We can see that the Moon has entered Virgo on the 10th of June at 11:01, and after that it will enter the next sign, Libra, on the 12th of June at 23:27, or 11:27 pm. This means that if our example person was born on the 11th of June, it doesn't matter at which time she was born, her Moon Sign will be Virgo anyway.

Now let's imagine that another person was born on the 12th of the same month. If he doesn't know his birth time at all, it will be reasonable to assume that his Moon Sign is most probably Virgo, as the Moon was in Virgo on that day until very late in the evening.

However if a person was born on the 10th of June instead, we wouldn't be so sure about his or her Moon Sign. The Moon was in Virgo for about 13 hours during that day, and in Leo for 11 hours. I'd suggest that person to read the chapters about the Moon in Leo and the Moon in Virgo and decide which sign is the most appropriate. In many cases that will work.

Using The Moon Sign Calculator

Let's consider the same examples as in the previous section but this time use the Moon Sign Calculator. I will be using the online version but pretty much the same can be done with a smartphone version too.

The idea is to calculate the Moon Sign for the very beginning of the date of birth (12 am or 0.00, depending on which time format you are used to), then for the very end of it (like 11:59pm, or 23:59), then compare the results. I will be paying attention both to the calculated Moon Sign, and the degree of that sign.

The first example, the 11th of June 1970 birth, London. The 12am time gives Virgo, 6.23. The 11:59pm gives Virgo, 18.14. We can see that the sign in the very beginning of the day was the same as in the very end of the day, which means the whole day the Moon was in Virgo.

Now let's do the calculations for the 12th of June. 12am gives Virgo, 18.15. 11:59pm gives Libra, 0.16. You can see that there was a change of sign during the day but the Moon has just entered Libra after spending most of the day in Virgo.

I hope you've got the idea, and I believe that following my explanations, the greatest majority of those people who don't know their time of birth will still be able to figure out what their Moon Sign is.

The Limitations of the Moon Sign Calculator, and of the Moon Sign App

Unfortunately, both the online calculator and the smartphone apps have their limitations, and in some (relatively rare) cases the result offered by them can be wrong. The reason for this is that all my solutions use the time zone definitions provided by their respective computing platform. Unfortunately, the history of the time zones is very complex, and none of the contemporary computing platforms reflects that history well.

This means that your calculations will be all right in the great majority of cases, especially for those people who were born in the last 30 years or so, but for some years and regions there can be a mistake of about one hour because the daylight saving time wasn't taken into account properly or, vice versa, it was taken into account while in that particular county it wasn't observed then.

Let me give you a real life example. Once I was contacted by a person who did know his Moon Sign. He used my calculator, and the result was wrong. When I investigated that case, I found out that the man was born in the 1950s in Florida, very close to the time when the Moon crossed over from one sign to another. The problem was that in those years daylight saving time wasn't observed in the place where the man was born, but it is observed there now. So the computing platform gave the calculator a one hour correction, which was wrong in that particular case, and the error of one hour was sufficient, again in that particular case, to give a wrong Moon Sign.

There is still a way to find out the correct Moon Sign even in problematic cases, and I will tell you about it in the next section.

A Precise Method of Finding Out Your Moon Sign

The most reliable and precise way to calculate your Moon Sign is using an astrological charting software. The benefit of doing that is that such a software uses a copy of ACS Atlas. That atlas was created by competent astrologers, and it uses the most reliable historical data for all the time zones around the world.

Unfortunately, these days the licensing of the ACS Atlas is prohibitive. However, there are a few places on the Internet where you can calculate your precise astrological chart for free, and from it you can figure out your Moon Sign, and your Sun Sign, and your Rising Sign, and pretty much everything else there is in astrology.

One very convenient version of such calculator is made available on my website What-Is-Astrology.com[510]. The calculator is very easy to use, just enter the date and the time and the location of birth, and a colourful chart will be generated for you. Then just find the symbol of the Moon (a crescent) and click on it. You will see a wealth of information - not only about the sign the Moon is in but also about the Moon in general, and lots of other interesting things as well.

---

[510] http://what-is-astrology.com/natal-chart-calculator.html

Appendix B. How to Find Out Your Sun Sign

The Sun Sign is very easy to find, in most cases, because the movement of the Sun is quite regular, and year after year it travels through the same sign of the zodiac on more or less the same days. Different books offer tables that will help you to figure out your Sun Sign from your birth date. Here is one popular version of such a table:

Sign	Dates
Aries	21 March - 20 April
Taurus	21 April - 21 May
Gemini	22 May - 21 June
Cancer	22 June - 22 July
Leo	23 July - 22 August
Virgo	23 August - 23 September
Libra	24 September - 23 October
Scorpio	24 October - 22 November
Sagittarius	23 November - 21 December
Capricorn	22 December - 20 January
Aquarius	21 January - 19 February
Pisces	20 February - 20 March

This table is very easy to use, and many people who are interested in astrology know it by heart. Unfortunately, it isn't very reliable in those cases when the person was born close to the border of signs, like on the 21st of January or the 22nd of June.

For example, if you were born in San Francisco on the 20th of January 1981 you might decide that your Sun Sign is Capricorn as that is what the table above says. However, you will be wrong as on that particular day the Sun has entered Aquarius on the 19th of

January, at least in the Pacific Standard Time, so everyone born on the 20th of January had *Aquarius* for their Sun Sign.

You will find the detailed explanations, as well as an advice on what to do to verify your Sun Sign, in my online article What is Sun Sign and Why It Is Important[511].

---

[511] http://lucklab.com/sunsign/index.html

Appendix C. Moon Sign Celebrities

You will find here plenty of examples, most of which were mentioned somewhere in the book. Most of the information comes from the Astro-Databank[512], a great resource for everyone who is interested in astrology.

I made sure that the tables below list the Sun Sign for each celebrity. This can be useful when reading *The Moon Sign and the Sun Sign - How They Work Together* chapter. Also, it might be interesting to think which of the signs is better noticeable in the personality and life of this or that celebrity - the Moon Sign or the Sun Sign?

I wish you to make many discoveries when studying these tables.

Aries

Name	Birth Date and Time	Sun Sign
Adenauer, Konrad	Jan 5, 1876, 10:30am	Capricorn
Agrippa, Henri Cornelius	Sep 15, 1486 Julian, 3:15am	Libra
Alexander, F.M.	Jan 20, 1869, 7:54pm	Aquarius
Anderson, Pamela	Jul 1, 1967, 4:08am	Cancer
Arden, Elizabeth	Dec 31, 1878, 11:20am	Capricorn
Armstrong, Louis	Aug 4, 1901, 10:00pm	Leo
Auguin, Christophe	Dec 10, 1959, 1:15pm	Sagittarius
Banderas, Antonio	Aug 10, 1960, 9:00pm	Leo
Bechstein, Carl	Jun 1, 1826, 4:00am	Gemini
Bell, Marilyn	Oct 19, 1937, 6:00am	Libra

---

[512]http://lucklab.com/sunsign/index.html

Appendix C. Moon Sign Celebrities

Bergman, Ingrid	Aug 29, 1915, 3:30am	Virgo
Bernhardt, Sarah	Oct 23, 1844 8:00pm	Scorpio
Bernstein, Leonard	Aug 25, 1918, 1:00pm	Virgo
Bissell, Patrick	Dec 1, 1957, 3:11am	Sagittarius
Brando, Marlon	Apr 3, 1924, 11:00pm	Aries
Braque, Georges	May 13, 1882, 9:00pm	Taurus
Brown, Arthur	Jul 23, 1886, 11:00pm	Leo
Capone, Al	Jan 18, 1899, 9:30am	Capricorn
Carreras, José	Dec 5, 1946, 4:00am	Sagittarius
Cellini, Benvenuto	Nov 2, 1500 Julian, 9:10pm	Scorpio
Chekhov, Anton	Jan 29, 1860, 0:10am	Aquarius
Clifford, John Charles	Jun 12, 1947, 9:51pm	Gemini
Commons, Kim	Jul 23, 1951, 2:46am	Cancer
Dali, Salvador	May 11, 1904, 8:45am	Taurus
De Gaulle, Charles	Nov 22, 1890, 4:00am	Scorpio
Delon, Alain	Nov 8, 1935, 3:25am	Scorpio
Doolittle, James	Dec 14, 1896, 4:25pm	Sagittarius
Ely, Ron	Jun 21, 1938, 8:10am	Gemini
Espy, Willard R.	Dec 11, 1910, 6:05am	Sagittarius
Fermi, Enrico	Sep 29, 1901, 7:00pm	Libra
Fossett, Steve	Apr 22, 1944, 1:58am	Taurus
France, Anatole	Apr 16, 1844, 7:00am	Aries
Fürstenberg, Diane Von	Dec 31, 1946, 3:00am	Capricorn
Galileo, Galilei	Feb 15, 1564 Julian, 3:31pm	Pisces
Galland, Adolf	Mar 19, 1912, 12:30pm	Pisces
Garcia Marquez, Gabriel	Mar 6, 1927, 9:00am	Pisces
Gates, Bill	Oct 28, 1955, 10:00pm	Scorpio
George, Peter	Jun 29, 1929, 1:30pm	Cancer
Hahnemann, Samuel	Apr 10, 1755, 11:59pm	Aries
Hamilton, Ashley	Sep 30, 1974, 7:14pm	Libra

Henry VIII, King of England	Jun 28, 1491 Julian, 8:45am	Cancer
Hillary, Edmund	Jul 20, 1919, 4:00pm	Cancer
Houston, Whitney	Aug 9, 1963, 8:55pm	Leo
Jackson, Janet	May 16, 1966, 7:00pm	Taurus
Jarre, Jean-Michel	Aug 24, 1948, 4:00am	Virgo
Jobs, Steve	Feb 24, 1955, 7:15pm	Pisces
Jolie, Angelina	Jun 4, 1975, 9:09am	Gemini
Joliot-Curie, Irène	Sep 12, 1897, 10:00pm	Virgo
Kant, Immanuel	Apr 22, 1724, 5:00am	Taurus
Kennedy Onassis, Jacqueline	Jul 28, 1929, 2:30pm	Leo
Leo, Alan	Aug 7, 1860, 5:49am	Leo
Leopold, Prince of England	Apr 7, 1853, 1:10pm	Aries
Luther, Martin	Nov 10, 1483 Julian, 10:46pm	Scorpio
MacKenzie, Gisele	Jan 10, 1927, 11:46am	Capricorn
Messinger, Rena	Feb 16, 1956, 4:55pm	Aquarius
Nobile, Umberto	Jan 21, 1885, 3:15pm	Aquarius
Pavarotti, Luciano	Oct 12, 1935, 1:40am	Libra
Petty, Richard	Jul 2, 1937, 8:45am	Cancer
Renoir, Pierre-Auguste	Feb 25, 1841, 6:00am	Pisces
Robespierre, Maximilien	May 6, 1758, 2:00am	Taurus
Sand, George	Jul 1, 1804, 3:00pm	Cancer
Sarkozy, Nicolas	Jan 28, 1955, 10:00pm	Aquarius
Scholem, Gershom	Dec 5, 1897, 0:15am	Sagittarius
Schweitzer, Albert	Jan 14, 1875, 11:50pm	Capricorn
Silva, Jose	Aug 11, 1914, 2:14am	Leo
Stewart, Jackie	Jun 11, 1939, 2:50pm	Gemini
Strauss, Johann Sr.	Mar 14, 1804, 2:00am	Pisces

Tagore, Rabindranath	May 7, 1861, 4:02am	Taurus
Turgenev, Ivan	Nov 9, 1818, 12:00pm	Scorpio
Twain, Mark	Nov 30, 1835, 4:45am	Sagittarius
Voight, Jon	Dec 29, 1938, 11:50am	Capricorn
Wonder, Stevie	May 13, 1950, 4:15pm	Taurus
Woolf, Virginia	Jan 25, 1882, 12:15pm	Aquarius
Zola, Émile	Apr 2, 1840, 11:00pm	Aries

Taurus

Name	Birth Date and Time	Sun Sign
Adams, Samuel	Sep 27, 1722, 12:00pm	Libra
Adler, Alfred E.	Feb 7, 1870, 2:00pm	Aquarius
Aguilera, Christina	Dec 18, 1980, 10:46am	Sagittarius
Andersen, Hans Christian	Apr 2, 1805, 1:00am	Aries
Antonioni, Michaelangelo	Sep 29, 1912, 9:45pm	Libra
Ashmole, Elias	May 23, 1617 Julian, 3:28am	Gemini
Bach, Anna Magdalena	Sep 22, 1701, 5:30am	Virgo
Bosch, Robert	Sep 23, 1861, 5:00am	Libra
Braun, Wernher von	Mar 23, 1912, 9:15am	Aries
Calvin, John	Jul 10, 1509 Julian, 10:00pm	Cancer
Castañeda, Carlos	Dec 25, 1925, 2:00pm	Capricorn
Cayce, Edgar	Mar 18, 1877, 3:03pm	Pisces
Clausewitz,	Jun 1, 1780, 3:30pm	Gemini

Carl von		
Clinton, Bill	Aug 19, 1946, 8:51am	Leo
De Broglie, Louis	Aug 15, 1892, 1:00am	Leo
Diaz, Cameron	Aug 30, 1972, 2:53am	Virgo
Diesel, Rudolf	Mar 18, 1858, 3:43pm	Pisces
Dumas, Alexandre	Jul 24, 1802, 5:30am	Leo
Dylan, Bob	May 24, 1941, 9:05pm	Gemini
Fischer, Bobby	Mar 9, 1943, 2:39pm	Pisces
Fitzgerald, F. Scott	Sep 24, 1896, 3:30pm	Libra
Fleming, Ian	May 28, 1908, 0:10am	Gemini
Garbo, Greta	Sep 18, 1905, 7:30pm	Virgo
Gaultier, Jean-Paul	Apr 24, 1952, 7:00pm	Taurus
Geiger, Hans	Sep 30, 1882, 8:30am	Libra
Heyerdahl, Thor	Oct 6, 1914, 4:40pm	Libra
Hilton, Conrad	Dec 25, 1887, 5:20am	Capricorn
Ibsen, Henrik	Mar 20, 1828, 2:45pm	Pisces
Iggy Pop	Apr 21, 1947, 11:34am	Taurus
Jagger, Mick	Jul 26, 1943, 2:30am	Leo
John, Elton	Mar 25, 1947, 2:00am	Aries
Jung, Carl Gustav	Jul 26, 1875, 7:29pm	Leo
Lehar, Franz	Apr 30, 1870, 10:00pm	Taurus
Madoff, Bernie	Apr 29, 1938, 1:50pm	Taurus
Marceau, Marcel	Mar 22, 1923, 8:00am	Aries
Marx, Karl	May 5, 1818, 2:00am	Taurus
Mathieu, Mireille	Jul 22, 1946, 10:00pm	Cancer
Milton, John	Dec 19, 1608, 6:30am	Sagittarius
Montaigne, Michel de	Feb 28, 1533 Julian, 11:30am	Pisces
Moore, Demi	Nov 11, 1962, 2:16pm	Scorpio
Novalis	May 2, 1772, 10:00am	Taurus
O. Henry	Sep 11, 1862, 9:00pm	Virgo
Peck, Gregory	Apr 5, 1916, 8:00am	Aries
Petipa, Marius	Mar 11, 1818, 9:00am	Pisces
Proust, Marcel	Jul 10, 1871, 11:30pm	Cancer

Appendix C. Moon Sign Celebrities

Reagan, Ronald	Feb 6, 1911, 4:16am	Aquarius
Reno, Jean	Jul 30, 1948, 5:00am	Leo
Roberts, Jane	May 8, 1929, 11:27pm	Taurus
Ross, Diana	Mar 26, 1944, 11:46pm	Aries
Rousseau, Jean Jacques	Jun 28, 1712, 10:00am	Cancer
Saint-Saens, Camille	Oct 9, 1835, 7:00am	Libra
Shaw, George Bernard	Jul 26, 1856, 0:55am	Leo
Silver, Queen	Dec 13, 1910, 3:30pm	Sagittarius
Spinoza, Baruch	Nov 24, 1632, 2:00pm	Sagittarius
Swedenborg, Emanuel	Jan 29, 1688 Julian, 5:45am	Aquarius
Teresa, Mother	Aug 26, 1910, 2:25pm	Virgo
Zeiss, Carl	Sep 11, 1816, 6:00pm	Virgo

Gemini

Name	Birth Date and Time	Sun Sign
Abell, Sam	Feb 19, 1945, 2:46pm	Pisces
Achard, Marcel	Jul 5, 1899, 8:00pm	Cancer
Andreotti, Giulio	Jan 14, 1919, 7:00am	Capricorn
Bardot, Brigitte	Sep 28, 1934, 1:15pm	Libra
Baruch, Bernard	Aug 19, 1870, 1:50pm	Leo
Ben-Gurion, David	Oct 16, 1886, 12:24pm	Libra
Bolivar, Simon	Jul 24, 1783, 10:34pm	Leo
Catherine the Great	May 2, 1729, 2:30am	Taurus
Capablanca, Jose Raul	Nov 19, 1888, 1:45am	Scorpio
Chan, Jackie	Apr 7, 1954, 9:45am	Aries

Connolly, Billy	Nov 24, 1942, 4:30am	Sagittarius
Culpeper, Nicholas	Oct 28, 1616, 12:12pm	Scorpio
Douglas, Kirk	Dec 9, 1916, 10:15am	Sagittarius
Dürer, Albrecht	May 21, 1471 Julian, 11:00am	Gemini
Dvorak, Antonin	Sep 8, 1841, 11:00am	Virgo
Earhart, Amelia	Jul 24, 1897, 11:30pm	Leo
Fourier, Charles	Apr 7, 1772, 6:00am	Aries
Freud, Sigmund	May 6, 1856, 6:30pm	Taurus
Gabin, Jean	May 17, 1904, 2:00am	Taurus
Garibaldi, Giuseppe	Jul 4, 1807, 6:00am	Cancer
Graf, Steffi	Jun 14, 1969, 4:40am	Gemini
Haydn, Franz Joseph	Mar 31, 1732, 3:56pm	Aries
Karajan, Herbert von	Apr 5, 1908, 10:30pm	Aries
Kepler, Johannes	Dec 27, 1571 Julian, 2:37pm	Capricorn
Kohl, Helmut	Apr 3, 1930, 6:30am	Aries
Marx, Groucho	Oct 2, 1890, 8:35am	Libra
Obama, Barack	Aug 4, 1961, 7:24pm	Leo
Prada, Miuccia	May 10, 1948, 4:30am	Taurus
Rodin, Auguste	Nov 12, 1840, 12:00pm	Scorpio
Rockefeller Sr., John D.	Jul 8, 1839, 11:55pm	Cancer
Sharif, Omar	Apr 10, 1932, 5:30pm	Aries
Shields, Brooke	May 31, 1965, 1:45pm	Gemini
Teilhard De Chardin, Pierre	May 1, 1881, 7:00am	Taurus
Teller, Edward	Jan 15, 1908, 0:55am	Capricorn
Turner, Tina	Nov 26, 1939, 10:10pm	Sagittarius
Wren, Christopher	Oct 30, 1632, 7:44pm	Scorpio

Appendix C. Moon Sign Celebrities

Cancer

Name	Birth Date and Time	Sun Sign
Armani, Giorgio	Jul 11, 1934, 7:20am	Cancer
Baudelaire, Charles	Apr 9, 1821, 3:00am	Aries
Becker, Boris	Nov 22, 1967, 8:45am	Scorpio
Besant, Annie	Oct 1, 1847, 5:29pm	Libra
Besson, Luc	Mar 18, 1959, 1:45pm	Pisces
Cobain, Kurt	Feb 20, 1967, 7:20pm	Pisces
Debussy, Claude	Aug 22, 1862, 4:30am	Leo
Derek, Bo	Nov 20, 1956, 2:13pm	Scorpio
Dior, Christian	Jan 21, 1905, 1:30am	Aquarius
Heifetz, Jascha	Feb 2, 1901, 3:00am	Aquarius
Iglesias, Julio	Sep 23, 1943, 11:00am	Virgo
Kübler-Ross, Elisabeth	Jul 8, 1926, 10:45pm	Cancer
Mann, Thomas	Jun 6, 1875, 10:15am	Gemini
Maupassant, Guy de	Aug 5, 1850, 8:00am	Leo
Minnelli, Liza	Mar 12, 1946, 7:58am	Pisces
Moschino, Franco	Feb 27, 1950, 2:20pm	Pisces
Newton, Isaac	Jan 4, 1643, 1:38am	Capricorn
Oppenheimer, Robert	Apr 22, 1904, 8:15am	Taurus
Orwell, George	Jun 25, 1903, 11:30am	Cancer
Paganini, Niccolo	Oct 27, 1782, 10:30am	Scorpio
Pio, Padre	May 25, 1887, 4:10pm	Gemini
Puccini, Giacomo	Dec 22, 1858, 2:00am	Sagittarius
Ramana Maharishi	Dec 30, 1879, 1:00am	Capricorn
Reeves, Keanu	Sep 2, 1964, 5:41am	Virgo
Rice, Condoleezza	Nov 14, 1954, 11:30am	Scorpio
Roosevelt, Eleanor	Oct 11, 1884, 11:00am	Libra
Roosevelt, Franklin D.	Jan 30, 1882, 8:45pm	Aquarius
Roosevelt, Teddy	Oct 27, 1858, 7:45pm	Scorpio
Rothschild, Edmond de	Sep 30, 1926, 12:00pm	Libra

Sai Baba, Sri Sathya	Nov 23, 1926, 6:22am	Scorpio
Schumacher, Michael	Jan 3, 1969, 1:43pm	Capricorn
Shakira	Feb 2, 1977, 10:08am	Aquarius
Stravinsky, Igor	Jun 17, 1882, 12:00pm	Gemini
Wozniak, Steve	Aug 11, 1950, 9:45am	Leo
Yo-Yo Ma	Oct 7, 1955, 6:00pm	Libra

Leo

Name	Birth Date and Time	Sun Sign
Abbado, Claudio	Jun 26, 1933, 2:00am	Cancer
Albertus, Frater	May 5, 1911, 3:42am	Taurus
Bach, Richard	Jun 23, 1936, 12:36pm	Cancer
Becquerel, Alexandre	Mar 24, 1820, 1:00pm	Aries
Bessel, Friedrich	Jun 21, 1784, 4:00pm	Cancer
Braille, Louis	Jan 4, 1809, 4:00am	Capricorn
Cousteau, Jacques-Yves	Jun 11, 1910, 1:06pm	Gemini
Dietrich, Marlene	Dec 27, 1901, 9:15pm	Capricorn
Disraeli, Benjamin	Dec 21, 1804, 5:30am	Sagittarius
Dumas, Alexandre fils	Jul 27, 1824, 6:00pm	Leo
Eastwood, Clint	May 31, 1930, 5:35pm	Gemini
Fonda, Jane	Dec 21, 1937, 9:14am	Sagittarius
Gandhi, Mohandas	Oct 2, 1869, 7:12am	Libra
Gann, W.D.	Jun 6, 1878, 10:34am	Gemini
Hanks, Tom	Jul 9, 1956, 11:17am	Cancer
Hilton, Paris	Feb 17, 1981, 2:30am	Aquarius
Hoover, Herbert	Aug 10, 1874, 11:15pm	Leo

London, Jack	Jan 12, 1876, 2:00pm	Capricorn
Marconi, Guglielmo	Apr 25, 1874, 9:15am	Taurus
McCartney, Paul	Jun 18, 1942, 2:00am	Gemini
Medici, Cosimo de	Jun 12, 1519, 9:19pm	Gemini
Michael, George	Jun 25, 1963, 6:00am	Cancer
Monet, Claude	Nov 14, 1840, 7:27pm	Scorpio
Peugeot, Jean Pierre	Jun 16, 1896, 5:51am	Gemini
Pininfarina, Battista	Nov 2, 1893, 6:30am	Scorpio
Saint-Exupéry, Antoine de	Jun 29, 1900, 9:15am	Cancer
Santana, Carlos	Jul 20, 1947, 2:00am	Cancer
Schiller, Friedrich von	Nov 10, 1759, 8:00am	Scorpio
Sibelius, Jean	Dec 8, 1865, 0:30am	Sagittarius
Starr, Ringo	Jul 7, 1940, 0:05am	Cancer
Streisand, Barbra	Apr 24, 1942, 5:08am	Taurus
Thatcher, Margaret	Oct 13, 1925, 9:00am	Libra
Ustinov, Peter	Apr 16, 1921, 11:00am	Aries
Verlaine, Paul	Mar 30, 1844, 9:00pm	Aries
Vivaldi, Antonio	Mar 4, 1678, 5:50pm	Pisces
Vlaminck, Maurice	Apr 4, 1876, 4:00pm	Aries
Vonnegut, Kurt	Nov 11, 1922, 8:00am	Scorpio
Wilde, Oscar	Oct 16, 1854, 3:00am	Libra
Yogananda, Paramahansa	Jan 5, 1893, 8:38pm	Capricorn

Virgo

Name	Birth Date and Time	Sun Sign
Adams, Douglas	Mar 11, 1952, 11:10am	Pisces
Assagioli, Roberto	Feb 27, 1888, 12:00pm	Pisces
Bell, Alexander Graham	Mar 3, 1847, 7:00am	Pisces
Brahe, Tycho	Dec 14, 1546 Julian, 10:47am	Capricorn
Britten, Benjamin	Nov 22, 1913, 7:00pm	Scorpio
Bunin, Ivan	Oct 22, 1870, 7:00am	Libra
Carlyle, Thomas	Dec 4, 1795, 4:00pm	Sagittarius
Chopra, Deepak	Oct 22, 1946, 3:45pm	Libra
Cocteau, Jean	Jul 5, 1889, 1:00am	Cancer
Connery, Sean	Aug 25, 1930, 6:05pm	Virgo
Cromwell, Oliver	May 5, 1599, 3:00am	Taurus
Druon, Maurice	Apr 23, 1918, 3:15am	Taurus
DuPont, Pierre Samuel	Jan 22, 1935, 12:00pm	Aquarius
Engels, Friedrich	Nov 28, 1820, 9:00pm	Sagittarius
Faulkner, William	Sep 25, 1897, 10:30pm	Libra
Flammarion, Camille	Feb 26, 1842, 1:00am	Pisces
Gandhi, Rajiv	Aug 20, 1944, 6:34am	Leo
Gauguin, Paul	Jun 7, 1848, 10:00am	Gemini
Heineken, Alfred	Nov 4, 1923, 12:00pm	Scorpio
Hoffman, Dustin	Aug 8, 1937, 5:07pm	Leo
Johnson, Amy	Jul 1, 1903, 1:30am	Cancer
Kaas, Patricia	Dec 5, 1966, 10:25am	Sagittarius
Kennedy, John F.	May 29, 1917, 3:00pm	Gemini
Kurosawa, Akira	Mar 23, 1910, 12:00pm	Aries
Lollobrigida, Gina	Jul 4, 1927, 3:00am	Cancer
Lumière, Auguste	Oct 19, 1862, 3:30pm	Libra
Madonna	Aug 16, 1958, 7:05am	Leo
Mendelssohn Bartholdy, Felix	Feb 3, 1809, 8:00pm	Aquarius
Messerschmitt, Willy	Jun 26, 1898, 7:00am	Cancer

Messner, Reinhold	Sep 17, 1944, 1:00am	Virgo
Nabokov, Vladimir	Apr 22, 1899, 4:26am	Taurus
Pfeiffer, Michelle	Apr 29, 1958, 8:11am	Taurus
Pininfarina, Sergio	Sep 8, 1926, 12:30pm	Virgo
Schmidt, Helmut	Dec 23, 1918, 10:15pm	Capricorn
Schopenhauer, Arthur	Feb 22, 1788, 12:00pm	Pisces
Simenon, Georges	Feb 13, 1903, 0:10am	Aquarius
Steiner, Rudolf	Feb 25, 1861, 11:15pm	Pisces
Stendhal	Jan 23, 1783, 1:00am	Aquarius
Travolta, John	Feb 18, 1954, 2:53pm	Aquarius
Van Damme, Jean-Claude	Oct 18, 1960, 6:45am	Libra
Weinberger, Caspar	Aug 18, 1917, 3:10pm	Leo
Welch, Jack	Nov 19, 1935, 10:30am	Scorpio
Wordsworth, William	Apr 7, 1770, 10:00pm	Aries

Libra

Name	Birth Date and Time	Sun Sign
Adjani, Isabelle	Jun 27, 1955, 1:00am	Cancer
Alzheimer, Alois	Jun 14, 1864, 4:00am	Gemini
Austen, Jane	Dec 16, 1775, 11:45pm	Sagittarius
Bellini, Vincenzo	Nov 3, 1801, 10:15pm	Scorpio
Belmondo, Jean-Paul	Apr 9, 1933, 9:00am	Aries
Bergman, Ingmar	Jul 14, 1918, 1:00pm	Cancer
Bhutto, Benazir	Jun 21, 1953, 7:21pm	Gemini
Blavatsky, Helena	Aug 12, 1831, 2:17am	Leo
Bohr, Niels	Oct 7, 1885, 10:00am	Libra
Boyle, Susan	Apr 1, 1961, 9:50am	Aries
Brecht, Bertold	Feb 10, 1898, 4:30am	Aquarius
Bush, George H. W.	Jun 12, 1924, 10:30am	Gemini
Bush, George W.	Jul 6, 1946, 7:26am	Cancer

Cage, Nicolas	Jan 7, 1964, 5:30am	Capricorn
Castro, Fidel	Aug 13, 1926, 2:00am	Leo
Child, Julia	Aug 15, 1912, 11:30pm	Leo
Christie, Agatha	Sep 15, 1890, 4:00am	Virgo
Dalida	Jan 17, 1933, 9:00pm	Capricorn
De Staël, Madame	Apr 22, 1766, 5:58pm	Taurus
DiCaprio, Leonardo	Nov 11, 1974, 2:47am	Scorpio
Dirac, Paul	Aug 8, 1902, 6:48am	Leo
Disney, Walt	Dec 5, 1901, 12:35am	Sagittarius
Dr. Dre	Feb 18, 1965, 10:56am	Aquarius
Eisenhower, Dwight D.	Oct 14, 1890, 3:00am	Libra
Elgar, Edward	Jun 2, 1857, 2:30pm	Gemini
Fonda, Henry	May 16, 1905, 2:00pm	Taurus
Gaudi, Antoni	Jun 25, 1852, 9:30am	Cancer
Givenchy, Hubert de	Feb 20, 1927, 11:30am	Pisces
Grimaud, Hélène	Nov 7, 1969, 11:30am	Scorpio
Heisenberg, Werner	Dec 5, 1901, 4:45am	Sagittarius
Hilfiger, Tommy	Mar 24, 1951, 2:59am	Aries
Joel, Billy	May 9, 1949, 9:30am	Taurus
Leadbeater, Charles	Feb 16, 1854, 10:30am	Aquarius
Legrand, Michel	Feb 24, 1932, 12:21pm	Pisces
Maeterlinck, Maurice	Aug 29, 1862, 8:30am	Virgo
Mitchell, Joan	Feb 12, 1925, 10:31pm	Aquarius
Mitterrand, François	Oct 26, 1916, 4:00am	Scorpio
Nureyev, Rudolph	Mar 17, 1938, 1:00pm	Pisces
Prokofiev, Sergei	Apr 23, 1891, 5:00pm	Taurus
Russell, Bertrand	May 18, 1872, 5:45pm	Taurus
Seagal, Steven	Apr 10, 1952, 1:54pm	Aries
Stallone, Sylvester	Jul 6, 1946, 7:20pm	Cancer
Tesla, Nikola	Jul 10, 1856, 12:00am	Cancer
Toulouse-Lautrec, Henri	Nov 24, 1864, 6:00am	Sagittarius
Vivekananda, Swami	Jan 12, 1863, 6:33am	Capricorn

Scorpio

Name	Birth Date and Time	Sun Sign
Amundsen, Roald	Jul 16, 1872, 5:00am	Cancer
Assange, Julian	Jul 3, 1971, 3:00pm	Cancer
Bebel, August	Feb 22, 1840, 8:30pm	Pisces
Berlioz, Hector	Dec 11, 1803, 5:00pm	Sagittarius
Borodin, Alexander	Nov 12, 1833, 3:00am	Scorpio
Clapton, Eric	Mar 30, 1945, 8:45pm	Aries
Cronin, A.J.	Jul 19, 1896, 3:45am	Cancer
Curie, Pierre	May 15, 1859, 2:00am	Taurus
De Bergerac, Cyrano	Mar 6, 1619, 3:00pm	Pisces
Depardieu, Gérard	Dec 27, 1948, 8:00am	Capricorn
Domingo, Plácido	Jan 21, 1941, 10:00pm	Aquarius
Geller, Uri	Dec 20, 1946, 2:30am	Sagittarius
Goldberg, Whoopi	Nov 13, 1955, 12:48pm	Scorpio
Hallyday, Johnny	Jun 15, 1943, 1:00pm	Gemini
Hitchcock, Alfred	Aug 13, 1899, 3:15am	Leo
Joliot-Curie, Frederic	Mar 19, 1900, 9:00am	Pisces
Krupp, Alfred	Apr 26, 1812, 6:00pm	Taurus
Lady Gaga	Mar 28, 1986, 9:53am	Aries
Lanza, Mario	Jan 31, 1921, 9:45am	Aquarius
Lavoisier, Antoine	Aug 26, 1743, 9:30am	Virgo
Livingstone, David	Mar 19, 1813, 10:30pm	Pisces
Mandela, Nelson	Jul 18, 1918, 2:54pm	Cancer
Morricone, Ennio	Nov 10, 1928, 10:25pm	Scorpio
Nostradamus, Michel de	Dec 14, 1503 Julian, 12:00pm	Capricorn
Ohm, Georg	Mar 16, 1789, 3:00am	Pisces
Pompidou, Georges	Jul 5, 1911, 7:30am	Cancer
Rockefeller, Nelson	Jul 8, 1908, 12:10pm	Cancer
Scriabin, Alexander	Jan 6, 1872, 2:07pm	Capricorn

Spencer, Herbert	Apr 27, 1820, 11:59pm	Taurus
Spielberg, Steven	Dec 18, 1946, 6:16pm	Sagittarius
Steinbeck, John	Feb 27, 1902, 3:00pm	Pisces
Taylor, Elizabeth	Feb 27, 1932, 2:30am	Pisces
Toscanini, Arturo	Mar 25, 1867, 2:00am	Aries
Weber, Carl Maria von	Nov 18, 1786, 10:30pm	Scorpio

Sagittarius

Name	Birth Date and Time	Sun Sign
Adamo, Salvatore	Oct 31, 1943, 2:00am	Scorpio
Armstrong, Neil	Aug 5, 1930, 12:31am	Leo
Aurobindo, Sri	Aug 15, 1872, 5:00am	Leo
Balzac, Honoré de	May 20, 1799, 11:00am	Taurus
Benetton, Carlo	Dec 26, 1943, 12:00pm	Capricorn
Bogarde, Dirk	Mar 28, 1921, 8:30am	Aries
Brahms, Johannes	May 7, 1833, 3:30am	Taurus
Buchwald, Art	Oct 20, 1925, 1:00pm	Libra
Carroll, Lewis	Jan 27, 1832, 3:45am	Aquarius
Casanova, Giacomo	Apr 2, 1725, 8:00pm	Aries
Coelho, Paulo	Aug 24, 1947, 12:05am	Virgo
Copernicus, Nicolaus	Feb 19, 1473 Julian, 5:13pm	Pisces
Edison, Thomas Alva	Feb 11, 1847, 1:30am	Aquarius
Einstein, Albert	Mar 14, 1879, 11:30am	Pisces
Fairbanks Sr., Douglas	May 23, 1883, 5:00am	Gemini
Fleming, Alexander	Aug 6, 1881, 2:00am	Leo
Ford, Gerald	Jul 14, 1913, 12:43am	Cancer
Fromm, Erich	Mar 23, 1900, 7:30pm	Aries
Gounod, Charles	Jun 17, 1818, 4:00am	Gemini

Hugo, Victor	Feb 26, 1802, 10:30pm	Pisces
Kasparov, Garry	Apr 13, 1963, 11:45pm	Aries
Krishnamurti, Jiddu	May 12, 1895, 12:30am	Taurus
Legrand, Alexandre	Jun 6, 1830, 6:00pm	Gemini
Lindbergh, Charles	Feb 4, 1902, 1:30am	Aquarius
Lorca, Federico Garcia	Jun 5, 1898, 12:00am	Gemini
Manilow, Barry	Jun 17, 1943, 9:00am	Gemini
Matisse, Henri	Dec 31, 1869, 8:00pm	Capricorn
Mozart, Wolfgang Amadeus	Jan 27, 1756, 8:00pm	Aquarius
Murdoch, Rupert	Mar 11, 1931, 11:59pm	Pisces
Nietzsche, Friedrich	Oct 15, 1844, 10:00am	Libra
Norris, Chuck	Mar 10, 1942, 3:00am	Pisces
Pacino, Al	Apr 25, 1940, 11:02am	Taurus
Peter I, Czar of Russia	May 30, 1672 Julian, 1:00am	Gemini
Picasso, Pablo	Oct 25, 1881, 11:15pm	Scorpio
Ram Dass	Apr 6, 1931, 10:40am	Aries
Van Gogh, Vincent	Mar 30, 1853, 11:00am	Aries
Woods, Tiger	Dec 30, 1975, 10:50pm	Capricorn

Capricorn

Name	Birth Date and Time	Sun Sign
Aznavour, Charles	May 22, 1924, 12:15am	Gemini
Bismarck, Otto von	Apr 1, 1815, 1:30pm	Aries
Boccherini, Luigi	Feb 19, 1743, 10:00am	Pisces
Bon Jovi, Jon	Mar 2, 1962, 8:45pm	Pisces
Bonaparte, Napoleon I	Aug 15, 1769, 11:30am	Leo
Bruckner, Anton	Sep 4, 1824, 4:15am	Virgo
Chopin, Frédéric	Mar 1, 1810, 6:00pm	Pisces
Clooney, George	May 6, 1961, 2:58am	Taurus
Damon, Matt	Oct 8, 1970, 3:22pm	Libra
Dayan, Moshe	May 4, 1915, 4:50am	Taurus
Fellini, Federico	Jan 20, 1920, 9:00pm	Capricorn
Ferrari, Enzo	Feb 18, 1898, 3:00am	Aquarius
Gandhi, Indira	Nov 19, 1917, 11:11pm	Scorpio
Gore, Al	Mar 31, 1948, 12:53pm	Aries
Hemingway, Ernest	Jul 21, 1899, 8:00am	Cancer
Herschel, William	Nov 15, 1738, 1:15am	Scorpio
Holiday, Billie	Apr 7, 1915, 2:30am	Aries
Kennedy, Robert F.	Nov 20, 1925, 3:11pm	Scorpio
Lowell, Percival	Mar 13, 1855, 7:45am	Pisces
Makarios III, Archbishop	Aug 13, 1913, 7:21pm	Leo
Menuhin, Yehudi	Apr 22, 1916, 11:30pm	Taurus
Nansen, Fridtjof	Oct 10, 1861, 11:30am	Libra
Osbourne, Ozzy	Dec 3, 1948, 6:00am	Sagittarius
Picasso, Paloma	Apr 19, 1949, 7:45pm	Aries
Pitt, Brad	Dec 18, 1963, 6:31am	Sagittarius
Rubens, Peter Paul	Jul 9, 1577, 6:15am	Cancer
Saint Laurent, Yves	Aug 1, 1936, 7:45pm	Leo
Schwarzenegger, Arnold	Jul 30, 1947, 4:10am	Leo
Shostakovich, Dmitri	Sep 25, 1906, 5:00pm	Libra
Sun Yat-Sen	Nov 12, 1866, 4:00am	Scorpio
Washington, George	Feb 22, 1732, 10:00am	Pisces

| Zeppelin, Ferdinand Graf von | Jul 8, 1838, 10:30am | Cancer |

Aquarius

Name	Birth Date and Time	Sun Sign
Ali, Muhammad	Jan 17, 1942, 6:35pm	Capricorn
Allen, Woody	Dec 1, 1935, 10:55pm	Sagittarius
Bartók, Béla	Mar 25, 1881, 8:50am	Aries
Becquerel, Antoine	Dec 15, 1852, 3:00pm	Sagittarius
Blair, Tony	May 6, 1953, 6:10am	Taurus
Bronte, Charlotte	Apr 21, 1816, 2:41pm	Taurus
Camus, Albert	Nov 7, 1913, 2:00am	Scorpio
Copperfield, David	Sep 16, 1956, 7:02am	Virgo
David-Néel, Alexandra	Oct 24, 1868, 4:50am	Scorpio
Diana, Princess of Wales	Jul 1, 1961, 7:45pm	Cancer
Ford, Henry	Jul 30, 1863, 7:00am	Leo
Gallo, Ernest	Mar 18, 1909, 7:15pm	Pisces
Gershwin, George	Sep 26, 1898, 11:09am	Libra
Jimenez, Juan Ramon	Dec 24, 1881, 11:59pm	Capricorn
Koresh, David	Aug 17, 1959, 8:49am	Leo
Leary, Timothy	Oct 22, 1920, 10:45am	Libra
Lennon, John	Oct 9, 1940, 6:30pm	Libra
Lilienthal, Otto	May 23, 1848, 11:30am	Gemini
Linnaeus, Carolus	May 24, 1707, 12:26am	Gemini
Lucas, George	May 14, 1944, 5:40am	Taurus
Machiavelli, Niccolo	May 2, 1469 Julian, 11:07pm	Taurus
Monroe, Marilyn	Jun 1, 1926, 9:30am	Gemini
Piccard, Auguste	Jan 28, 1884, 11:00pm	Aquarius

Rothschild, Mayer Amschel	Feb 23, 1743, 7:45pm	Pisces
Rudhyar, Dane	Mar 23, 1895, 12:42am	Aries
Sabatini, Rafael	Apr 29, 1875, 2:20am	Taurus
Stout, Rex	Dec 1, 1886, 10:30pm	Sagittarius
Voltaire	Nov 21, 1694, 5:30pm	Scorpio
Wagner, Richard	May 22, 1813, 4:11am	Gemini
Willis, Bruce	Mar 19, 1955, 6:32pm	Pisces

Pisces

Name	Birth Date and Time	Sun Sign
Alkan, Charles Valentin	Nov 30, 1813, 3:00pm	Sagittarius
Balanchine, George	Jan 22, 1904, 12:58pm	Aquarius
Berke, William	Oct 3, 1903, 6:00am	Libra
Brennan, Barbara	Feb 19, 1939, 7:30am	Pisces
Caruso, Enrico	Feb 27, 1873, 3:00am	Pisces
Celentano, Adriano	Jan 6, 1938, 7:00am	Capricorn
Cézanne, Paul	Jan 19, 1839, 1:00am	Capricorn
Citroën, André	Feb 5, 1878, 12:30am	Aquarius
Cohen, Leonard	Sep 21, 1934, 6:45am	Virgo
Crawford, Cindy	Feb 20, 1966, 12:56pm	Pisces
Da Vinci, Leonardo	Apr 14, 1452 Julian, 9:40pm	Taurus
Davies, Fredrick	Sep 1, 1936, 3:25am	Virgo
De Niro, Robert	Aug 17, 1943, 3:00am	Leo
Dufy, Raoul	Jun 3, 1877, 7:00am	Gemini
Franklin, Benjamin	Jan 17, 1706, 10:30am	Capricorn
Glinka, Mikhail	Jun 1, 1804, 3:30am	Gemini
Gluck, Christoph Wilibald	Jul 2, 1714, 12:45am	Cancer

Goethe, Johann Wolfgang von	Aug 28, 1749, 12:00pm	Virgo
Guevara, Che	May 14, 1928, 3:05am	Taurus
Handel, George Friedrich	Mar 5, 1685, 5:45am	Pisces
Hoover, J. Edgar	Jan 1, 1895, 7:30am	Capricorn
Jackson, Michael	Aug 29, 1958, 12:00pm	Virgo
Lamborghini, Ferruccio	Apr 28, 1916, 5:00pm	Taurus
Maserati, Ernesto	Aug 4, 1898, 2:00pm	Leo
Melies, Georges	Dec 8, 1861, 12:05am	Sagittarius
Michelangelo	Mar 6, 1475 Julian, 1:45am	Pisces
Morse, Samuel F.B.	Apr 27, 1791, 10:30am	Taurus
Nijinski, Vaslav	Mar 11, 1888, 10:30pm	Pisces
Petrarch	Jul 20, 1304 Julian, 4:33am	Leo
Presley, Elvis	Jan 8, 1935, 4:35am	Capricorn
Ramakrishna	Feb 18, 1836, 5:00am	Aquarius
Ravel, Maurice	Mar 7, 1875, 10:00pm	Pisces
Richelieu, Cardinal	Sep 9, 1585, 9:28am	Virgo
Roddenberry, Gene	Aug 19, 1921, 1:35am	Leo
Schubert, Franz	Jan 31, 1797, 1:30pm	Aquarius
Segovia, Andres	Mar 17, 1893, 6:30pm	Pisces
Shelley, Percy Bysshe	Aug 4, 1792, 10:00pm	Leo
Sinatra, Frank	Dec 12, 1915, 3:00am	Sagittarius
Stevenson, Robert Louis	Nov 13, 1850, 1:30pm	Scorpio

Printed in Great Britain
by Amazon